Theodulf of Orléans:
The Verse

MEDIEVAL AND RENAISSANCE
TEXTS AND STUDIES

VOLUME 450

Theodulf of Orléans:
The Verse

Translated and introduced by
Theodore M. Andersson

in collaboration with
Åslaug Ommundsen
and
Leslie S. B. MacCoull

Tempe, Arizona
2014

Published by ACMRS (Arizona Center for Medieval and Renaissance Studies)
Tempe, Arizona
© 2014 Arizona Board of Regents for Arizona State University.
All Rights Reserved.

Library of Congress Cataloging-in-Publication Data

Theodulf, Bishop of Orléans, approximately 760-821, author.
 [Poems. English]
  Theodulf of Orléans : the verse / translated and introduced by Theodore M. Andersson in collaboration with Åslaug Ommundsen and Leslie S. B. MacCoull.
      pages cm -- (Medieval and renaissance texts and studies ; volume 450)
   ISBN 978-0-86698-501-7 (alk. paper)
 1. Poetry, Medieval--Translations into English. I. Andersson, Theodore Murdock, 1934- II. Title. III. Series: Medieval & Renaissance Texts & Studies (Series) ; v. 450.
  PA8440.T33A2 2014
  871'.03--dc23
                                                                              2013050720

Cover Art:
Germigny-des-Prés. Mosaic in the central apse, early ninth century (detail).
Photograph by Hubert Denies
Reproduced with permission under the Creative Commons Attribution-Share Alike 3.0 Unported license
http://creativecommons.org/licenses/by-sa/3.0/deed.en

∞
This book is made to last. It is set in Adobe Caslon Pro,
smyth-sewn and printed on acid-free paper to library specifications.
Printed in the United States of America

TABLE OF CONTENTS

Preface   *xi*

Introduction   1

The Poems

Religious and Moral Poems

1. Fragmentum de vitiis capitalibus   17
    Fragment on the Mortal Sins

2. Ad episcopos   27
    To the Bishops

3. De gratia dei   37
    On God's Grace

4. De his qui aliud corde retinent, aliud ore premunt   37
    On Those Who Guard One Thing in Their Hearts and Say Another

5. Quale ieiunium et quae parsimonia deo acceptabilis sit et possit   38
    impetrare postulata
    *What Fasting and What Frugality Are Acceptable to God and Can Obtain
    What is Asked*

6. Contra simulatores et subdolos   38
    Against the Hypocrites and Deceivers

7. De eo quod avarus adglomeratis diversis opibus satiari nequit   39
    *About the Fact That a Grasping Man Cannot Be Satisfied with Any
    Agglomeration of Various Riches*

8. De eo quod plerumque reprobis prospera sunt   40
    About the Fact that False People Often Prosper

9. Quod dominus imitandus sit nobis ac penitus amandus et timendus   42
    That We Should Imitate the Lord and Love and Fear Him Deeply

10. De simulatorum et stultorum socordia, qui nesciunt a sua pravitate 42
per bonam exhortationem converti
*On the Indolence of Dissemblers and Fools Who, Despite Good Exhortations,
Decline to Convert from Evil*

11. Quamobrem cicatrices, quas dominus in passione suscepit, 43
in Resurrectione obductae non sint
*Why the Wounds That the Lord Received in His Passion Were Not Hidden
at His Resurrection*

12. De fide et spe et caritate 45
On Faith, Hope, and Charity

13. De dispensatione divina, quae saepe occulta est, numquam 46
tamen iniusta
On Divine Dispensation, Which Is Often Obscure but Never Unjust

14. Quod multis indiciis finis proximus esse monstretur 47
It May Be Shown by Many Signs That the End Is Near

15. Ex epistola ad Corintios Carmen ad precem cuiusdam monachi factum 48
*A Poem Composed at the Request of a Certain Monk from the Epistle
to the Corinthians*

16. De fructu centeno sexageno et triceno 50
On the Hundred-fold, Sixty-fold, and Thirty-fold Yield

17. De hypocritis et quod apostolorum temporibus sive eorum successorum 51
magis ecclesiae virtutes viguerunt quam his novissimis temporibus
*Concerning Hypocrites and the Fact That in the Times of the Apostles
and Their Successors the Virtues of the Church Prospered more Than in
These Very Recent Times*

18. Quod plerumque mali mala patiuntur et de tempore Antichristi 54
That the Wicked Often Suffer Evil and Concerning the Time of the Antichrist

19. De eo quod temporis status et locus et causa et motio ingenium 55
tractatoris adiuvat
*That the Fixing of Time, Location, Cause, and Direction Aid the Mind
of the Interpreter*

20. De contemptu mundi 57
On the Contempt of the World

21. Consolatio de obitu cuiusdam fratris 57
Consolation for the Death of a Certain Brother

22. Quae sint dicenda amico cum conspicit bona amici 61
What a Friend Should Say to a Friend When He Sees His Friend's Riches

23. Teudulfus episcopus hos versus conposuit 62
Bishop Theodulf Composed These Verses

Table of Contents vii

Secular and Historical Poems

24. Epitaphium Fastradae Reginae 65
    Epitaph for Queen Fastrada
25. Ad Carolum regem 65
    To King Charles
26. Super sepulcrum Hadriani papae 73
    Inscribed on the Tomb of Pope Hadrian
27. [To Corvinianus] 75
28. Versus Teudulfi episcopi contra iudices 79
    Bishop Theodulf's Verses against the Judges
29. [Comparatio legis antiquae et modernae 107
    Comparison of the Old and New Law]

Poems Attached to Historical Events

30. Ad monachos Sancti Benedicti 111
    To the Monks of Saint Benedict
31. Ad reginam 113
    To the Queen [Liutgard]
32. Ad regem 114
    To the King [Charlemagne]
33. Ad Fardulfum abbatum Sancti Dionysii 116
    To Abbot Fardulf of Saint-Denis
34. Quod potestas impatiens consortis sit 119
    That Power is Reluctantly Shared
35. Ad Carolum regem 120
    To King Charles [son of Charlemagne]
36. [no title] 121
37. De adventu Hludowici augusti Aurelianos 122
    On the Arrival of Emperor Louis at Orléans
38. Versus scripti litteris aureis de Sancto Quintino 124
    Verses Written with Gold Letters about Saint Quentin
39. Eiusdem ad Hluduicum valedictio 126
    A Farewell from the Same [Theodulf] to Louis
40. Epitaphium Helmengaldi 127
    Epitaph for Helmengald
41. Versus Theodulfi 127
    Theodulf's Verses

viii *Table of Contents*

42. A foris in prima tabula bibliothecae ·   136
    Outside on the First Tablet of the Bible Compilation
43. Ad Gislam   137
    To Gisla

Personal and Miscellaneous Poems

44. Cur modo carmina non scribat   139
    Why He Should Not Now Write Poems
45. De libris quos legere solebam et qualiter fabulae poetarum a   140
    philosophis mystice pertractentur
    On the Books That I Used to Read and How the Stories of Poets Should
    be Interpreted Allegorically by Philosophers
46. De septem liberalibus artibus in quadam pictura depictis   142
    On the Seven Liberal Arts Shown in a Certain Picture
47. Alia pictura, in qua erat imago terrae in modum orbis comprehensa   146
    Another Picture in Which There Was an Image of the Earth Formed as a Circle
48. [Itinerarium]   148
49. In sepulcro Sancti Nazarii   149
    On the Headstone of Saint Nazarius
50. De vulpecula involante gallinam   150
    On a Fox Attacking a Hen
51. De equo perdito   152
    Concerning a Lost Horse
52. De bilingue   153
    On a Chatterer
53. Ad quendam de muneribus   154
    To a Gift-Giver
54. De passione Domini   154
    On the Passion of the Lord
55. In die resurrectionis   154
    On the Day of Christ's Resurrection
56. De tabella   155
    On a Tablet
57. De talamasca   155
    On a Mask
58. Versus in altari   157
    Verses on an Altar

Table of Contents   ix

59. In xenodochio   157
    In an Inn

60. In fronte domus   158
    On the Front of a House

61. In fronte domus   158
    On the Front of a House

62. In faldaone episcopi   158
    On the Bishop's Throne

63. Super ianuam   159
    Above the Doorway

64. Super propinatorium   159
    Over a Drinking Hall

65. In altare Sancti Aniani   159
    On the Altar of Saint Anianus

66. In obitu Damasi   160
    On the Death of Damasus

67. Quod deus non loco quaerendus sit, sed pietate colendus   160
    *That God Should Not Be Sought Out in a Place but Should Be
    Worshipped Piously*

68. Die sollemni anniversario   160
    On a Solemn Festival Day

69. [Versus facti ut a pueris in die palmarum cantarentur   161
    Verses to be Sung by Boys on Palm Sunday]

70. [untitled poem to Emperor Louis]   164

The Exile Poems

71. Ad Aiulfum episcopum   167
    To Bishop Aiulf

72. Incipit epistola Theodulfi episcopi ad Modoinum episcopum   170
    scribens ei de exilio: Theodulfus Modoino suo salutem
    *Here Begins the Epistle of Bishop Theodulf to Bishop Modoin Writing
    Him from Exile: Theodulf Greets His Modoin*

73. Incipit rescriptum Modoini episcopi ad Theodulfum episcopum.   177
    Modoinus indignus episcopus Theodulfo suo.
    *Here Begins the Reply of Bishop Modoin to Bishop Theodulf. Modoin,
    the Unworthy Bishop, to His Theodulf.*

Poems of Doubtful Attribution

74. [De paradiso — 183
    On Paradise]

75. [De resurrectione carnis — 184
    On the Resurrection of the Flesh]

76. [untitled] — 188

77. [untitled] — 189

78. [untitled] — 190

79. [untitled — Prudens to Prudentius] — 190

Textual Notes — 195

Appendix — 201

Bibliography — 203

Indices — 213

PREFACE

Charlemagne's long shadow obscured even the most conspicuous figures in his entourage. One of these was Theodulf, a close adviser, especially in theological matters, and the most distinguished poet in Charlemagne's court circle. He is nevertheless very little known beyond the confines of medieval Latin studies, and there is no published translation of his verse. The present volume is therefore intended as an introduction to this verse for a broader readership. It is not a literal, word-by-word translation, but attempts to catch something of the flavor of Theodulf's original distichs by rendering them in English with a fairly even flow of stressed and unstressed syllables ending in a trochaic cadence in the odd lines and an iambic cadence in the even lines. In order to achieve this effect I have had to take small liberties such as substituting Father for God and Savior for Christ where a trochee is required, or change the word order slightly to save the trochee for the end of the line, or replace an active construction with a passive construction to preserve the rhythm. Those readers who prefer a literal prose translation should procure Nikolai Alexandrenko's excellent version in his unpublished Tulane dissertation from 1971 (see the Bibliography). Our translation includes all the poems printed by Ernst Dümmler in his MGH edition of 1881, although a number of them are of doubtful authenticity, and three at least (nos. 66, 73, 79) are certainly not by Theodulf. We have elected to translate Dümmler's collection as a whole rather than entering into the debate on what is genuine and what is open to question. We also follow Dümmler's order so that the user can refer easily to the Latin originals.

A general introduction surveys what is known, and not known, about Theodulf's life and summarizes the types and varieties of his verse. We avoid asking the non-Carolingianist to embark on a reading cold by prefacing each poem, or group of poems, with a headnote on the content and earlier commentary. Only a few textual notes are appended on particularly troublesome passages. I am above all grateful to my collaborators Åslaug Ommundsen and Leslie Mac-Coull, who have made many corrections and improvements and have expanded my collection of biblical echoes and bibliographical references very significantly. We are also much indebted to Stephen A. Barney for a close reading of the long poem "Contra iudices," which has gained greatly from his attentions. We are also much indebted to our forerunner, Nikolai A. Alexandrenko, whose translations and copious commentary have lent us constant assistance. Specific debts to this dissertation are acknowledged along the way.

Theodore M. Andersson
January 2013

INTRODUCTION

More than a century ago Charles Cuissard outlined a chronology of the chief moments he thought could be established in Theodulf's lifetime (1892:102–3), but there is not a great deal of bedrock in our information. It is especially the early years that remain unillumined and can only be accounted for hypothetically. Theodulf identifies himself as a Geta (Goth or Visigoth — 25.165) and refers to his native country as Hesperia, which may be understood as either Italy or Spain. A number of early investigators opted for Italy (notably Rzehulka 1875:1–8), but most critics now agree that it must have been Spain. De Riquer (1994:25) suggests that the use of Hesperia instead of Hispania may have been a matter of metrical convenience. There have also been voices that favored a birthplace in what is now southern France, Septimania or Aquitaine, but these voices have also died down. The choice of Spain rests to some extent on statements in the poems and most importantly on evidence deduced from Theodulf's theological treatise known as the *Libri Carolini* or the *Opus Caroli Regis contra Synodum*.

Alejandra de Riquer (1994:20–23) once more sifted the evidence of the poems carefully and concluded convincingly that, though nothing is certain, the relevant passages point overall in the direction of Spain. The most often cited of these passages is one in "Contra iudices" (28.137–40):

> Then, Narbonne, we reach your site and beautiful city,
> Where a joyful crowd presses forward to me;
> The remnants of the Gothic people and the Spanish population .
> [Hespera turba]
> Are overjoyed to see me as their countryman [consanguineus] and
> chargé d'affaires.

"Remnants of the Gothic people" (reliquiae Getici populi) would fit well with an immigration of Spaniards into Septimania in the period 778–82 (Freeman 1992:185; Dupont 1965). In his *carmen figuratum* (23.28) Theodulf refers to himself as "immensis casibus exul" (banished by enormous misfortunes). Freeman therefore surmises that he could have been one of these Spanish exiles and would have been recognized as such by his countrymen twenty years later when he returned to Narbonne as Charlemagne's *missus dominicus* in 798. Rouche (1979) provides a survey of the politically unstable situation before 780 in and around Narbonne before Frankish rule was imposed.

There are a certain number of references to "Hesperia" elsewhere in the poetry, but they do not seem to favor Spain over other areas. Theodulf is not as distinctively a Spaniard as Alcuin is an Englishman. On the other hand, there may be a certain Spanish bent in his reading. In his poem "On the Books that I Used to Read" (45.16) he addresses Prudentius as a kinsman (*parens*), and he is fond of citing Isidore of Seville (e.g., Fuhrmann 1980). Spanish origin is also supported by two verse epitaphs of unknown provenance printed in Dümmler's edition (*PLAC* 1: 443–44). The first states that Theodulf was born in Spain but "nurtured" in Gaul ("Protulit hunc Speria, Gallia sed nutriit"). According to the second he was born in "Hesperia" and is credited with words to the effect that, caught up by the sweetness of Charlemagne, he left fatherland, people, home, and hearth and spent many happy years in his service until his downfall under Louis the Pious.

Ann Freeman (1992:185; 1994:186), like Cuissard before her (1892:46), located Theodulf's birth and training in Zaragoza, which had been a significant center of learning as early as the seventh century (Orlandis 2003:304–12). Scholars have traditionally placed the poet's birth around 760, but, as de Riquer emphasizes (1994:14), the evidence is vague. It rests on a letter addressed to Theodulf by Alcuin in 801 (*Epistolae*, pp. 368–69), in which, among many flattering epithets, the recipient is assigned an "aetas florida" (blossoming age). One problem with this passage is that the compliments are so overwrought. Alcuin could be praising early maturity or persistent youth in advancing age. In other words, he could be suggesting an age of forty or fifty, though probably not thirty or sixty. The usual guess seems to be around forty, and that would square with a birth ca. 760. If Freeman is right to place him in the emigration from Zaragoza in 778–782, he would have been about twenty years of age. De Riquer (1994:28) pinpoints the importance of his age at the time of emigration and takes seriously the indication in the first epitaph telling us that Theodulf was "nurtured" in Gaul. She finds not unattractive an old surmise that he might have been a monk in Benedict's monastery at Aniane, where a substantial library may have been available.

The case against an education in Gaul lies in the extensive evidence accumulated by Ann Freeman (e.g., 2003:23–33) showing that Theodulf had very fully developed Spanish habits recorded in the Vatican manuscript of the *Libri Carolini*. Spanish liturgy, Spanish Bible redactions, and Spanish orthography appear to have been firmly implanted in his mind. That might consort better with an education completed in Spain rather than an education reformed in a Frankish monastery.

Cuissard (1892:102) was inclined to push Theodulf's chronology further back in time, assuming that he was born about 750. He thus places him in Lorsch as early as 774 (see the headnote to poem 49) and assumes he could have been a bishop as early as 881 (1892:64). But the more we retreat in time, the more difficult it becomes to account for his whereabouts and activity in the 770s. The first

Introduction 3

datable poem we have is the little epitaph for Queen Fastrada, who died in 794, but Schaller (1962:22) doubts that it was written by Theodulf. The next is the epitaph for Pope Hadrian from 795, but Charlemagne would not have commissioned it unless Theodulf already had a considerable reputation as a poet. He was clearly at the height of his poetic powers when he wrote "Ad Carolum regem" in 796 (with a reference to the submission of the Avars in 795) and, a couple of years later, his masterpiece "Contra iudices." His poetic apprenticeship must therefore go back to the 780s, but poets may have begun early in this period (e.g., Godman 1987:130) and there is no need to go farther back in time. That Theodulf had real ease in poetic composition is confirmed by a poem that he wrote to aspiring young poets (44.7).

If we adopt Ann Freeman's chronology and accept that Theodulf arrived in Septimania ca. 780, the mystery 70s in Cuissard's chronology evaporate, and we can theorize that Charlemagne recruited him not very long after his arrival, that is, not so many years after he had recruited Alcuin in Parma in 781 (on Alcuin in Parma see Bullough 2004:33–36). Also open to doubt is the date at which Theodulf became a bishop. Cuissard (1892:62–64) thought that he must already have been a bishop in order to command enough authority to compose his early admonition to the bishops ("Ad episcopos"); he therefore dates his episcopal dignity from 781, but we will see below (headnote to poems 1–2) that it is not certain that "Ad episcopos" is an early poem.

Others have thought that Theodulf must have been a bishop and participated in the discussion of Adoptionism at the Council of Frankfurt in 794. Bishop or not, it is plausible that he participated, but there is no documentation (de Riquer 1994:37). The first reference to Theodulf as bishop is in a letter of Alcuin's from July of 798 (*Epistolae*, ed. Dümmler, 243–44; trans. Allott 1974:95–96). The letter is addressed to Charlemagne and refers to Paulinus of Aquileia, Richbod of Trier, and Theodulf as bishops. Cuissard (1892:64–65) made a calculation that would suggest that Theodulf was also abbot in the monastery at Fleury a little east of Orléans from 801 to 821. De Riquer (1994:39–40; cf. Freeman and Meyvaert 2001:125 and note 9) pointed out that he was divested of his offices in 818 and therefore adjusted his abbacy back to 797/798 to 818. If abbacy and episcopate were coterminous, this would also provide the date at which he became bishop.

The years around 798 were thus pivotal. Theodulf had reached the culmination of his ecclesiastical career and had become Charlemagne's trusted adviser in theological matters. Ann Freeman's exacting researches have taught us that he was the chief author of the *Libri Carolini*, a treatise directed against the supposed iconodulism of the Second Council of Nicaea, which concluded in October of 787. Theodulf was engaged in the drafting of the Frankish opposition to the *Nicene Acts* in the years 791 to 794 (see especially Freeman 1985). The study of the *Libri Carolini* has in itself become a specialized subfield too complex to rehearse here (see Noble 2009). The debate over the last fifty years may be followed in Freeman's collected papers in the volume *Theodulf of Orléans: Charlemagne's Spokesman against the Second Council of Nicaea* (2003). Particularly helpful for the outsider is the initial paper (with Paul Meyvaert), a translation (or rather the English original) of the introduction to Freeman's new MGH edition of the *Libri Carolini* in 1998 (1–123).

From the mid-790s we also have a surprising amount of personal information about Theodulf. We know that he was at the center of Charlemagne's court life. He was well acquainted with all the leading figures of the realm, as we learn from his spicy panegyric "Ad Carolum regem" (poem 25), which can be dated to 796. Indeed, he must have known the courtiers very well because he could afford to engage in some rather audacious banter at their expense. An indication of the esteem in which he was held is his selection as a *missus dominicus* to the law courts of Provence in 798. The long poem (28) inspired by this journey not only provides interesting information on judicial matters but also gives a rare insight into Theodulf's personal life, where he was, what he was doing, and, above all, what he was thinking. If we had similar poems from the 780s, we would be wonderfully well informed.

That Theodulf continued to enjoy favor after the turn of the century is illustrated by a dispute between him and Alcuin ca. 801 (see Meens 2007 and Greeley 2006). A monk condemned and imprisoned in Orléans by Theodulf made good his escape and sought sanctuary with Alcuin in Tours. Theodulf sent men to recapture the fugitive, and the upshot was a riot involving both the monks and the citizenry of Tours. Both Theodulf and Alcuin appealed to Charlemagne, who came down decisively in favor of Theodulf. The matter is described at some length in Alcuin's letters (nos. 245–49, [392–401]; parts translated by Allott 1974:120–26), and Wallach (1959:103–40; also Werner 1990:38–39 and note 123) provided a legal analysis, which is now updated by Rob Meens (2007) in his thorough exposition of the case.

At about the same time a congratulatory letter from Alcuin to Theodulf (no. 225 [368]) indicates that the latter had risen to the rank of archbishop of Orléans (Wallach 1959:112; de Riquer 1994:42). We also know that Theodulf was apprised of the crisis pertaining to Pope Leo III in 799, an event to which Theodulf refers in poem 32. In the same letter in which Alcuin congratulates Theodulf on his appointment as archbishop he refers to a report that Theodulf had eloquently testified to the truth in a public meeting. De Riquer (1994:42) understands this to mean that Theodulf was present and active in the proceedings during which Charlemagne's mission in Rome reinstated Pope Leo in December of 800. Freeman and Meyvaert (2001:125–39) also assume that Theodulf was in attendance in Rome and found inspiration for his mosaic in the church of Germigny-des-Prés in the mosaics of Santa Maria Maggiore.

Between 800 and 818, at which time Theodulf was exiled, there are half a dozen poems connected with events in his life, but the information that can be deduced from them is quite problematical. In poem 30 Theodulf requests

Introduction 5

additional help from Benedict of Aniane, who apparently had already provided two monks to help with the restoration of the church of Micy (Germigny). The mission is specified in 30:5–8:

> Then return many thanks for the gift already given,
>> And eagerly pray that he be willing to send more,
> So that the pious work shall arise on the initial foundation,
>> Which already delights me, which my heart desires.

Cuissard devoted a chapter to this church in Germigny and recorded inscriptions preserved in earlier documents. One reads as follows (1892:119):

> Haec in honore dei Thedulfus templa sacravi,
>> Quae dum quisquis adis, oro, memento mei.

> I Theodulf dedicated this church in God's honor;
>> Whoever approaches it, I pray, be mindful of me.

The church had already succumbed to fire in the ninth century and fell into ruin at an early date. In the modern reconstruction the only remnant of Theodulf's renovation is a remarkable mosaic above the altar in the apse. It may be viewed in the richly illustrated anthology of Carolingian art and architecture in Hubert, Porcher, and Volbach (1970:12–13) or in the plates and figures of Freeman and Meyvaert in "The Meaning of Theodulf's Apse Mosaic" (2001).

The mosaic is referred to in another inscription recorded by Cuissard (1892:120):

> Oraculum sanctum et Cherubim hic aspice spectans,
>> Et testamenti en micat arca Dei.
> Haec cernens precibusque studens pulsare Tonantem
>> Theodulfum votis jungito, quaeso, tuis.

> Gaze here at the holy sanctuary and Cherubim,
>> Lo, the ark of the witness of God shines bright.
> Viewing this and eagerly besieging God with prayers,
>> Join Theodulf to your prayers, I entreat.

Freeman found a precursor of the mosaic's design in the *Libri Carolini* (1957:700–01), Meyvaert elaborated the point (1979:52–56), and both together provided a full account (2001:125–39). As a result there appears to be a close link between Theodulf's thinking and the mosaic in the church at Germigny. Yet another inscription provides a date (Cuissard 1892:123):

ANNO: INCARNATIONIS:DOMINI: DCCC: ET VI

6   *Introduction*

The added "VI" struck Cuissard as peculiar, however, and he apparently did not credit it. Paul Meyvaert showed how justified Cuissard's suspicions were (2001; repr. 2008:12–13). The dates of Theodulf's restoration, and therefore the date of his poem, are consequently uncertain (see also Shaffer 2006 and Treffort 2007).

Poem 33 is addressed to Abbot Fardulf, about whom a few things are known (see the headnote to 33). He died in 806 and Theodulf's poem must therefore be earlier. Poem 34 "That Power Is Reluctantly Shared" has attracted a good deal of interest because it is so overtly political. It has been associated both with the "Divisio Regnorum" of 806, in which Charlemagne contemplated a division of the realm among his three sons, and Louis the Pious's "Ordinatio Imperii" of 817, which favored his eldest son Lothar. In the former case Theodulf's strong advocacy of a unified realm would seem to run against imperial policy; in the latter case it would seem to support imperial policy. Peter Godman (1987:97–100) therefore thought it more likely that the poem was in the spirit of the "Ordinatio Imperii" of 817 and designed to elicit Louis' favor. It would indeed require a strong argument to convince us that Theodulf took the initiative in opposing Charlemagne in 806.

The following poem (35) in praise of Charlemagne's eldest son Charles has also been assigned political importance because it could have led to Theodulf's dissension with Louis the Pious after Charles died in 811. But there is little doubt that Theodulf did his best to please Louis when the time came, and poem 37, a celebration of Louis, would be an important link in that effort if it was really composed by Theodulf. Both Schaller (1962:28–29) and Alexandrenko (1971:180) thought it probably was not Theodulf's work and was more likely written by his successor in Orléans, Jonas. If so, it does not describe a visit made by Louis in Orléans in 814, as Alexandrenko argues, but rather a later visit in 818 when Theodulf had already been deposed. On the other hand, de Riquer (1994:48) did not hesitate to attribute the poem to Theodulf. Whatever the answer, the poem is peculiarly general and impersonal. The remaining poems, classified as "Personal and Miscellaneous," are of considerable interest but shed no light on the chronology of Theodulf's life.

We pick up the trail again in "The Exile Poems." The last note before Theodulf's exile is an entry in the Astronomer's *Life of Louis the Pious* (364–66) to the effect that Theodulf accompanied the new pope Stephen IV to Rheims in 816:

> The emperor had learned of his [the pope's] arrival in advance and commanded his nephew Bernard to accompany him. As the pope approached, he [Louis] sent other delegates to accompany him with the requisite honor, while he decided to await his arrival in Rheims. He dispatched to him Hildebald, the chief chaplain of the holy palace, Theodulf the bishop of Orléans, John of Arles, and a host of other servants of the church in full priestly regalia.

Introduction   7

Such august company certainly suggests that Theodulf still enjoyed the emperor's full favor in the summer or fall of 816. But Cuissard (1892:93; cf. Schaller 1992b:116) speculated that this mission was the beginning of Theodulf's downfall. His hypothesis was that the meeting with Bernard led to a warm affection that was the first step in Theodulf's embracing of Bernard's cause.

Bernard did indeed suffer an unhappy fate. Thegan (210–12) tells the story as follows:

> In the same year Bernard, Pippin's son by a concubine, incited by evil men, rose against his uncle and wished to exclude him from rule, for he had wicked counselors on all sides. When the lord emperor heard of this, he came from the palace in Aachen to the town of Chalon-sur-Saône where Bernard together with his wicked counselors made his way to him, and they were taken into custody. At the same place the emperor celebrated Christmas. From there he returned to his seat in Aachen and after Easter held a great assembly and investigated all the most wicked conspiracies of people involved in this matter. Some were found to have fallen into this rebellion, both among the Franks and the Langobards; all of them were condemned to death except the bishops, who confessed and were subsequently deposed. These were Anselm of Milan, Wolfhold of Cremona, and Theodulf of Orléans. The death penalty meted out to the others the emperor did not wish to impose, but his counselors deprived Bernard of his eyes . . . . On the third day after the loss of his eyes Bernard died.

The Astronomer gives largely the same account, including Theodulf's participation, but in somewhat greater detail (380–86). On the basis of these chronicles and the very specific inclusion of Theodulf among the conspirators, it is not surprising that Bernard's revolt has been used to explain Theodulf's fall from favor and exile, though his actual guilt is an open question. Indeed, Theodulf protests his innocence in a poem to Bishop Aiulf of Bourges (71) and, most vigorously, in a poem to Bishop Modoin of Autun (72). Rzehulka (1875:53–57) argued strongly against Theodulf's guilt and Peter Godman (1987:101–5) made an ingenious and challenging case for believing that he was as innocent as he claimed and was the victim of unidentified detractors hinted at in 71.85. Godman (1987:97; see also Werner 1990:39, 46–47 and Fried 1990:253) suggests that Count Matfrid in Orléans, who might have profited from Theodulf's demise, could have been the leader of these detractors. Modoin (73.109) refers to Matfrid in his reply to Theodulf, and Godman takes this to be an effort at conciliation (1987:104).

Matfrid had figured prominently in the discussion of Theodulf's deposition before Godman. Elisabeth Dahlhaus-Berg (1975:17–19) argued that he moved against Theodulf for territorial gain and that his move was characteristic of tensions between secular and ecclesiastical lords in the ninth century. Thomas F. X. Noble (1981:32), on the other hand, found this argument to be a case of *post hoc ergo propter hoc*; the fact that Matfrid later acquired Theodulf's properties, presumably from Louis after Theodulf's exile, cannot be used to show that Matfrid had always had designs on these properties. Noble finds it more likely that Theodulf's adamant poem on the indivisibility of the realm was tantamount to a case of disloyalty since the "Ordinatio Imperii" was a carefully crafted compromise between the unity and divisibility of the realm. He speculates that, though the poem was written in 806 on the occasion of Charlemagne's "Divisio Regnorum," Theodulf may have produced another poem or equivalent document in the same vein in 817 and thus have provoked Louis' ire. But if we judge it unlikely that Theodulf would have stood in overt opposition to Charlemagne in 806, we must consider it equally unlikely that he would have opposed Louis in 817, especially because he would perhaps have been on a less secure footing with the new emperor than he had been with Charlemagne. What Dahlhaus-Berg, Noble, and Godman may well have established is that Theodulf's participation in Bernard's rebellion is too simple a solution for Theodulf's exile. On the face of it, rebellion seems to be an unlikely move on Theodulf's part, and, as a result, the mystery has only deepened.

The uncertainty persists in his last years. Theodulf may have redacted the acts of the Council of Châlons in 813 (Meens 2007). Apart from the legend that he sang the hymn "Gloria, laus" at an open window in Louis' hearing and was released (see the headnote to poem 69), there has been uncertainty about his location. It was generally assumed that he spent his exile years in Angers, where he seems to have composed "Gloria, laus," but Schaller published a paper (1992a:91–101) pointing out that the way he describes his situation at the intersection of the rivers Huisne and Sarthe in 72.121–122 places him rather in Le Mans. We are not even sure of his death date; Cuissard (1892:99–100) located two necrologies, one recording his death on 18 September, 821, and another on 10 October 821. Theodulf's birth and death are thus both clouded in some obscurity. Consequently we are largely dependent on what Ann Freeman has extracted from the *Libri Carolini* and what the poems tell us. There are doubts about the authenticity of some poems, which were published by Jacques Sirmond in 1646 from a manuscript that is now lost. Thanks, however, to the philological labors of Dieter Schaller (1962) the larger number can confidently be attributed to Theodulf. These poems were carefully translated into English prose by Nikolai Alexandrenko in an unpublished Tulane dissertation with very full bibliography in 1971, but because his work remained unpublished, it has been unknown to many scholars and presumably even less known to other readers. The present volume tries to make a readable English version available to a larger audience.

For practical purposes Theodulf's body of verse has been sorted into six groups:

1. religious and moral poems
2. historical poems
3. poems attached to historical events

Introduction 9

4. personal and miscellaneous poems
5. exile poems
6. poems of doubtful attribution

This arrangement follows exactly what the reader will find in Ernst Dümmler's MGH edition of 1881 — which gives most, but not all, of the biblical and classical references — and thus ensures that there will be no difficulty in locating the original texts. On the other hand, the grouping is misleading in some ways. For example, some of the "historical poems" are no less focused on moral and religious issues (e.g., 28 and 29) than the poems in the first group, although they happen to have a historical context. Nor are the "personal and miscellaneous poems" any more personal than the historical and exile poems. Other groupings are therefore just as good. For example, Alejandra de Riquer (1994:70–75) settled on the following categories:

1. poems on ethical and Christian themes
2. social and political poems
3. panegyrics
4. epitaphs and inscriptions
5. fables and tales
6. iconographic poems
7. personal poems

But neither our six categories nor de Riquer's seven are adequate to suggest the variety in Theodulf's production. The following eighteen subdivisions might come closer to a proper differentiation, but eighteen is a distinctly unwieldy number:

1. social and religious critiques 1, 2, 28, 29
2. religious poems 3, 9, 11, 13, 18, 19, 20, 54
3. moral poems 4, 6, 7, 10, 17, 22, 67
4. paraphrases 5, 8, 15
5. allegories 12, 16, 45, 46, 47
6. elegy 14
7. personal communications 21, 30, 33, 43, 44, 53, 71, 72
8. *carmen figuratum* 23
9. epitaphs 24, 26, 40
10. panegyrics 25, 31, 32, 35, 37, 39, 70
11. diatribe 27
12. *facetiae* 33ii and iii, 50, 51, 52, 57, 72ii, iii, iv
13. political poem 34
14. prefaces 36, 41
15. hagiography 38
16. inscriptions 42, 56, 58, 59, 60, 61, 62, 63, 64, 65
17. travelogues 28, 48, 49
18. hymns 55, 68, 69

This grouping, though more differentiated, may not be much less misleading because the long poems in particular combine several types. It also fails to indicate how Theodulf's interests are weighted. The most numerous group is assembled under "inscriptions" (ten in number), but these poems are among the shortest and are in some cases quite trivial. On the other hand, the social and religious critiques, with only four examples (1, 2, 28, 29), amount to an aggregate of 1634 verses, rather more than a third of Theodulf's output. They are also the poems with the greatest weight and moral thrust, so that a reading of Theodulf might well begin with them.

These poems also show Theodulf at his most virtuoso. "Contra iudices" (28) in particular runs a gamut from light-hearted satire on bribery, to a colorful account of Theodulf's mission to southern France in Charlemagne's employ, to a lampooning of judicial practices, to an early example of the *memento mori*, and finally to a powerful critique of capital justice and an equally powerful denunciation of the exploitation of the poor by the rich. This all-embracing variety of tones and types makes it quite pointless to categorize the poem under a single heading. It is indeed the multiplicity of registers and themes that contributes significantly to Theodulf's special standing among the Carolingian poets. He exhibits more energy, more innovation, even more whimsy than his brother poets either in his own generation or the next. One consequence is that it is sometimes difficult to pinpoint the precise tonality that he intends. This is true, for example, of the little episodes that are classed here as *facetiae*. Are they just entertaining anecdotes or do they have a covert agendum? Theodulf toys with his readers to an extent not matched among his contemporaries.

Although Theodulf was a bishop not only by appointment but clearly also by inclination, as his "Ad episcopos" and his capitularies illustrate, he cannot be defined as a primarily religious poet. Only eight of the seventy or so poems reasonably ascribed to him are classified here as religious. To these should no doubt be added three paraphrases of Scripture (5, 8, 15), five allegories (12, 16, 45–47), one poem about Saint Quentin (38), and three loosely defined hymns (55, 68–69). The religious total might therefore be twenty, leaving another fifty or so to be classified differently. These fifty can, however, by no means be lumped as secular.

It is one of the salient features of Theodulf's verse that religious and secular issues are constantly intermingled. Theodulf's dominant concern is with social values, and in his age such values could not be separated from the religious framework. In this sense all his poems are religious in nature, but what may strike the modern reader is the frequency with which Theodulf focuses on issues that we consider to be primarily social or institutional. Thus the anger and pride condemned in the first poem are, to be sure, cardinal sins, but they are just as surely aspects of social behavior. The admonition of bishops in the second poem focuses to some extent on religious deficiencies, but it is also a critique of an administrative class. The admonition of judges in "Contra iudices" (28) identifies no lack of personal foibles in the judges themselves, but it is more largely

Introduction 11

directed against the defects in the judicial system. Thus the major poems take aim at major problems in the fabric of governance.

This orientation is not confined to the major poems. The attack on pride in the first poem (vv. 167–168, 185–186, 239–240) is a wider concern, for example in 2.249–250. It culminates in a long diatribe in "Contra iudices" (28.457–516) and echoes in the late epistle to Bishop Aiulf (71.48–49):

> No matter how high you are, remember to be correspondingly humble,
>> So that by the sweet grace of exalted God you may be enriched.

Nor is the concern with justice limited to the full-scale treatment in "Contra iudices." It recurs in 36.23–26, 45.23 and 27, 46.53–56, and 71.83–86. It also figures in larger terms in Theodulf's preoccupation with the apparent problem that the unjust fare well in this life, a problem to which he adverts twice (poems 8 and 13). Closely allied with the issue of justice is the more purely secular concern with honesty. The theme is sounded in 2.153:

> Let the deeds of faith be manifest and those of probity honest.

A full admonition is found in 4.15–20 with scriptural support in Leviticus 19:36 and Proverbs 11:1:

> "Let your measure be not deceptive, nor your scale wicked,"
>> Let it be pure in mind and honest, and matching in words.
> Let your peck be just and your pint in order
>> So that we will not suffer deceit.
> To God false representations are always displeasing,
>> The just Judge loves a just and straightforward heart.

Poem 6 as a whole comes to grips with several forms of dishonesty, again with a basis in Scripture (Proverbs 6:16–19), and poem 12.37–38 concludes with a broad condemnation of dishonesty (*improbitas*). Poem 17 elects to flag its critique of modern times with a prefatory condemnation (17.1–4):

> Feigned virtue prospers, true virtue declines to no purpose;
>> The latter stood tall, the former, groaning, seeks the depths.
> For as true probity avails, feigned honesty will injure;
>> One is ready to counsel, the other eager to deceive.

"Contra iudices" also begins with an imperative to avoid crooked ways. Poem 46.41–42 provides Lady Ethica with a branch from which to preside over honest norms, and in the poem to Bishop Aiulf Theodulf twice adverts to the value of honesty (71.21 and 56).

Also verging on the secular sphere is an emphasis on and advocacy of kindness. Christ is established near the outset of the collection (9.1–4) as the quintessence of kindness and responsiveness, and this model is always near the surface in Theodulf's verse. At the conclusion of poem 13 God is depicted as the perfect balance between justice and kindness, and in "Contra iudices" Theodulf sums up the priorities in a particularly telling distich addressed to the judges (28.845–846):

> Let judgment come first, kindness [*pietas*] come second, bribes come never
>> In the judicial process, where Christ is also at hand.

But even this injunction, though explicit, yields to a more powerful formulation in Theodulf's reprise of the judicial issues in the following poem (29.61–66):

> But with limbs stretched on the wood of the cross, the Creator
>> Drove out the old wrongs with new light.
> He judged kindly that the body of the robber should remain living
>> And that crime should pass away through remorse,
> That dire crime should not avenge crime nor evil avenge evil,
>> Nor does the Lord compel reciprocal wounds.

The modern world did not begin to catch up with Theodulf's teaching until the last decades of the twentieth century, and then not fully (Megivern 1997).

That kindness was also the rule in Theodulf's social and personal dealings is indicated by the inscription on his throne. Here he admonishes himself (62.6):

> Address those standing about with kindly speech.

"Sweet words" are accordingly recommended to Bishop Aiulf as well (71.55). The social implications of kindness are realized on a grand scale at the end of "Contra iudices," where Theodulf appears to have reached his goal but cannot refrain from adding an eloquent plea on behalf of the poor (28.887–954). The message is condensed in several pointed distichs (28.893–894, 935–936, 942–943):

> You who are charged with the poor, be gentle;
>> You will know that you are their equal in kind.

> Be not violent to the poor but all the kinder,
>> For their prayers are possibly better than yours.

> For if your mercy does not raise a poor man,
>> When you ask for mercy yourself, you will be denied.

It is clear that there is an important instructive component in Theodulf's verse. The long poem of which "Ad episcopos" is a part and the 956 verses of "Contra iudices" are sometimes given the label "paraenesis" to underline their admonitory

Introduction 13

nature. The same exhortatory mission emerges in Theodulf's capitularies and theological writings as well. It was his obligation to teach in his capacity as bishop, and he seems to have embraced this responsibility (Brommer 1974:57–62). Traces of this proclivity can be found here and there in his verse, where women as well as men are encouraged in the pursuit of learning. Queen Liutgard, for example, is not relegated to household administration (25.89–90):

> She attends studiously to the business of learning
>   And absorbs noble arts in the vault of the mind.

But, like everyone else, she must be subordinated to Charlemagne himself (25.113–114):

> Should she ask that the crossroads of Scripture lie open,
>   Let the king be her teacher, whom God himself taught.

Earlier in the poem (25.21–26) the king is credited with wisdom wider than the Nile, the Danube, the Euphrates, and the Ganges, but we must bear in mind that hyperbolic praise of Charlemagne's learning was part of Carolingian court idiom.

In poem 43 the mysterious Gisla, who is presented with a double psalter, is urged to read them "with studious and assiduous spirit" and extract from them their significance (43.9–10). In his poem about a waning interest in versifying Theodulf urges younger aspiring poets to learn so that they may be held to be learned (44.19). In 2.269–276 he addresses a bishop's obligation to teach, and in poem 10 he fulminates at some length against those who are inaccessible to learning (10.3–4):

> In whomever it is vain to instill teaching,
>   The more you teach him, the greater fool he will be.

The fullest statement on learning and teaching may be found in the verse epistle to Bishop Aiulf, whom Theodulf remembers as an exceptionally promising boy, now mature and ready to take on the task of transmitting his knowledge (71.13–16):

> Now your task is to transmit holy teaching
>   And to inculcate in the people holy laws.
> You who once sipped cups from the grammatical fountain
>   Now excellently moisten minds with ambrosial dew.

Theodulf reinforces the message in 71.43–44 but catches himself in schoolmasterly mode and mocks himself with the words (71.58): "I have now become like a teacher in school."

This ironizing at his own expense is indicative of a certain self-awareness in Theodulf. His authority does not cross the line into preachy postures. On the contrary, he is at pains to be moderate. In poem 5, for example, he urges his readers to care for the poor, but at the same time he advises (5.9–10): "disdain not your own requirements, / for you share the same state." In poem 19 he singles out Jesus's mild reproval of the woman taken in adultery in John 8:11 as a model of enlightenment. The major statement on moderation, however, is "Contra iudices," in which Theodulf recommends cautious speed (28.611–614), non-threatening discipline (28.639–645), and, above all, a restrained and proportionate hand in meting out penalties (28.857–864).

Although many of the emphases in Theodulf's verse can be seen as matters of social policy, the underlying outlook remains religious. This may be seen most clearly in the constant reminders that our goal is heaven and that this goal should guide our actions. Theodulf, who is adept at rounding off poems, chooses as his most frequent summation the wish that the recipient of his poem may have a smooth transition to the next life (e.g., 20.4, 26.31–38, 31.21–22, 35.35–36, 40.22, 44.25–26 and 30, 46.45–46, 50.16, and 71.98). As so often, "Contra iudices" contributes disproportionately to this theme. The trajectory toward heaven serves as a kind of epigraph (28.1–4):

> Magistrates, choose the road of just judgment,
> And may your feet disdain crooked ways.
> One road leads to heaven, the latter drags down to the shadows,
> Pious life follows the former, for the latter death waits.

Theodulf goes on to wax eloquent on the delights of heaven (28.9–24) and returns to the promise of heavenly rewards later in the poem, celebrating our spiritual ascent (28.555–588). The rise to heaven is ubiquitous in the poems, but the alternative must also be kept in mind. It is remarkable, however, how lightly the alternative is touched on. There is no fire and brimstone and only two traces of the blazing inferno of Christian tradition. Poem 11 on the wounds of Christ suggests (11.38) that those responsible for Christ's crucifixion "will justly suffer a fiery fate," and the four-line "De contemptu mundi" (20.1–2) counterposes "the perpetual fires with which the Creator / justly threatens" to the rewards of heaven. Otherwise Theodulf neutralizes the eternal fires by substituting the shades of the classical underworld, most often Styx (1.102, 7.3–4, 8.16, 17.101, 28.6) but also Acheron (28.5–6), Avernus (1.189, 7.3–4), Cocytus (28.6 and 85–87), Phlegethon (11.3, 28.85–87), and Tartarus (1.243, 21.81). That Theodulf chooses to minimize and classicize hellfire in this way surely belongs in the context of his general taste for moderation and his urging of a proportionate penal code. There is no trace of a hectoring or browbeating tone. Censure is directed not at the people but at the clergy and officials. Nor are the people admonished to obey their superiors; on the contrary, Theodulf seems to suggest a direct and personal relationship between the individual and God. The relationship surfaces particularly in "Contra iudices," with its repeated reminders that God sees all

Introduction   15

things (28.46, 339–342, 779–780, 789, 90, 835–836). This warning is echoed in 17.43–44 and 60.5–6 and is spelled out most explicitly in 28.339–342:

> Consider, for the Lord on high observes you from heaven,
>   And will note all you do with divine mind,
> He who is judge and witness at once, and avenger of evil,
>   Who rewards worthy action with good, and evil with ill.

The compact is not with any arm of the state, civil or ecclesiastical, but between the individual Christian and God.

What emerges from this sketch of Theodulf's poetic personality is a devout servant of the church but also a man of active social conscience, as much a moralist as an ecclesiastic (Raby 1957:1:187; Weinberger 1982:276). He values justice, honest dealing, duty, and personal relations, and he has a pronounced streak of moderation. And yet what readers who have a passing acquaintance with him may remember most vividly is his departure from these values in his tirades against his colleague Cadac-Andreas in "Ad Carolum regem" and "Ad Corvinianum." That he taxes his victim with not being able to pronounce Latin might be allowed to pass as no more damaging than Heinrich Heine's notorious accusation, in the early nineteenth century, that Hans Ferdinand Massmann knew no Latin, but the ensuing heaping of invectives goes beyond the limits of a witticism. This anomaly is all the more striking because of Theodulf's eloquent critique of anger in his first poem, reinforced by a comment in his second capitulary (ed. Brommer 1984:177: "For anger that remains in the heart and generates hate and craves vengeance is considered to be among the chief sins."). We might suppose that humor was perhaps broader in the eighth century than it is now, but there is a good deal of poetry from the period and no indication that this was the case. We must perhaps conclude that Theodulf, like many of us, could now and then fly into a rage, but unlike most he had a gift with words that allowed him to dramatize his anger in a particularly memorable way.

Religious and Moral Poems

Poems 1–2

The poems numbered I. ("Fragmentum de vitiis capitalibus") and II. ("Ad episcopos") in Dümmler's edition are parts of a longer poem in four books pertaining to ecclesiastical matters. I. is part of the third book on the cardinal sins (drawing on Prudentius: see O'Sullivan 2004:6–20) and II. appears to be the complete fourth book, which is cast as an admonition (sometimes titled "paraenesis") to the bishops. We have 314 lines of the first book, dealing fully only with acedia (*tristitia*, vv. 1–44), anger (*ira*, vv. 53–167), and pride (*superbia*, vv. 168–254). In the lost portion Theodulf seems to have dealt with gluttony, lust, avarice, and envy, which he lists in verses 265–266. If he dealt with these at the same length as acedia, anger, and pride, the whole book would have numbered rather more than 600 verses, but he may have been briefer on some sins. Hagen (1882:XI) surmised that some 400 verses were missing from the third book. At the beginning of the fourth book (vv. 7–10) Theodulf tells us that the first book was about faith and the second book about how faith should be practiced and about heaven and hell. It is not possible to estimate the total length accurately, but since the 594 extant verses are probably less than half the poem, we can readily imagine a total of 1500 verses or more, that is, easily the longest of Theodulf's poems.

The treatment of *tristitia* and *ira* distinguishes between a destructive form and a more benign form. Thus *tristitia* is, with the support of the Bible, preferable to frivolous merriment (vv. 1–14), but there is another exaggerated and damaging variety resulting in mental confusion or delusion (vv. 15–20), and yet a third variety fomented by *ira* (vv. 21–38) and leading to helpless disorientation. To combat these effects Theodulf recommends conversation with benevolent brothers, prayer, and the reading of Scripture (vv. 39–52). The treatment of *ira* is structured in a similar way, but it begins with wrath in its worst form (vv. 53–87), which, like acedia, culminates in a sort of mental breakdown. There is, however, a lesser wrath (*ira levis*, v. 98), *zelus* or zeal (v. 91), which is tantamount to justifiable indignation and can serve to combat evil as long as it does not degenerate into hateful fury (*ira gravis*, v. 100). The remedies against *ira* are fraternal affection and, above all, patience (vv. 117–166). The chief sin is pride (*superbia*, v. 167), which is not given the benefit of greater and lesser degrees. It can only be countered by emulating the humility of Christ (vv. 245–250). Theodulf also includes a reminiscence of Ovid's *Metamorphoses* (Lendinara 1998:177).

Book 4 begins with a summary of what has gone before and then takes the form of a personified letter apostrophized by the poet and ordered to appear before the bishops, one of Theodulf's favorite conceits. The letter is charged to pay obeisance to the bishops in the form of personal attentions, a parody of the services showered on a lady by her wooer in the Roman circus in Ovid's *Ars Amandi* (2.35–52). When the book turns serious, it pinpoints the failings of bishops who advocate one thing in words but conduct themselves in quite a different way (vv. 75–120). Theodulf is nonetheless careful (or diplomatic enough) to distinguish between good bishops and bad (vv. 121–140). The former are duly praised (vv. 141–166) and only the latter are excoriated (vv. 167–200). Book 4 concludes with an emphasis on the role of bishops as teachers, with Moses as the great prototype.

Dümmler placed these fragments at the beginning of his collection, believing that they date from Theodulf's youthful period. This belief seems to have been based to a large extent on his reading of verse 31 in the fourth book: "Although I am an insignificant part in the great priestly crowd, etc." Dümmler added a footnote to this effect: "He indicates that when he wrote this he was no more than a deacon or a cleric of inferior rank. Therefore he excuses himself, given his rank, for daring to admonish the bishops." But this reading has been challenged, for example by Elisabeth Dahlhaus-Berg (1975:183). She believes that the "clerical crowd" refers not to the hierarchy to which Theodulf is immediately connected but rather to the great panoply of priests throughout the centuries. She would rather place the poem in the context of Theodulf's other long hortatory poem "Contra iudices" (or "Paraenesis ad iudices") from around 800 (number 28 in Dümmler's edition).

This contextualization is reinforced by the fact that there are more motival reminiscences of "Contra iudices" in the "Fragmentum" and "Ad episcopos" than in any other of Theodulf's poems. We may note the following: Moses as key figure (28.27–32, 387–388; 2.225–234), the image of medical healing (28.75, 354–356; 1.289–294), a fringe bordering a robe (28.83; 2.40), references to the church as mother (28.109; 2.147); the image of a siege engine breaking down the spirit (28.169; 1.150), vacuity compared to empty winds (28.310; 2.103), the avoidance of food and drink (28.399–410; 2.89–92), lust tied to eating and drinking (28.411–412; 1.265), the avoidance of proud behavior (28.457–480; 1.173–204), the fall of Satan (28.465, 489–492; 1.241–244), clouds receding before the sun (28.504; 1.42), the superiority of spirit over body (28.566–567; 2.74). These echoes might suggest that the poems are also adjacent in time.

Placing the "Fragmentum" and "Ad episcopos" late rather than early would also serve to alleviate certain other anomalies. We would not have to believe that Theodulf began his poetic career with his magnum opus. We would not have to believe that he took it on himself as a young priest to lecture senior bishops, not

Religious and Moral Poems 19

only to lecture them but to lampoon them with a satirical edge borrowed from Ovid's *Ars Amandi*. We may prefer to associate Theodulf's satirical vein with his court poetry, particularly the "Ad Carolum regem" (number 25) probably from 794. "Ad episcopos" seems a better fit in this later period.

1. Fragmentum de vitiis capitalibus (Fragment on the Mortal Sins)

———

To prepare the devotion of a contrite heart for God.
Therefore this sadness is bound by law and flourishes by reason;
    It prepares great joys for holy minds.
"Blessed," said the Lord, "are you who weep in the present,
    For later you will have great joy."[1]
The heart of the wise man resides where there is great sadness,[2]
    Said the sage, and the foolish surely where there is joy.
Truly the glorious apostle has stated: "Be downcast
10   And give yourself over to plaints and tears.[3]
Let your laughter beget grief and and joy beget mourning."
    Imparting this, he gave holy advice.
Who will be able to compass all those things in his own writings
    That holy Scripture relates here and there on this theme?
Another form of sadness born of madness and mental confusion
    Is injurious dullness in the absence of wit:
This sadness does not purge the mind but disturbs it with wicked gyration;
    The mind that it muddles it cannot make clear.
This sadness is fostered by fear, it is born of desperation
20   Which nurses it with a flow of black milk.
A third evil aspect of sadness arises from abominable anger,
    Which even passing ills are apt to incite,
When the mind succumbs to ardent desire or apprehension,
    Or all unaware is carried off by blind burning desire.
It is often so blinded by disordered fury
    That it knows not what it says or does.
It suffers grief with no harm and mourns without reason,
    Dark clouds of error envelop its core.
Now sleep subdues it, now dull silence grips it,
30   It walks abroad and naps, murmurs or is mute.

———

[1] Luke 6:21; Matthew 5:5
[2] Ecclesiastes 7:5
[3] James 4:9

The man sits idly by and slumbers with eyes wide open;
    Saying nothing, he thinks he says much.
He is slow to action, absent of mind, of dull recollection;
    Nothing is fixed in his mind or conveyed in speech.
Like a ship at sea with no helmsman
    He has no certain course but wanders aimlessly on the deep.
Thus the spirit oppressed by the black gloom of sadness
    Drifts hither and thither through the seas of the mind.
In many exchanges with his brothers this illness decreases,
40   The assiduous devotion to prayer drives it out.
Speech also puts it to flight, and the reading of Scripture,
    The dark cloud flees the brightness of the sun.
The sickly repugnance of such vice will have no endurance
    If by the hand of these assembled virtues it is bestirred.
As wax melts in fire and ice in the sunlight,
    A trace of liquid in fire and fire in a stream,
Just so do the disquieting dangers of wasting disease
    Succumb completely to the power of good.
If reason animates, harmonizes, and adorns the spirit,
50   Then the diabolical monsters of the vices take to their heels.
In the members of our body our substance is lifeless,
    But in reason it thrives, for there is the image of God.
Furious wrath hot with foaming jaws pursues us,
    Rolls blood-red eyes that are gory with noxious bane.
To wrath was entrusted the fierce scourge of Bellona,
    With which she incites minds to cruel strife.
Putting comrades at odds, to both sides she hands weapons,
    With which she bitterly stifles the gift of peace.
In the process atrocious crime thrives and discord increases,
60   And sweet fraternal love in evil expires.
Thus savage nurture is given to bloody transgressions
    So that all manner of crime advances in force.
With this legion on the march the battle line of virtues weakens
    And the holy commandments of God lose effect.
These are known to inhabit only the mind that is peaceful
    And have no place at all where black fury abides.
Law observes the irascible man, but for the law he is sightless;
    It desires to take vengeance, but he wanders feckless and blind.
With fury at hand, modesty, peace, and devotion vanish;
70   It throws all goodness out of the stronghold of the mind.
As the dark clashing of winds heaves the waves of the waters
    And does not allow its elements to be still,

Religious and Moral Poems

Or as the calm grove is shaken by zephyr and east wind,
    And the trees whistle and the beaten trunks fall,
Just so does perfidious wrath stir human perceptions,
    Nor, wretched as it is, does it allow hearts to be still.
Its madness plunges minds headlong
    And keeps them from staying intact.
It cuts off the senses, not unlike brains in frenzy,
80   Maliciously preventing the victim from knowing what he does or says.
Thus spite covers the face and trembling dashes the members,
    The eyes shine more fiercely than the Gorgon's fire.
He growls, flails with hands, and rampages,
    He can no longer recall what he did.
Raving, he joins the Stygian choruses of Furies
    And madly joins the maidens of Phlegethon.
Wrath is alien to heavenly choruses, where Christ is ruler,
    Where the warrior gains great rewards for his deeds,
Where joyous peace, great love, blessed order prevail,
90   Where the holy citadel shines with ethereal domes.
But there is zeal too, such as is judged to be prudent anger
    When it is shown to support what is right.
Through it there is constant resistance to sinister evil;
    Struck down by its impact, evil is put to flight.
It is evil to nourish sin and worthy to resist it.
    The wrathful man repels vices, while the slothful man gives them force.
But if a zealous man wishes that a corrigible man be
    Subject to improvement, his ire will remain mild.
If good things dismay and the worst things give pleasure,
100   This kind of ire will be grave and exceedingly harsh.
It sinks in the foul pit of ill-disposed hatred
    That leads miserable men to the Stygian depths.
For ire is hate when it remains of long standing;
    Evil does not learn from evil but leads from bad to worse.
"You see," said the Lord, "a mote in the eye of your brother,[1]
    But you fail to see the beam in your own."[2]
Mild anger is the mote, a beam is inordinate hatred,
    The one passes quickly, the latter stays and weighs down.
One sounds a light note, the other oppresses the spirit;
110   The former seeks correction, the latter death too.
A frivolous mind creates wrath, wrath fosters dire hatred;
    A thistle begins as a blade, then is heavy with spikes.

---

[1] Matthew 7:3
[2] Luke 6:41

From careless speech flow crimes, momentous and dismal,
From a smooth egg is hatched a fierce snake.
Thus bad seeds long nurtured do damage,
But nipped in the bud, no longer do harm.
If there is love among brothers, it does not breed fury,
And if wrath is absent, no hatred remains.
This sin is tempered by the virtue of reason,
120 The love of justice treads sin, head and face, under foot.
Modest patience destroys this threatening misdeed;
She is the guardian of good and the destroyer of ill.
As mother, nurse, and able defender of virtues,
Patience prevails ably, it nurtures and helps in their midst.
It knows how to break the savage barbs of vices
And it crushes frightful weapons with its own.
Faith is the shield, hope the breastplate, where love is the helmet,[1]
On which the sword of dashed steel expires,
Which rebounds from impact, with its edge blunted,
130 The fierce sword lies shivered in pieces and parts.
The greater the blow, the greater the fragmentation,
And the farther the scattered pieces fly off.
After man forewent the joys of life immortal
The bitter blight of a miserable death took hold,
And until man returns to his previous essence,
We are always beset on all sides by fear and travail,
For which reason your powers restore us, beneficent patience,
And we are a throng protected by your arms.
Patience conferred lofty solace on all the blessed,
140 To whom a revered city was given so that they might be safe,
Whose sum the brevity of this poem forbids us to number,
Who patiently earned heaven's reward.
Among these Job was her most faithful companion;
The power of faith inhered in him as a peer.
The virtues flourished in him, and abundant possessions,
He stood out in distinction with all his goods,
Blessed with children, home, herds, and a crowd of servants,
And that which is greater than these, the law and fear of God.
But the inimical foe at close range directs darts against him,
150 And the battering ram strikes the wall of his mind.
Despoiled, with everything lost in an instant,
He ceased being a father, ceased being a lord.

---

[1] Ephesians 6:16

Religious and Moral Poems   23

Prosperity fled him, the benevolent gifts of good fortune,
 Of all he might bear or possess only illness remains.
In place of servants mere worms, for possessions was left only squalor,
 For offspring a dung heap, for raiment mere rags.
Torments oppress him, his wife's curses afflict him,
 His defenses suffer the darts of his friends.
Mindful of original crime, through the mouth of his helpmeet
160 You believed you could reduce this man like Adam of old.
But reason comes to his aid and so does mother patience;
 By virtue of these two his mind was in a safe port.
Whom prosperity made just, adversity made patient,
 On the one hand he gathers goods, on the other he undoes sin.
On whom reason bestows a helmet, to him a shield is provided by patience,
 With which your fury may be abated, O wrath.
On the heels of these sins vicious pride follows,
 Mother and queen of evil, leader and origin of guile.
She gives sustenance to all vices,
170 For without her no man can sin.
Still she rises divided in duple bisection,
 A single two-headed thing is twofold.
The first, overt pride, is a malignant infection,
 A second the empty evil of capricious praise.
Whether her sister, granddaughter, or daughter,
 A single menacing nature belongs to both.
O boasting, a fourfold vainglory prospers in you;
 Black at heart, you inflict blows in four spheres.
Some get a gift, but the crowd, not knowing the giver,
180 Refuses to render due thanks to God.
There are those who devise for themselves marks of merit
 And ascribe gifts only to them, not to God.
But others can claim no gift, nor will ever be able to do so,
 Though in their vain hearts they imagine they do.
Greater pride, I think, has no man than the person
 Who believes that only he is able or eligible.
An angel once fell, thinking himself to be lofty,[1]
 The only one mastering power and light.
In place of a cloudless heaven he gained gloomy Avernus,
190 Estranged from angelic honor he was doomed.
Swollen pride is torn in three portions,
 As three-headed Cerberus devours with three maws.

---

[1] Isaiah 14:12–15

Now the first of these is legal transgression,
    Which marks arrogance toward the law.
Law is abandoned as often as it is resisted;
    A man sins when doing what it forbids.
Thus pride is the beginning of sin according to Scripture,[1]
    Without pride no one can neglect the commandments of God.
What law prescribes let them do, and avoid what is foreign,
200   Then all dreaded works will be shunned.
Others affect to disdain all their fellows
    And think that what they have they alone own.
In another group of those to whom the maintenance of law is entrusted
    Pride causes the inflation of arrogant hearts even more.
Where humility is called for, they strive to be haughty
    And they give a high price for great sin.
You, O Pharisee, are guilty of this in the sanctum of the holy temple,[2]
    And, alas, many proceed in this way.
As the treasure remains safely secured with the wise keeper,
210   So a humble mind conserves all that is good.
Third is the group with inflated habits of thinking,
    Whom the pride of mounting ambition lifts high.
They disdain to submit to just supervision
    And are zealous in scorning the words and deeds of their spiritual
    guides.
Because they refuse the company of honest behavior,
    They become a crowd teaching what is false.
They know not their own ignorance because they think they're
    enlightened;
    Thus wandering wits drive them out of control.
One thing all arrogant men have in common:
220   They always think themselves of great worth;
They never give assent to the words of their brothers
    And they think they speak better than anyone else;
They rely on their own minds and perceptions, not others',
    And disregard the support of better advice.
Trumpeting false praise in their own interest
    And despising the words and deeds of other men,
Despising their peers, their inferiors, and their betters,
    They believe that nothing is equal to them and theirs.
They manage nothing with quiet reason, and thus pursuing
230   Devious byways they have lost the straight path.

---

[1] Ecclesiasticus 10:14–15

[2] Luke 18:11

Religious and Moral Poems

But the healing of God cures wicked diseases
    And causes agreeable health to return.
While the spirit fears to forego the light of the virtues
    And fears to be cloaked in the evil blackness of sin,
Your illness, O vanity, is expelled in a moment
    And vainglory does not besmirch the pure heart.
Fear bars the sickly contagions of illness,
    The sharp broom drives out dirt from the house.
And you, arrogant filth and fickle fury, are banished
240   By the example of the humble King and his love,
And fear of the angel's tumble from the citadel of heaven,[1]
    From whence the wretch with a swollen heart fell below
Uttering arrogant words, plunged into Tartarus from heaven.
    He is now an odious demon who was angel before.
But the humble Lord from the ethereal city
    Joins the terrestrial hosts to the dwellers above.
Let the race of men take an example from his dark downfall
    And be soothed by the ascent of the redeeming Lord.
The soaring mind of man falls, and the humble mind rises;
250   The closer to earth, the closer it is to bliss.
By descending it advances, ascending it is subject to falling;
    All things go in order and by degrees.
All things are determined by higher judgment,
    Which brings low the ambitious and raises the meek.[2]
You, O Muse, who have wandered a little through the meadows of vices,
    Call a halt at the end of this moderate book.
With the ravaging of these seven Satan wreaked devastation,
    And with them he conquered the earth.
With these vices the fierce foe held captive all people
260   And with these arms he brought them to heel.
As the wicked one overcame the first forebear,
    He then took up arms against the whole race.
With the arms used to subdue him with wicked malice
    He now heinously strives to master his heirs.
There is voracious gluttony, followed by foul adultery,
    The deceit of avarice and envy's crime,
The inertness of acedia, the sickness of furious anger,
    And in command of these looms pestilent pride.
But God brought arms against these specters,
270   With which their work may be wisely annulled.

---

[1] Isaiah 14:12–15
[2] Luke 1:52; cf. James 4:6, 1 Peter 5:5

Thus the wise healer takes up arms against illness
    Of various kinds, so that sweet health may be restored,
Neutralizing coldness with heat, moisture with dryness,
    Softness with hardness, smoothness with a rough counterpart.
Devout fasting counters the foul greed of gluttony,
    Which besets, impels, and controls the mortal race.
The maiden modesty, adorned with brilliant beauty,
    Extinguishes your flames, O baleful lust.
The blessed practice of giving counteracts avarice
280   When the generous hand does piety's work.
The love of the Lord and the brethren overcomes envy,
    And through its practice the works of envy decline.
Fraternal converse puts to flight slothful acedia, as do
    Devotion to prayer or reading holy words.
Safe and moderate patience suppresses dire anger
    And blunts its savage spears.
Inflated pride is allayed by Christ's example;
    Fear of judgment and gentle love dissolve its effect.
Thus the healer often heals by opposing prescriptions,
290   Often restores to health by applying contrary means.
He frequently also cures by applying similar healing,
    Brought to bear on wounds by a gentle hand,
Applying to long wounds long plasters, to round wounds circular plasters,
    And adjusting these plasters to fit the wound.
The tree of Eden brought death, with the wood of the cross life was replen-
    ished;
    Death was brought on by taste, life by the honor of the cross.
A maiden of old brought death, a new Virgin salvation,
    The former by persuading her husband, the new one by bearing God.
The woman of old brings death to the man, the new one announces the Savior,
300   To his pious disciples and, lo, that he lives.[1]
The speaking serpent brought illness, the one overhanging healing;[2]
    The scaly and monstrous serpent does one thing, the bronze snake
    the reverse.
Food gave death, but it also gives life's renewal;
    Once wicked Eve bestowed it, now you provide it, powerful Christ.
The rod became a serpent and was then reinstated,[3]
    Christ succumbs to death, then returns to life.

---

[1] John 20:18
[2] Numbers 21:9
[3] Exodus 4:2–4

Religious and Moral Poems

The rod signifies power, the serpent is fatal;
 Each succeeds the other just as it should.
Power divides the earth and works fearful wonders,
310 Power that you, great Moses, retain in the "type" of your law;
Fit to convey the "figura" of death is the serpent,
 For through him accursed death supervenes.
O Muse, you who have wandered a bit through the meadows of vices,
 It is time to bring your steps to a halt with this end.

2. Ad episcopos
(To the Bishops)

Follow, fourth book, on the heels of the three now completed,
 Go where the brothers gone before you call.
He who gives words to the mute and steps to the crippled,
 Who lent them support, ask that he help you here.
In those books general teaching was conveyed for all people,
 But this book is intended expressly for you.
The first book underpins holy religion
 And matters by which is known highest faith.
The second relates briefly how it should be practiced,
10 What place is prepared for the wicked and which for the good.
The third book explains the war to be waged against horrid opponents,
 And it arms allies to the extent that it can.
The groundwork of faith, the growth of the work of salvation,
 These books set out, and assign pious laws to their place.
They oppose vices, arm the citizens with virtues,
 Order the city with arms, laws, and faith.
You yourself should summon priests to our bastions,
 Their devoted service should be in your care.
Remember to lead the way and kneel before them
20 And that you may be blessed make humble request.
When received by holy hands and warm welcome,
 Prepare to plant kisses on countenance and neck.
Having once bestowed kisses, beg for mutual kisses,
 And declare that you have something to say.
When license to speak has been granted,
 Excuse the writer to the extent that you can,
Because I take up this matter with no rash ambition,
 Nor does a presumptuous mind urge my work.
Nor do I aspire to be a teacher of our holy bishops,
30 Whose life is the measure of salvation to me.

Although I am insignificant in the great crowd of clerics,
    I yearn to help the fathers in any way that I can.
I, who with true devotion wish, am accustomed, and am desirous
    To serve them humbly and assist them with zeal.
That the father's chair may stand straight on the ground, and the cushion
    in order,
    Is my concern, that it may be well adjusted for prayers;
That the linen should properly cover the shins, feet, and ankles,
    To which should be added a good pair of boots.
Alert to pour water on his hands and carry his towels
40   When he is unkempt; we attach long borders to the robes,
So that, with the wrinkles smoothed out, the tunic shines brightly
    And the light fringe does not fall askew.
I strive that pallium and cloak hang well and neatly
    And a hand with great care addresses his head.
There is work for the fingers, to remove any defilement,
    And with his feet washed, the father's lower reaches shine too.
If wax or oil from a lit lamp spills over,
    Let it be expunged from the clothing by hand.
If perspiration appears on the brow, we wipe it,
50   If dust stains the clothing, off it is flicked.
To ward off the cold we wrap the feet warmly,
    The breeze of a fan dispels the heat.
"If a blind man tries," said the Lord, "to lead a blind man,
    Both will fall together into the ditch."[1]
The wicked and unenlightened should both be excluded,
    For one does evil, the other ignores holy words.
A single guide by both afflictions is often obstructed
    If he can really be called a guide:
He who sets bad examples and who fails to help with instruction,
60   By which neither his own nor any mind can be ruled.
Holy Isaiah reproves the unenlightened guide as follows,
    Intoning the holy words of the Lord:
"The shepherds themselves do not know you, O wisdom,
    An assembly of watchmen deprived of light and blind,
All of whom are gravely afflicted by being unknowing,
    A pack of dogs without the power to bark."[2]
O, outrage and great crime when he who is destined
    To be the norm of salvation becomes the conduit and leader of sin.

---

[1] Luke 6:39
[2] Isaiah 56:10

Religious and Moral Poems 29

However many have perished by his example,
70   He himself, I think, will pay for all their evil deeds.
Guiltier is he than the thief, more than the black-hearted bandit,
      For he injures minds more than material things.
The former seizes material goods, the latter destroys the inner person,
      For who will deny that the spirit is superior to the flesh?
There are those who teach right, but by doing evil
      They destroy in deed what they foster in words.
By perverse deeds they contradict themselves wildly,
      Their mouths condemn the evils of which they are guilty in fact.
They help others but refuse their own rescue,
80   They are alive for others but are death to themselves.
They admonish others what to be but are themselves mindless;
      Being a lamp to others, you become ash to yourselves.
It is a sorry method for driving out evils;
      None can do right while carrying out wrongs.
In what way, I ask, can filth be cleansed by the filthy?
      How can a man in deep sleep be on guard?
What prostrate man can contrive to raise those who are supine,
      And how can a wounded man set about doctoring wounds?
A bishop ceases to restrain people from a gluttonous belly
90   If he himself is swollen by delicacies.
He can hardly forbid wine if he swills it freely,
      "Be sober" are not the words of a drunk.[1]
A man cannot denounce vices to which he is subject,
      A man unfamiliar with virtues does not smooth their path.
A man given to avarice is not improved by the words of another
      Who is bound by the cramped hand of that plague.
He will not loose the biting knots of hatred
      Whose mind harbors the evil monsters of hate.
He cannot instill quiet peace in the people
100   Who is not bound to the people by peace,
With what arms will he be able to break the goads of anger
      Whom ghastly wrath has enslaved?
Can one calm the vacuous wind that vain pride elicits
      If one is oneself beset by its blasts?
In what way can one inspire contempt for the world?
      Unless one disdains it, one will in turn be disdained.
When human favor has trained a man to flatter the mighty,
      How will he advise judges to maintain the law?

---

[1] 1 Peter 5:8

How can he say that the poor should be protected by the law of devotion
110   If he afflicts them with whatever afflictions he commands?
Whomever boasting draws up on a rope to the high heavens
      The plague of ambition will plummet to earth.
A boastful man will hardly restrain the boaster,
      Nor can he tell anyone not to aspire.
How will he declare that the great judgment should be dreaded,
      Which, alas, he himself perchance does not fear?
The man whose tongue has been restricted by the curb of his own misdeeds
      Is silent about the evils of others lest he hear of his own.
He does not inspire to good deeds that he has not accomplished,
120   Nor does he inhibit ill deeds of which he is guilty himself.
While I write on the lives of wicked bishops
      Or confer honor on the pious or on you, my Muse,
I do not burn lilies with overgrown nettles,
      Nor, O fierce thorns, do I burn the crops with your weeds.
Soft crops are mixed with the harsh in agreeable meadows,
      The field bears noxious seeds along with the sweet.
In the loveliest garden redolent with herbs aromatic
      Your fragrance, O hemlock, is often conveyed.
For that evil is mixed with good, and good with evil,
130   Who will deny or in doubt disbelieve?
For the Lord commands that the garden be weeded and proper,
      Free of ill plant life until it matures.[1]
Young goats stay in Christ's pen with lambs gentle in nature.
      The right hand awaits the pious, the sinners are culled by the left.[2]
Mystical nets caught all types of fishes.
      The good are taken and thrive, the bad are thrown back and die.
What the field of the church, the pen, and nets gather,
      Why should this poem not undertake to embrace?
Why should it not strive to depict the mores
140   Of all, intending to filter their ways?
The outstanding vestment of the church shone brightly,
      The church provided allurements to the sight of men.
But let the adornments of virtue give you honor,
      You should favor the eyes of the heart as you can.
Surpassing reverence was in sacred religion
      And honor in the vestments of ecclesiastical wealth.
In holy mother church is joined for you holy reverence,
      And in the zeal and pious deeds of your life.

---

[1] Matthew 13:30
[2] Matthew 25:33–41

Religious and Moral Poems

Gold leaf encircled the forehead of the high priest,[1]
150   By which a fourfold crown gave a lordly name.
But let the forehead of your mind be encircled with kindness,
    And let your voice sound the name of Christ with scriptural words.
Let the deeds of faith, integrity, and justice be manifest,
    And may the order of four virtues be yours.
They observe at close hand the deeds of all people,
    As the attentive shepherd is wont to inspect his fold.
Thus they love the good and profess that by law they should be held in
    affection,
    And those they thus strengthen they call to higher things.
By contrast those whom the huge weight of sin burdens,
160   These they are able to lighten however they can.
But if they cannot relieve them of the burden of vices,
    They urge them patiently to bear them and to persist.
In whatever way life or patience profits,
    While they improve some, they brace to endure the rest.
These men are blessed, but, O, how they differ from the others
    Who breathlessly pursue their rewards, not the Lord's.
The men who refuse to be beneficial only strive for advancement:
    The latter sleep at the task, the former hold vigilant watch.
Those whom the fierce sins of people never sadden
170   Will not be cheered by the goodness achieved by their flock.
As they never deplore that their crimes will adhere to the wicked,
    This crowd will never gladden [others] by encouraging them.
He who strives to be richer, refusing to be more religious,
    Gains the rewards of war but shuns the actual fray.
Not the work, alas, but the wealth, not onus but honor attracts him;
    Splitting what is well joined, he clings to one, rejecting its mate.
In seeking only what is good for themselves, not the people,
    They seek only to be called shepherds, not to serve.
They have no thought of grazing or guarding the sheep herd
180   But have their eyes fixed on what can be gained.
I am mistaken if this is not said by the excellent prophet
    When he declares with divine words:
"Wicked, alas, are the shepherds of Israel[2]
    When they provide food for themselves and none for the flock,
For the flock offered milk as nourishment for your consumption,
    And your woolen clothing was shorn from its backs.

---

[1] Exodus 28:36
[2] Ezekiel 34:2–6

If it was fat, a ravening crowd devoured it,
　　But your labor did not strengthen the weak.
You applied no cures to the sickly livestock,
190　　And your hand did not mend what was undone.
No one attempted to return a lost sheep to the fold,
　　And you took no care to seek out those that were lost.
You imposed harsh rule with malevolent measures.
　　And to your flock you were a powerful mob to be feared.
The herds of my bleating sheep therefore are scattered,
　　For there was hardly a shepherd to look to their care.
The fury of predatory beasts devours them,
　　They become prey for the monsters that roam in the fields."
With the dire weight of sins not yet lifted
200　　They sought out the place for profitable gain,
Those who cannot precede their subjects on the path of the righteous
　　And to whom the right way is not well known.
In what way, I ask, can anyone guide his companions,
　　Not knowing the way that he takes?
If it is hot, we seek shade, if frosty, a fireplace;
　　In whatever way I am able I can strive to help.
Who will refuse to adorn with words the spirit of his master,
　　Whose body our hands adorn with attire?
Why will I not undertake to offer clean living
210　　If even now I do not tolerate the stains his clothing reveals?
Why will I not choose to facilitate life eternal
　　When now I can provide so much ease?
The people should submit to the church in all matters,
　　Which the people must exalt at all times,
Which is their honor and splendor, founder and guardian,
　　Following the twelve names of great men.
The stout order of columns is itself fixed in the Savior,
　　Of whom the diligent crowd is duly in awe.
The shining gate is his heavenly station,
220　　Through which he who wishes enters joyfully to approach Christ.
Those to whom is given the care of governing the spiritual person,
　　To whom are allotted the people, carry great weights,
As well as those who offer prayers for the sins of the people
　　And deplore sins of others mixed with their own.
They turn the wrath of the great Judge away from the people,
　　A task carried out by Moses and his kin.
This noble choir reveals His will and conveys it,
　　With whose guidance devout people ascend to the heavenly heights;

Religious and Moral Poems   *33*

The defender of truth and the foe of false teaching
230   Declares and maintains truth, expels and drives out what is wrong.
By their guidance the people perceive what is evil, what they must shrink
          from,
        Also what is good and honeyed within.
Guardian of the oppressed people, kindhearted avenger,
        He is called father by the whole Catholic Church.
They promise the high rewards of the light-flooded kingdom,
        Where the angelic choir and the crowd of church fathers reside.
It is won by the holy warrior, taking up arms and striving,
        Triumphing over the dread foe, he flies up on high.
Performing good deeds, they give proof of good labors
240   And become a good measure and an honor for the people of God.
Here is the assemblage of priests with kindly keys of admission,
        Who both lock and unlock and bind and unbind.[1]
Dispensing holy religion of the highest Ruler,
        The dutiful assemblage shines in their ranks.
Not ambition but the glory of life propelled them
        To the more exalted place of the highest seat.
The wings of human favor did not guide them,
        But, beneficent God, your generosity raised them aloft.
Those who do not applaud themselves for their high position
250   Are possessed by a humble and pious mind.
Honor conferred does not inflate these minds with vain bluster
        But the lordly weight of an imposed yoke weighs them down.
Their minds are not occupied by distinction but by burdens,
        Not by how high is their honor but how weighty their task.
Thus a horse fitted with magnificent trappings and adornments
        Groans when his rider applies the spurs.
If goodness is apparent and hypocrisy is absent,
        It is well when a man offers to follow a lead.
For the Redeemer commanded that men observe your example
260   So that they may glorify the Father on high.[2]
As a resplendent crown once covered his forehead,
        So may law and piety envelop your mind.
The mind is the stronghold of the soul; if it clings to the love
        Of the Creator, what greater thing has a man?
In the soul the image of divine goodness is patent,
        And in holy morals, if the spirit is well aligned.

---

[1] Matthew 16:19
[2] Matthew 5:16

If we may take an example from minor matters,
　　In this way does a little ring fix an image on wax.
Let the teaching of mystery be a prized obligation,
270　　That the authority of your limited power may adopt.
If many things are dangerous when revealed to the uneducated,
　　Many others do harm if not properly set out.
Thus a food that is harmful to some helps others;
　　There is a time and order for each, and appropriate sites.
May circumspection in teaching gird your tunic,
　　And may the multi-colored ephod of virtues be above.[1]
Let the gentle cloak be pure, devoid of all cunning,
　　And let it be varied with the good the virtues commend,
For David, the most holy hero, urges[2]
280　　That the priests may don the pious vestments of the just.

Poems 3–20

Charles Cuissard (1892:6) echoes a reviewer of his predecessor Louis Baunard in criticizing a lack of chronological sequence in the poems and tries to remedy the lack by discussing the poems chronologically. The result, however, is that Cuissard foregrounds the historical poems, in which a dating is possible, and neglects the religious poems, in which there are very few dating indices. Dümmler (1881:444–45) noted that he places the poems from Theodulf's time as deacon first, followed by the poems that show no dating criteria but seem, with respect to subject and style, to belong to the same period. This ordering seems to have led Manitius (1911:540) to the view that Theodulf's early poems were characterized by seriousness. If the parody of Ovid in "Ad episcopos" is early, however, it certainly mitigates the serious tone. On the other hand, a clustering of the moral and scriptural poems in the early period could persuade us that Theodulf began by establishing his ecclesiastical credentials, a not unreasonable approach for a young cleric. There is a good deal of translation from the Bible in these poems, and we could also surmise that he is honing his skills through the exercise of translation, but we cannot exclude the possibility that such poems were scattered throughout his career.

　　Poem 3 is a short but elegant statement on God's sharing his goodness in the form of grace, without which nothing can be accomplished. Poem 4 partakes more of Theodulf's trenchant style and wishes suitable rewards for the hypocrites who think one thing but say another. Poem 5 paraphrases Isaiah but illustrates some of Theodulf's central themes in the long "Contra iudices," for

---

[1] Exodus 25:7, 28:6, 39:2
[2] Psalm 132:9

Religious and Moral Poems   35

example his concern for feeding and sheltering the poor. It is also indicative of his moderate stance and eagerness to harmonize extremes: "Clothe the naked and disdain not your own requirements, / For you share the same state." Poem 6 returns to the assault on hypocrisy, but, based on Proverbs 6:16–19, it condemns a broader range of sins.

Poem 7 belongs to a different type altogether and is a cross between ostentatious learning and a satire of learning. It is nominally aimed at the greedy man who can never accumulate enough wealth, but that is merely a pretext for a catalogue poem on all the known ends of the earth and the riches they produce. Cataloguing is a favored device in Theodulf's verse and is just as likely to be late as early. Poem 8 (misnumbered 7 in Dümmler's edition) is pure paraphrase in three parts. The title suggests that it is about the anomaly that wicked people are prosperous, but in fact there are distinct variations.

The first part from Psalm 144:7–15 catalogues the manifestations of prosperity and happiness but concludes with a line stating that the only true happiness is devotion to God. The second part from Jeremiah 12:1 asserts that such happiness is an illusion because God sees all, and prosperity will evaporate at the last judgment. The third part from Job 21:13 is very much in the same vein, listing the apparent benefits of false prosperity but holding out the prospect of doom in the next life. Poem 9 is a succinct admonition to love and fear God.

From here Dümmler's order moves on to a number of mid-sized poems. Number 10 is directed against deceitful people who remain incorrigible and impervious to instruction. Teaching, and therefore also the inability to learn, is a theme in Theodulf's verse and can be found not only in the concluding lines of "Ad episcopos" but elsewhere as well. In his late exile poem to Modoin Theodulf suggests that his only consolation is teaching and conducting services (72.19). Number 11 is a commentary on Luke 24:39–40 and John 20:25–29, explaining why Christ's wounds were still visible to his disciples. As Alexandrenko points out (1971:89), the poem was translated by Helen Waddell, who ranked it at the apex of Carolingian poetry (1947:21–22). Theodulf provides a fourfold explanation: 1. The visible marks confirm the mystery to the apostles, 2. they are a constant reminder of Christ's human suffering on our behalf, 3. they make palpable that Christ's death assured life everlasting for humans, and 4. that the wounds keep ever present our mistreatment of Christ, so that anything short of worshipful devotion will entail eternal damnation. Freeman and Meyvaert (2001:134–35) connected this poem with the picture in Theodulf's apse mosaic of Germigny of a hand possibly showing a wound, and Meyvaert and Davril (2003) demonstrated in what detail Theodulf borrowed his motifs from Bede's *Commentary on Luke* and his homily 2.9. See also Shaffer 2006 and Treffort 2007 on this building.

Number 12 on faith, hope, and charity develops Luke 11.11–12 allegorically: "What father among you, if his son asked for a fish, would hand him a snake? Or if he asked for an egg, hand him a scorpion?" Theodulf states that substituting a stone for bread would betoken a heart of stone, not charity. The fish represents faith, and the substitution of a serpent death. The egg signifies hope because it promises a chick, but the scorpion is disabling despair. Without all three we are condemned to grief. Number 13 deals with the apparent injustice entailed in the success of the wicked and the failure of the good. Theodulf argues that the perfect alignment of success with the good and failure with the wicked would foreclose the function of the last judgment. Divine judgment can never be unjust, merely deferred.

Number 14 on the unreliability of the seasons, the failure of the earth's cultivation, and the decline of human values as indications that the end is near is sometimes connected with Theodulf's despair in exile (Baunard 1860:316–17; Cuissard 1892:98), but this may be a case of forcing a standard elegy into a biographical frame. Number 15 returns to the paraphrase style of 8 and provides a free rendering of 2 Corinthians 6, prefaced by a praise of Saint Paul. Number 16 on the parable of the sower in Matthew 13 is once more allegorical rather than periphrastic. It interprets the thirty-fold yield as marriage, the sixty-fold yield as widowhood, and the hundred-fold yield as virginity. These associations are found in Saint Jerome's letter 123 (*PL* 22.1052). Of special interest is the rendering of numbers with finger signs; on this tradition the reader may consult Umiker-Sebeok and Sebeok (1987), Williams and Williams (1995:esp. 588), and Bruce (2007:esp. 56).

Number 17 is a longer poem of 110 verses, though it is incomplete at the end and may have been considerably longer. It is a sharp attack on present-day deceit and hypocrisy in contrast to the honesty of old; the acerbic tone may be sampled in vv. 15–24. The style is reminiscent of the critique of bishops in "Ad episcopos," and if that poem belongs in the period around 800, this one may also belong in the same context. Theodulf's three orders are not the same as those in Duby 1980 (and cf. *PL* 105.280C-282D, "De omnibus ordinibus hujus saeculi"). Number 18 is a rather awkward poem on Christ's role in remedying Antichrist and the time of Antichrist. The awkwardness is not surprising given the dearth of specifics on this matter, but the poem ends with a very precise calculation of the duration of Antichrist's onset extracted from Daniel and Revelation (see Alexandrenko 1971:111). Number 19 is also a curious poem on the aid afforded the interpreter of Scripture by the specification of time, place, or season. Thus Jesus's coming from the Mount of Olives (John 8:1) and his gentle chiding of an adulteress makes the Mount of Olives an allegory of mercy, that he comes at dawn signals a new light, and so forth. The final piece (20) is a four-line poem on the unimportance of this life and the paramount promise of a heavenly reward.

Religious and Moral Poems　　　　　　　　　　　　　　　　　　　　　*37*

3.　　**De gratia dei**
　　　　(On God's Grace)

So great is the goodness of God that edifies and adorns us who are feeble
　　　That he transfers his merits into our own;
And whatever accrues from grace, without which nothing good is accomplished,
　　　Let these things be counted among our own gifts.
In devotion he gives good will and its fulfillment,
　　　Here he leads the way and there his work follows us.
Hence a beginning is made, and thence completion should follow,
　　　An offering in every respect is pleasing to God.
For the goodness conferred by himself, he mercifully proffers prizes,
10　　　Provided our effort harmonizes with him.

4.　　**De his qui aliud corde retinent, aliud ore premunt**
　　　　(On Those Who Guard One Thing in Their Hearts and Say
　　　　Another)

An evil person pays no heed to the words of the excellent psalmist
　　　When he wishes to be set apart from such men:
"Do not lump me," he said, "along with the sinner,[1]
　　　Nor condemn me with those who always do ill.
Their confidant hears peaceful pronouncements,
　　　But in their hearts lurk savage thoughts.
Give them, O God, just rewards for their actions,
　　　According to their dire connivances with sin.
May their wishes be aligned with their conduct,
10　　　And I pray that they may receive commensurate rewards.
Because they did not know the work or the holy deeds of the Master,
　　　Destroy them, do not build them up."
The excellent judgment of sacred law enjoins this
　　　When the terrible voice sounds such words:
"Let your measure be not deceptive, nor your scale wicked,"[2]
　　　Let there be pure honesty in mind and word.
"Let your peck be just and your pint be in order[3]
　　　So that we will not suffer deceit."
To God false representations are always displeasing,
20　　　The honest judge loves a just and straightforward heart.

---

[1] Psalm 28:3–5
[2] Leviticus 19:36
[3] Proverbs 11:1

5. Quale ieiunium et quae parsimonia Deo acceptabilis sit et possit impetrare postulata
(What Fasting and What Frugality Are Acceptable to God and Can Obtain What is Asked)

For God the King himself approves in the words of the great prophet
 That holy fasting is accepted by him.
"Loose the bonds," he said, "of wicked irreverence,[1]
 Loosen the burdens that often press hard.
Allow the man to go free who was formerly fettered,
 And may your whole burden now be laid down."
For the man who hungers disdain not a shared portion,[2]
 May the homeless and poor be brought to your house.
Clothe the naked and disdain not your own requirements,
10 For you share the same state.
Then, as in the morning, the glory of your light emerges,
 And swiftly your certain salvation appears.
The pious laws of the Lord precede you
 And the holy glory of God imposes constraint.
Then when you ask, the devotion of the dear Lord will hear you,
 He will tell you, 'I am here when you call'."

6. Contra simulatores et subdolos
(Against the Hypocrites and Deceivers)

You hold nothing fixed but convert all things to fictions,
 O hypocrite, you who only feign the semblance of good.
He who commits certain evil or feigned goodness is wicked,
 He who hates what God loves and loves what God hates.
"Those things that God hates," said the wise king, "are six in number;
 The seventh is what his mind detests:[3]
Eyes fixed on high, the words of mendacious language,
 The hands by which flows innocent blood,
The unclean heart visited by evil intentions,
10 The wicked feet hastening to sin,
The deceitful witness speaking wild falsehoods,
 And the man who sows dire strife among kin."
Of all these, the mad and dishonest man is, was, and will be guilty;
 His mind is full to o'erflowing with infamous acts.

---

[1] Isaiah 58:6–9
[2] cf. Isaiah 58:7
[3] Proverbs 6:16–19

Religious and Moral Poems

7. De eo quod avarus adglomeratis diversis opibus satiari nequit (About the Fact that a Grasping Man Cannot Be Satisfied by Any Agglomeration of Various Riches [Ecclesiastes 5:9])

Whatever the world, filled with various nations, possesses,
    It would never be enough for him, were it all his.
The man greedy for grasping is ever a sinkhole,
    And the foul chasms of Styx cannot be filled.
Not what Chryse and Argyra and the land of Ceylon hold,
    The riches of which are said to be huge.
Not what gem-rich India boasts, with spices and ivory objects,
    Nor the region of Ophir rich in precious metal and refined gold.[1]
If Assyria full of fragrant balsam is added
10   And Persia itself brings her wealth.
If distant Sheba were near with her incense
    And the Arab of Arabia Felix brought gifts,
And if Baghdad, loaded with Agarenian goods, were added
    And the city raised high in Persian lands;
What the Tigris and Euphrates hold, and also the Jordan,
    And what the blessed fields of Palestine bring forth,
Whatever things of beauty Bactria has, whatever worth Hyrcania may
    dispose of,
    And the teams that the Bosphoran plow guides,
What the Asian oceans convey and the Caspian regions,
20   And what the Chinese, rich in fleece, own,
What the cruel Scythian, the fierce Geta and tough Sarmatian,
    Whatever the Hydaspes has, whatever, O Araxes, is yours,
Whatever the wild Gelonian or the Rhodopeian Hebrus have in assets
    And the fields always cloaked in Riphaean frost,
And what the Hyperborean people dwelling under the Great Bear
    Or the Don or the Black Sea or the Danube display,
What the flowing-haired Dane loves, and the flaxen Swabian,
    Or the people residing in the far north,
Or what the Hungarian, the Dacian, the Thracian, Athenian, Arcadian
    assemble,
30   Or whatever in your city, O Constantine, thrives;
What wise Greece produces, or powerful Germany,
    What the misformed Avar or Pannonian Gepid have,
And that city long ago promised to the blessed fathers,
    Whatever Jerusalem, dear to God, boasts,

---

[1] 2 Chronicles 9:10; 1 Kings 10:11

What is peculiar to those people burned by Pelusian vapors,
    What the black Troglodyte, what the Ethiopian has,
If the whole dark troop of the Ethiopians contribute,
    And the people residing under the sign of the Crab,
What the tribes of nomads and what your realms hold, Jugurtha,
40   What coastal areas reap and African fields bear,
What the Libyan orbit and the Mauritanian earth abound in,
    Or the place of Antaeus [Libya] or the gardens of the Hesperides,
What their country affords to the fortunate Galauli,
    Whose island brings forth multiple wealth,
Whatever the hot shore of the Atlantic Moor can muster,
    And your people, if familiar with your source, O Nile,
Whatever Latium or fertile Calabria,
    The Veneti and Ligurians and pleasant fields of the Po,
And the city formerly sworn to the devil and now yours, our Savior,
50   What the joyful capital of the world and the church have,
A city disdaining the walls sprinkled with brotherly bloodshed,
    Which now seeks out heavenly realms and flees pagan fanes,
And does not worship the man nursed by a wolf, but the son of the Virgin,
    And stands gloriously fixed in apostolic might;
What wealthy Gaul and fair Spain engender,
    Whatever Cordoba, rich in possessions, owns,
What Britain boasts and what Ireland raises,
    And, if anything useful, whatever Thule might bear,
And whatever goods formidable Asturias may offer,
60   Who is the pride of the Hesperides, a warrior mighty in arms,
And if the tiller of Galician soil should visit,
    Who confers on his neighbors his beautiful goods;
If all these, gathered together at once, were given,
    Still his grasping hand would be less than content.

8.   De eo quod plerumque reprobis prospera sunt (About the Fact that False People Often Prosper)

"Pluck me from all the waters," said David in prayer,
    "From your strange hand, harsh sons.[1]
Those who are madly given to false prating,
    Their right hands are the right hands of wrong.
As the new planting of their children blossoms
    That quickened from the day of its delicate seed,

---

[1] Psalm 144:7–15

Religious and Moral Poems

On every side and ubiquitously the girls are fit and embellished
  Like the courtly splendor of God's illustrious hall.
In one and the other the pantries are full to o'erflowing
10   And delight with wine and plentiful stores.
The artless and prolific sheep wander hither and thither
  With the fattened bodies of bovine stock.
No wall shows signs of present ruin,
  Nor does any passing vexation affect their affairs.
This is a cause for many to say that people are happy,
  But he is blessed for whom the Lord God is king."

ii. De eadem re in Hieremia
(Concerning the Same Matter in Jeremiah)

Jeremiah delights to have addressed God with these prayers
  And, with respect to these matters, to speak these words:
"O most just Guide, why does the way of sinners prosper?[1]
  For all are well off who commit all manner of wrong.
The people planted by you grow from a fair inception,
  And they ripen the fruit on their own.
With false speech you are close to their language,
  Though you are far from the workings of their minds.
To you, exalted God, to whom all that is hidden lies open,
10   They appear transparently to your eye.
Gather them as a flock that is an offering to you,
  Sanctifying them justly at the time of their death."

iii. De eadem re in Iob
(Concerning the Same Matter in Job)

Job too, your warrior, O Patience, professes,
  And casts the matter thus in his book:
"Why does the company of evildoers live in splendor?[2]
  Why, O Treasure, are they consoled by your wealth?
Their unspeakable seed remains in their circle,
  A crowd of relations surrounds them on all sides.
They preside over safe and sturdy houses,
  And your rod, Lord God, is not a threat.
Their cows give birth and are not subject to harmful miscarriage,
10   Nor is the heifer deprived of her calf.

---

[1] Jeremiah 12:1
[2] Job 21:7–13

A little crowd joins the moderate family
    Delighting in various pastimes and games.
Indeed they hold tambourines in their hands, and sonorous cithers,
    And the sound of an organ gives them joy.
They pass the time of life with manifold pleasures,
    But in an instant they seek out the foul chasms of the Styx."

9.   Quod dominus imitandus sit nobis ac penitus amandus et timendus (That We Should Imitate the Lord and Love and Fear Him Deeply)

For one imitates him in devotion and pious actions,
    He who is both our kind father and lord.
He is possessed of immeasurable devotion, sweet mercy,
    He who is always open to proper prayer.
He grants not only forgiveness of sins but rewards,
    Always loving, and gently sparing those who appeal.
If exalted God is our lord and father,
    We should follow his devotion and deeds in heart and faith.
Children will learn to love their father, a servant to fear him,
10   Let love befit the child and the servant know fear.
If unnatural the offspring, arrogant the servant,
    They commit great disgrace on both counts.

10.   De simulatorum et stultorum socordia, qui nesciunt a sua pravitate per bonam exhortationem converti (On the Indolence of Dissemblers and Fools Who, Despite Good Exhortations, Decline to Convert from Evil)

Intelligence does not inform the one, nor wisdom the other;
    Teaching does not subdue one, nor intelligence his mate.
In whomever it is vain to instill teaching,
    The more you teach him, the greater fool he will be.
Thus, whoever tries to wash rough brickwork,
    The more he washes, the more dirt it accrues.
What good are good words where there is no inclination,
    Or what good are seeds cast in weeds?[1]
What good is yellow honey poured in foul ditches,
10   Or what can be done with liquid or oil mixed with filth?
What good is a lyre running on to a long-eared donkey,
    What good is a trumpet if artfully sounded to a horned ox?

---

[1] Matthew 13:24–30

Religious and Moral Poems

Your vision, O blind man, thrives as much in the first light of morning
    As his mind prospers after good words.
Poems can do many things, though not all, albeit
    Writings, both pagan and sacred, so claim.
It is said that Circe converted the companions of famous
    Ulysses into various beasts by intoning the art of song.
Although songs can do many things, they will not cure rashes,
20   Nor will ringworm be healed from their sound.
As, however, they avail nothing for those who have hernia,
    When they are chanted, the whole work is for naught.
Thus your work is wasted, wicked deceiver,
    Even if your effort is to introduce something good.
Although the wise king says much on the subject,
    It is good to extract only one thought:
If the fool is crushed in the swirl of the mortar[1]
    Like spelt, his dullness will not submit.
I have set down the words of Solomon; now to what the rustics
30   Are accustomed to saying about similar things:
Not in this way and not with a whip will you ever be able
    To change an owl into a hawk, that puts claws to cranes.
Or, O falcon, for your ways to be those of a vulture,
    For it is slow, voracious, and heavy in flight.
He wishes to learn no good, and nothing but evil.
    Do you wish to know why he does so? He's a fool.
He who is worse than Judas wishes to appear better than Peter.
    It is his lot to disguise many evils by feigning high rank.
He thinks trivial good is great, and many evils mean nothing.
40   Though he wishes to deceive many others, disabled he deceives only
      himself.

11.   **Quamobrem cicatrices quas dominus in passione suscepit, in resurrectione obductae non sint**
    (Why the Wounds That the Lord Received in His Passion Were Not Hidden at His Resurrection)

For the wounds that in the name of the Lord were inflicted
    Will be the source of honor for the martyred saints.
As the Savior returned from Phlegethonian shadows,
    This is signaled by his feet, his side, and his hands.

---

[1] Proverbs 27:22

Not because he could not cover over all the wounds he suffered,
      As dull pagan error often assumes,
He who could conquer all of death's afflictions,
      But because his actions are filled with kindly aid.
These mysteries include four far-famed causes,
10   Because the Author of life bears the stigmata of death.
First that the disciples may recognize that it is his body,
      Not a mere delusion, and lock it in the shrine of the heart,
So that certain faith in the arising Lord may adorn them,
      That they may celebrate the hope of resurrection evermore.
Then that, as he prays in his human nature for us,
      He may in himself show our wounds to God,
And what travails he has suffered for us humans
      And mercifully show in constant care
How he, whom forgetfulness never troubles. should remember,
20   And how he always takes pity with devout love.
It earnestly reminds us how he was ever mindful of human beings
      And always wished to take pity with kindly love,
So that his only child would share our mortal nature,
      We for whom he was willing to suffer such wounds.
Thirdly, so that the elect should never grow weary
      Of rendering praise when, O Passion, they see your marks,
And seeing their own salvation in his grievous afflictions,
      And in his descent to hell their subsequent climb to the stars,
By dint of his death themselves gloried in life everlasting
30   And owing to his thorns their own golden crowns.
Fourthly, that the crowd of sinners seeing him at the ultimate moment,
      May be saddened, oppressed by strong grief.
As Scripture relates: "They will see whom they were guilty of piercing."[1]
      And on the page of another passage again:
"Every beholder will recognize him, and the crowd that pierced him,
      And all the tribes of the earth will mourn for themselves and his death."[2]
And they will know that they are condemned to just judgment
      And will justly suffer a fiery fate.
The crowd will not be saved that wickedly mistreated
40   The Lord, or the crowd bent on scorning commands,
Either flouting vows or refusing to undertake them,
      Or railing against those with obedient minds.
O cruel wickedness of men, O mad ravings,
      O huge delirium, O satanic sin!

---

[1] Zechariah 12:10; John 19:37
[2] Revelation 1:7

Religious and Moral Poems   45

That God is not worshipped, or is worshipped only
    Under great duress, this does not go unavenged.

12. De fide et spe et caritate
(On Faith, Hope, and Charity)

Lo, finally sweet faith, hope, and concord hold power
    In the minds of the people all at once.
God established these foundations of the ancestral
    Church, by which provision the house of heaven may rise.
Faith grants us, hope bears us, great love unites us with others,[1]
    And this threefold good animates, guides, and dictates.
With them our minds prevail, are inspired, and are nourished;
    We ask and receive these things that God the Father gave.
"Will ever," said the Lord, "with prayer inverted,
10   Anyone get an evil return by praying to God?
Will anyone give the petitioner of bread the petrifaction
    Of stone, in response to a request?"[2]
For bread signifies God and the love of brothers,
    Which, if anyone lacks it, he possesses a heart of stone.
Will anyone give for fish the sinuous coils of a serpent,[3]
    Since, though a fish nourishes, the latter wickedly kills?
The first signifies faith, which matures in swirling waters,
    And in the tumult of winds thrives with delight.
Contrary to this, lack of faith, like a savage serpent,
20   Strikes and kills with a perfidious tongue.
Or if one seeks an egg, will one be given a scorpion[4]
    That strikes with a sharp curved tail or conveys fierce threats?
For the pious gifts of hope are signified by a round egg,
    Having what it carries inside obscured by a shell:
As eggs conceal a chick, thus hope is concealed in the present;
    In one case the content emerges, in the other the future is prepared.
Contrary to this is vexatious dejection;
    It wickedly repels a man, holding him back.
If it repels, let worthiness overcome what is forgotten
30   And apply yourself to what called you before.

---

[1] See Dümmler, p. 652
[2] Matthew 7:9; John 6:35, 15:17
[3] Luke 11:11
[4] Luke 11:12

With Paul you should grasp the high hand in heaven,
  Happily wearing a fair crown on high.[1]
As fish signifies faith, egg hope, bread love's substance,
  He who lacks all three is condemned to perpetual grief.
Since now justice retreats and sorry wickedness abounds with evil,
  These three are made lukewarm along with other good things.
Because dishonesty exists, impends, thrives, and prospers,
  Alas, the love of many is often left cold.[2]

13. De dispensatione divina, quae saepe occulta est, numquam tamen iniusta
(On the Divine Dispensation, Which Is Often Obscure but Never Unjust)

O power, O honor, O glory of exalted perception,
  Which all marvel at, yet no one can understand.
We who see many things in the human race variously governed,
  Though ignorant of why, what, and for what reason it is done,
For evil often shadows good people, and good singles out sinners,
  Or good things often follow the good, and evil often tracks the bad.
Often the good man is oppressed and the wicked exalted,
  The wicked man falls and the good man reaches the top.
All these things are managed by supernal judgments,
10 Some are often obscure, but never unjust.
The Lord decides individual cases with firm and gentle approval[3]
  For all ages, and governs all things.
For God neither judges nothing, nor always all details,
  Even if those wicked things are now done in despite of his law.
If he made no judgment in the present,
  Would not what dark fury commits escape unavenged?
Then thinking that God pays no attention to mortals,
  The wicked would madly commit all manner of sin;
And if well-deserved vengeance struck sinners,
20 And all blows of judgment were fixed:
The laws of the last day would be voided
  And the task of judgment would have no role.
Thus he judges some things so that we know that he heeds us
  And that God views what we do from heaven above.

---

[1] 1 Corinthians 9:25
[2] Matthew 24:12
[3] Wisdom 8:1

Religious and Moral Poems   47

Therefore he judges not all things but holds some in abeyance
 So that the last great day will have the task in hand.
The day that God's law, that prophecy, that the Lord himself has appointed,
 Which is known to all with rational powers,
The day on which to weigh the just scale of justice,
30 God will come borne on a red cloud.
He is devoted and just, will nurture one and inspire fear in the other;
 I fear his justice but must embrace his merciful love.
Because he loves us and because his justice curtails sinful instincts,
 On the one hand he soothes with oil, on the other he applies acid wine.[1]

14. Quod multis indiciis finis proximus esse monstretur (That It May Be Shown by Many Signs That the End Is Near)

It can be seen that the world declines and signals destruction,
 And that it announces its fall without words.
For it speaks by clear signs, even if we are silent on the teachings
 Of divine law, which declare all things that will come to pass.
The gentler climate of winter that used to prevail does not continue,
 The climate that may nourish the grass, woods, and seeds.
The abundance of hot sun is gone from the labor of summer
 And the spring seasons take no delight in their task.
The autumns scarcely overflow with sweet vintage
10 And do not thrive with the burden of fruits on the trees.
The earth does not now bear the good things that it used to
 And shows itself to be depleted and bare.
The abundance of all things decreases,
 There is more failure here and there, and overall less.
Altogether the worker attends less to his office
 Than once, and nothing stands firm as it did before:
The cultivator in the fields, the soldier in camp, the sailor on the ocean,
 The scales in judgment, scrupulousness in transacting affairs.
Is there concord in friendship? Who is skilled in artistic endeavors?
20 Where does gentle order prevail in our ways?
Lively youth does not thrive as it did lately,
 Overall hideous old age devours with a black maw.
For he diminishes necessarily, whoever approaches his limit
 And perceives that his death is not far off.
The sun descending gives off rays with less brilliance
 And the shrinking moon bears dusky horns.

---

[1] Luke 10:34

The tree that youthfully blossomed with foliage and flowers
      Drops occasional seeds on unsightly soil.
The water source accustomed to flood banks of rivers
30   Thus in the passage of time often becomes a thin drop.
A cracked wall portends future destruction,
      A wall that in youth stood firmly, embellished with art.
As the old man grows weary of sporting tumult,
      Of standing, riding, walking, and merry talk,
As frequent breathlessness oppresses his tremulous body,
      He sighs and utters many a groan.
Thus all sweetness has left the world as it ages
      And none of its strength remains as before.
Dire greed, squalor, perjury, and lust are enduring,
40   Consuming envy, fraud, strife, disputes, and deceit.

15. Ex epistola ad Corinthios carmen ad precem cuiusdam monachi factum
(A Poem Composed at the Request of a Certain Monk, from the Epistle to the Corinthians)

Thus quickened things are often properly settled
      When a single work made of many is joined.
In many things there is a beautiful order;
      This work also stands out in the art of discourse,
In which the ample fields of sacred Scripture are abundant,
      And the devout grove breathes with an ambrosial scent.
Wandering among them, as I amble through beds of violets,
      I pluck roses with my fingers, which a basket may bear;
Thus it culled from the holy teaching of Paul the Apostle
10   What he dispatched with his Arcadian pen.
He adorns holy and well-ordered speech with adroit expression
      After thus enumerating the virtues one and all.
Where the pronouncements are properly phrased in varied locution,
      The meaning and order of the better way is laid bare.
"We adjure you," he said, "O pious community of brothers,[1]
      That you not be deprived of God's holy grace.
Indeed," he said, "I heard you, prophet, in an auspicious moment,[2]
      And from that day I strove to bring salvation's help.
Now, now, look, the acceptable time is before us, really before us;
20   Lo, the day of salvation by grace is near.

---

[1] 2 Corinthians 6:1–7
[2] Isaiah 49:8

Religious and Moral Poems

Let staining offense by none and to none be given
  Lest our service be deservedly impugned.
Let us thus bend our efforts in all matters
  So that all our company may serve supreme God.
Let great patience grow strong in us
  So that by the tornado and winds of evil we be not overcome.
Let vexing distress and oppressive conditions,
  The impiousness of the wicked make us happy by proper trial.
In the gloom of the dungeons or black rebellions
30   It befits the cleansed to rise to heavenly realms.
Let our minds be exercised by laborious efforts,
  Let us be sleepless, let our hearts be awake.[1]
Let our stainlessness be pure, our learning accomplished;
  Let us be long-suffering and from squalor be freed.
May our quiet minds bear the yoke of the Lord softly[2]
  So that our minds may receive the gifts of the Holy Ghost.
May his love not be feigned but genuine affection
  So that a true note may then emit truth
In the power of God, by which all creation is governed,
40   Which embraces the vault of heaven, the land, and the seas."
He begins now to oppose certain contraries,
  With his pen thus variously adorning his speech:
"Let the arms of the just," he said, "be borne by right hand and left hand[3]
  So that the soldier of God may emerge as victor with both,
Through glorious honor at one time, through bridled disgrace at another,
  We are seen to be wicked, but may good report accrue to the good.
If we are judged by widespread opinion to be deceivers,
  It is still proper to tell the truth.
Although unknown, we are still a known people;
50   Though condemned to die, we live nonetheless.
A chastened cohort in combat, we remain unvanquished;
  Though saddened, we are ever a cheerful band.
We are a tearful and destitute group, but let us enrich many,
  And let us possess ample riches though we have nothing at all."

---

[1] cf. Song of Songs 5:2
[2] Matthew 11:30
[3] 2 Corinthians 6:7–10

16. De fructu centeno sexageno et triceno
(On the Hundred-fold, Sixty-fold, and Thirty-fold Yield)

The field of the church is divided into these sections,
    Being sprung from the good seed of the Lord.
The first part is a hundred-fold, the second part sixty-fold,
    The third part has a thirty-fold yield.[1]
With the first yield gone, the second cannot recover,
    But the third yield duly subvenes.
The third follows the first and the second the third one;
    To the first, however, none can return.
The third leaves the church in low estate, and the second falters,
10   Not at all will the first yield recur.

ii. De eadem re
(On the Same Matter)

For when properly the good seed fell in good earth,
    That the sower sowed for the love of a pleasing yield,
The thirty-fold, sixty-fold, and hundred-fold yields follow,
    And the field of the spirit sprouts from the seed of faith.
Thirty-fold glows in marriage, sixty-fold in the state of widows,
    But these two are surpassed in the third order of good;
The glory of a hundred-fold yield is given to virgins,
    And this sacred number corresponds to martyred saints,
Which is sufficiently conveyed in the bending of fingers,
10   A matter properly established by men of old.
For the top of the index finger joined to the thumb lightly
    Is able to signify thirty in numerical space.
The soft embrace of the fingers conveys sweet kisses
    Of marriage, which remain pleasing to each.
But the curved thumb pressed by a curved index finger
    Shows sixty, or the figure of widowhood;
As a finger compresses a finger, distress often presses widows,
    And the great sigh of the turtledove is their sign.
If a passage from left to right is made in order,
20   And the index finger is approached to the thumb,
And a full orb is formed with a smooth circle,
    This figure is a hundred in numerical terms.
It conveys the beautiful wreaths that are properly given
    To pious virgins and martyred saints.

---

[1] Matthew 13:8

Religious and Moral Poems

This passage counsels us to disdain what is fleeting and foolish
    And strive for good deeds from now on;
To follow no fallible course but fix our minds on what is enduring,
    To spurn the declining world and to love God;
To pursue heavenly things and put off earthly matters,
30   To seize holy work with words, hands, heart, and faith.

17. De hypocritis et quod apostolorum temporibus sive eorum successorum magis ecclesiae virtutes viguerunt quam his novissimis temporibus
(Concerning Hypocrites and the Fact That in the Times of the Apostles and Their Successors the Virtues of the Church Prospered More Than in These Very Recent Times)

Feigned virtue prospers, true virtue declines to no purpose;
    The former stands tall, while the latter, groaning, seeks out the depths.
For as true probity avails, feigned honesty will injure;
    One is ready to counsel, the other eager to deceive.
When the teaching of pious priests was in the ascendant,
    Their speech and character were the norm of salvation's grace.
Now the faithless hearts and treacherous words of deceivers are sovereign
    And deception alone holds the field.
At that time attention was paid to the honor and example of holy fathers,
10   To whom the order of apostolic law gave the throne.
To them was given the law of loosing and binding,[1]
    The realms of heaven could be opened by their keys.
To them the Shepherd of shepherds commends sheep and their offspring,[2]
    And whatever work the pledge of love has assigned.
Thus it was then; but now everything rushes apart on differing pathways;
    Everything has fallen heels over head, with the head underneath.
Then the pallium given by the apostolic see was sturdy
    And the law was the vestment and order of power;
Now the vestment is dissembling, and no less the giver;
20   Vestment and mind are a perfect match.
A flowing hood covers the head, ill will the spirit,
    Rough wool the limbs, sheep's clothing the wolf.[3]
A double cloak lies outside, a duplicitous heart inside,
    Decent honesty is far from them both.

---

[1] Matthew 16:19, 18:18
[2] John 21:15–17
[3] Matthew 7:15

Their bindings gape with swelling pieces
   And shabby shoes cover swift feet.[1]
On his left he also carries a knife, a double tablet,
   And is accustomed to have a good cover and pen.
Pallor suffuses his face, and panting sighs inhabit his body;
30   His sighing voice may sound thin,
But this sighing voice utters words sweet and deceitful
   So that the pure hearts of men will truckle to his will.
Because they are unable to weep, they wish to imitate weeping,
   With a false flow moistening their uncouth cheeks.
They seek to appear just, holy, and pious,
   So that the glory of human praise can be bought.
With such a cloak the likeness of piety veils their visage;
   They wish to be seen as holy more than they wish to be so.
This type of man knows not how to travel through cities,
40   Or cease to frequent crossroads, country, and homes.
He does this so as to be able to replenish his greedy coffers
   With ill-gotten gains and fill his grasp so voracious for things.
They do good ostentatiously and many evils in secret;
   The former are obvious to men, the latter are apparent to God.
Whoever has done worthy work for human approval,
   In wretchedness, alas, he receives his just reward.
The great trumpet of the word of the gospel is sounded
   And intoned auspiciously through the crossroads of the world:
"Let not your left hand know what your right hand discharges,[2]
50   Then all that you do will be accepted by God."
Thus may the mind not know man's admiration
   When excellent custom accomplishes positive work.
Present life is signified by the left hand, future life by the right hand;
   This the holy Scriptures of God advise.
For a certain high king and powerful wise man,
   Concerning such matters, once uttered these words:
"His long life is lodged on the right side,[3]
   On his left glory, preeminence, and wealth."
His left hand likewise is under our heads, and pious
60   Embraces are given to us by the holy right.[4]
For the left hand provides the comforts of present existence,
   But in the right hand he prepares perpetual life without end.

---

[1] Proverbs 6:18
[2] Matthew 6:3
[3] Proverbs 3:16
[4] Song of Songs 2:6

Religious and Moral Poems

For two disciples held the left and the right hand,[1]
    And by this they signify on which side of the Lord they wish to sit.
Thus exalted wisdom is on Christ's right hand,
    By which eternal rest is given to our souls;
The conduct of life remains in this left hand
    Until such time as we arrive at our eternal reward.
The true riches are the glory and guidance of religion
70   That properly protects us in this exiled state.
For your left hand, mighty Christ, mostly
    Signifies the church in this present life.
For, singing of those who, with respect to appearance, are holy,
    I would not wish to be accused as long as I sing the truth.
While rehearsing these matters, however, I do not derogate just brothers,
    Whose hearts thirst for heaven and whose devout minds thirst for God.
For those in whom faith is devoted, love sweet, and hope pious,
    To them to live is Christ and to die a blessed gain.[2]
They have abandoned all, who, having heard the voice of the Almighty,
80   Struggle to follow the Lord with spiritual love
And stand at the foundation of the life of apostolic example
    So that the way of the church, as it once was, may persist.
To them are all things common by virtue of outstanding devotion,
    That is, those to whom God himself gave a single spirit and mind.[3]
Many things run in an up-and-down rhythm;
    Good things are mixed with the bad and evil things with good;
Dregs are found in wine and watery residue in the oil of olives,
    And the ambrosial liquid of honey has grounds.
Indeed there are two in the field and as many under the covers,[4]
90   The Lord said there were two at the mill,
Of whom one will be taken and the other abandoned.
    The one that is taken will be raised on high, the one left behind will die.
Thus the bosom of the church harbors three classes,
    Which one faith binds in differing ways:
The clerical order is in the field; the monk has a quiet existence;
    The common people stand at the turning mill.
The first advises the people, the second enjoys holy quiet,
    The last runs in the cycle of worldly affairs.
According to merit the three are separated by twofold division;
100   The path of perdition is trodden by one;

---

[1] Matthew 20:21–23
[2] Philippians 1:21
[3] Acts 4:32
[4] Luke 17:34

The cherishing group goes to heaven, another to the Stygian shadows.
　　Thus life prepares different places for them.
This threefold life matched up with a threefold order
　　Is signified by three holy men.
In truth, the rescuer Noah is the model of leaders,
　　Who guided hope through the waters for beasts and men.
Thus the celibate and anchorite monk thrives in Daniel,
　　Who gloriously overcame gluttony and lust.
In Job are seen those who perform or regret worldly actions,
110　　Since Job performed deeds in the world without stain

18. Quod plerumque mali mala patiuntur et de tempore Antichristi (That the Wicked Often Suffer Evil, and Concerning the Time of Antichrist)

He who rules the world with virtue and governs with devotion
　　Exultantly benefited humankind at the time
When he declared war on the unspeakable, murderous monster[1]
　　So that he was unable to carry out spiritual crimes.
He applied healing medicine to wicked evil
　　And tempers fearful destruction with His help.
If a fierce scorpion is overcome by the oil of shining olives,
　　This balm overcomes his sting.
If a new wound is anointed with that fluid,
10　　The liquid brings about that the poison can do no harm.
Thus evil is driven out by evil and illness overcomes illness,
　　Thus one thing is often accustomed to yield to the same:
A wedge drives out a wedge, one nail presses out another;
　　Thus with the advent of one, the other passes away;
Thus one stone grinds down another and wood by wood is blunted,
　　And steel beats steel, artfully smoothing it out.
Christ offered solace for the containing of evil
　　Or in order, O Antichrist, to shorten your days.
Lest deadly evil should grow by vile increase,
20　　It is confined to a narrow moment of time.
The evil dangers of that time are signaled,
　　O devoted Christ the King, by your prophetic voice:
"Then there will be," said the evangelist, "a great tribulation[2]
　　Such as was not nor will be seen from chaos until now.

[1] Revelation 12:7–9
[2] Matthew 24:21–22

Religious and Moral Poems

The days will be shortened when the testing is over,
 For otherwise no flesh at all will be saved."
All things are well carried out by the Lord's provision
 So that the right sequence will run in due course,
So that the threatening plague and impious tempest
30 Will exceed the third year but not finish the fourth.
A time, said Daniel, or times and half of another,[1]
 Will turn as the savage times of that abuse.[2]
Thus with the passage of forty months and two others,
 He explains and relates these events,
Signifying a year by "time" and two years by "times" in the plural,
 And, by a "half time" he teaches another six months,
So that the sum of the months runs up to this number:
 Three years and a half, neither more nor less.

19. De eo quod temporis status et locus et causa et motio ingenium tractatoris adiuvat
(That the Fixing of Time, Location, Cause, and Direction Aid the Mind of the Interpreter)

Thus the timing, location, climate, and direction,
 The manner of action come to the aid of an apt mind.
In the evening the Lord and Creator of the earth seeks for[3]
 The sinner in a flowery location and asks where he is.
This is the timing, for, with the light of day receding,
 He has already withdrawn into the shadows of night.
He knows where to find him, for he knew him not to be present
 Where at his command he had ordered him to be.
He seeks as if not knowing where he is, but finally I know not
10 What he wishes to reprove unless it be not knowing God.
No less, however, do hour and place afford wisdom
 In the sacred writing that Scripture provides.
Christ coming from the summit of the Mount of Olives[4]
 In the morning approached the holy threshold of the temple of God.
He frees the adulteress turned over to deceivers,
 Kindly he teaches by her example how pious and just he is,

---

[1] Daniel 12:7; 7:25
[2] Revelation 12:14; 13:5
[3] Genesis 3:8–9
[4] John 8:1

Being pious he saves her, being just he condemns her errors;
"Go," he said, "and commit such sins no more."[1]
For the Mount of Olives represents the Lord's great pity
20   As he came from the citadel of heaven to examine our sins.
With pity he revives us anointed with holy unguent
        And provides the help of piety and light.
He arrives in the morning, recalling day with night vanished,
        Bringing new light, with the shadow of the law gone away.
The wafting of air often opens the mind in addition,
        For heat and cold are replete with mystical sense.
In Jerusalem there were once festivals of dedication,[2]
        But these, according to Scripture, were suppressed by cruel cold.
The frosts of winter are the disbelieving hearts of the Jewish people
30   Who were bereft of the warmth of the faith.
There was also a frost when the passion of Christ proceeded.
        O Peter, when you deny, you freeze, with tears you regain your warmth.[3]
The sitting or the standing of the Lord, or his movement,
        Bring our minds to life when perceptions are in place.
Stephen says that He stands, Mark that He is seated,[4]
        But there is no contradiction — He does both.
Sitting has the force of rule, standing marks the warrior;
        For some He fights, for others He rules — He does both at once.
The alert messenger angel says, in standing, that He is delivered[5]
40   And announces that He is risen as he sits.
Here it says that He is about to fight, there about to govern;
        He is born for the fight and rises to rule.
Standing pertains to the high priest, sitting to the teacher,
        And He is the father's offering for us, and He teaches us.
He observes two as he walks and heals their blindness standing;[6]
        Let moving pertain to man, standing to God.
If motion and place are seen in the deeds of the Lord in heaven,
        A great yield of intelligence will begin to accrue.
Finally, when he ascends high on the mountain or goes to the nether regions,
50   On the one hand he shows he is God, on the other a man.
Those whom he first heals, he afterwards fills with good nectar,
        First he heals with faith those whom he nourishes with law.

---

[1] John 8:11
[2] John 10:22
[3] Matthew 26:75
[4] Acts 7:55; Mark 16:19
[5] Luke 2:9; Mark 16:5
[6] Matthew 20:32–34

Religious and Moral Poems   57

He urged us to lie down on delicate hayricks[1]
  So that the work of perishable flesh be suppressed,
But he gave the disciples a feast, and they to the people;
  With the former feasted in learning, let the people join in.[2]

20. De contemptu mundi
   ## (On Contempt of the World)

If you happen to fear the perpetual fires with which the Creator
  Justly threatens, one and all of you will love his rewards.
The glory of this whole unstable world dwindles,
  But devout love mounts up within.

21. Consolatio de obitu cuiusdam fratris
   ## (Consolation for the Death of a Certain Brother)

Appended to the religious poems above are two of a more personal nature. The
first (21), on the death of a certain brother, has not received a warm reception.
Baunard (1860:215) wrote disparagingly: "Théodulfe est généralement plus
instructif qu'émouvant; il prêche plus qu'il ne chante." Baunard was in doubt
whether the brother in question was a blood brother or a monk. The locution
"cuiusdam fratris" would certainly suggest the latter, but that has raised the ques-
tion why Theodulf, if already a bishop, would have concerned himself with a
hundred-line obituary for a simple monk (Alexandrenko 1971:116). For this rea-
son some critics, including Alexandrenko and Schaller (1962:75–76), have dated
the poem late, in Theodulf's exilic years when he would have been relieved of
the burdens of his office. On the other hand, there is not a personal word in the
whole poem, which is a catalogue of no fewer than twenty-four biblical prec-
edents for the inevitability of death. This listing is reminiscent of Alcuin's long
enumeration of historical disasters intended in some curious way as a comfort to
the monks of Lindisfarne after a viking attack in 793 ("De clade Lindisfarnensis
monasterii," ed. Dümmler, *PLAC*, 1:229–35). It also anticipates Modoin's enu-
meration of exile precedents in his response to Theodulf's pleas from exile (poem
72 below), a formulaic tabulation that has been viewed as particularly chilly
(Cuissard 1892:97). Since Modoin echoes Theodulf elsewhere in his poem, one
may ask whether his enumerative model could have been Theodulf's "De obitu
cuiusdam fratris."

Much more engaging is 22 on the relationship of a man to his friends and
acquaintances. It emphasizes generous sharing and certain social niceties that
have not changed over the centuries: one should learn a person's name and use

---

[1] Matthew 14:19
[2] Luke 9:14–17

it. Should you have the misfortune to forget a name, you should not grieve the person by asking it directly, but try to ferret it out by listening to others or inquiring in secret. It is gratifying to get a glimpse of everyday manners from another world, although this tonality is not altogether isolated in Theodulf's poetry. One finds, for example, not a few indications on behavioral proprieties in a public context in "Contra iudices."

> If new beginnings were made in such crucial matters,
>> A new custom would be put on display.
> But because long ago a path of such import was beaten,
>> The ancient way of our ancestors should be maintained.
> The world from primordial chaos was subject to alternation
>> And remains to be completed in this condition as well.
> Great Adam, who dwelled in a flowery garden,
>> Bore the weight of this fate.[1]
> Though Abel's sacrifice was consumed by fires celestial,
>> He suffered blows from his brother and died here below.[2]
> Though bitter death was amazed at Enoch, snatched away from it,
>> Though long postponed, death seeks him out all the same.[3]
> Noah, hope of the world and second father, also perished,
>> He who triumphantly survived the great flood.[4]
> Shem too, with name changed, was a just leader,[5]
>> A proper renderer of true sacrifice.
> Abraham too, the standard and adornment of faith, was a victim;
>> Conquering Persian fire, he was himself overcome.[6]
> Holy Isaac, born of a barren mother,[7]
>> Was the type of your sacrifice, dear King Christ.
> No less mortal was Jacob, worthy to wrestle with the Lord as opponent,
>> Blessed by the aid of his father and God.
> Noble was his offspring and great his assembly,[8]
>> Among whom just Joseph in glory stood out;

---

[1] Genesis 5:5
[2] Genesis 4:4–8
[3] Genesis 5:21–24
[4] Genesis 9:29
[5] Genesis 11:11
[6] Genesis 25:7–8
[7] Genesis 21:1–7; 35:28–29
[8] Genesis 37:2–50:26

Religious and Moral Poems

After the ills that he suffered and the boons he provided
    Even he, dying, closed out his last day.
Lot, avoiding Sodom, could not avoid succumbing;[1]
    Death consumed him though he was safe from the sulphorous flames.
Moses died too, than whom none was more expert[2]
30   In communicating God's law and enjoying his words.
Priest and own brother [Aaron] died too, though crowned by gold and purple,
    His forehead bearing a holy weight.[3]
Nun's holy offspring [Joshua], prospering at the River Jordan,
    Distributes pious lands to pious men.[4]
His harsh lot is not unknown to the judges,
    By whose action the people were delivered from the foe.
Nor was excellent Samuel free from final payment,[5]
    Who from childhood excelled in learning, law, and faith.
David died too, who laid low Goliath,[6]
40   Outstanding in rule, arms, and sacred verse.
And wise Solomon died, the builder of the holy temple,[7]
    After surpassing honor, riches, and wealth;
In addition the pious order of ancient kings and prophets
    After their rule and holy pronouncement of divine words.
The famed high priests and the greatest of prophets, Isaiah,[8]
    After holy predictions followed this road.
You, Josiah, suffered the arms of the Egyptian ruler,[9]
    You who, alas, were apt in the worship of the Lord.
And Elijah too, though he was swept up to heaven,[10]
50   Though his death was delayed, still he was not spared.
Although a dead man arose from a touch of the bone of Elisha,[11]
    Dead the former arises, and the latter lies dead.
Lest he die, Jonah has a living interment;[12]
    The death he conquers arising, he meets to die.

---

[1] Genesis 19:15–29
[2] Deuteronomy 34:5
[3] Exodus 39:1–31; Numbers 33:38–39
[4] Joshua 3:13–17; 14:1; 24:29
[5] 1 Samuel 2:26; 25:1
[6] 1 Samuel 17:41–51; 1 Kings 2:10–11
[7] 1 Kings 3:11–13; 11:43
[8] 2 Kings 22:19–20
[9] 2 Kings 23:29
[10] 2 Kings 2:12
[11] 2 Kings 13:20–21
[12] Jonah 2:1

The holy man whom fierce lions shrank away from,[1]
    Him the dark day of death does not fear to attack.
With the fire of holy faith the boys extinguished the furnace,[2]
    But they cannot conquer the pyre of death.
Ezekiel dies after seeing the Lord's habitation[3]
60   And after seeing many mystical secrets of God.
Strong in the law of the priesthood and with blessed offspring,[4]
    Ezra, who rebuilt the temple and adorned it with love, died too.
Restorers of the walls of sacred Jerusalem[5]
    Were just Zerubbabel and pious Nehemiah's concern.[6]
They died who guarded the prophecies of the renewed people,[7]
    The prophet Zechariah and holy Haggai;
Also Esther and Mordecai, who overcame wicked Haman,[8]
    And who rescued the people of the Israelites.
Raphael saved Tobit and his daughter-in-law from horrid[9]
70   Demise, but not at all from the maw of death.
Judith with her sword reined in mad lewdness,[10]
    But, O wicked plague of death, not you.
Zechariah and the voluble woman overcame their mourning,[11]
    But not your blows, O bitter death.
Neither a heavenly man, nor an earthly angel [John the Baptist],[12]
    Preparing the way for the Lord, is a stranger to this fate.
But what, cruel death, do you do, fierce, vicious, and savage to others,
    When you perniciously seek out the Author of life?
He suppressed, bent, and drove you out with his passing
80   And, arising, laid open life's way.
He plunged the author of death into Tartarean shadows
    Deprived of courage and pious recruits.
Peter too died, venerated prince of apostolic standing,
    With whose key the heavenly realms can be reached.

---

[1] Daniel 6:17–23
[2] Daniel 3:19–24
[3] Ezekiel 40:1–4
[4] Ezra 7:6–22
[5] Ezra 3:8, etc.
[6] Nehemiah 2–3
[7] Ezra 5:1
[8] Esther 8:1–7
[9] Tobit 12:14
[10] Judith 13:1–10
[11] Luke 1:5–25
[12] cf. Matthew 11:11

Religious and Moral Poems

O Paul, you stand out in teaching, grasping the secrets of heaven,[1]
  You, adorned by great suffering, toil, and zeal, died.
John gives cups taken from the bosom of the Master,[2]
  John, whom pious virginity and the love of the Lord adorn.
The sublime and exalted apostolic order, brilliant
90   With its learned company and disciples, died too.
The outstanding company of martyrs in shining splendor,
  The crowd of believers and chorus of the pure.
Though created from mortal stock and supreme spirit,
  They pay their debt to you, O unlovely death.
It is difficult to record the names of all those
  Who are, were, or to whom the Lord may grant life.
Let the merits of each subsist, though none forever
  Will remain excluded from the condition of death.
Finally, the great king David, the holy prophet,
100   In inspiration and holy verse speaks thus:
"Is there a living man who does not incur you, O death, worst of fortunes,
  Or can be out of your sight?[3]
Or who can pluck his own soul from infernal possession,
  And who among them can be free of the savage hand?"
From the beginning of time this plight has borne down on mortals
  And has cruelly subjected the world to its law.
Therefore a brother pays the debt imposed by this condition
  And we compose songs for his death.

22. Quae sint dicenda amico cum conspicit bona amici (What a Friend Should Say to a Friend When He Sees His Friend's Riches)

When a sweet friend of yours surveys your riches,
  As one cheerful man to another, you will speak these words:
"The goods that you observe, let them be held in common;
  As beseems a good man, he will share in these things."
Be not chary in giving, believe me, for good is the practice of giving;
  Giving nothing, you acquire nothing; if you give, you yourself will receive.[4]
He who sows many seeds will reap a full harvest;
  Thus the owner will rejoice in the field.

---

[1] 2 Corinthians 12:2–4
[2] John 13:23
[3] Psalm 89:48
[4] Luke 6:38

Seeing a man not known by name, but whose face is familiar,
10   But if you know him by both, love him well.
Do not hesitate to give friendly words and kind kisses,
    And, as you do so, be attentive to his name.
Often you will remember it when another names him,
    Or on occasion he will name himself.
If the name is unknown, it is wrong and improper to ask it directly,
    But if you learn it in secret, no wrong or shame is incurred.
He who thinks he is known to you, or maybe once was familiar,
    Unless you call him by his own name, he will be grieved.
Learn to acquire the names and characteristics of people,
20   And, as you teach, call each by his name.
Be grand with the grand, and humble with the humble;
    As Paul said, he was all things to all men.[1]
In actions there should be the same correspondence;
    More things are done in public so that others may stay opaque.

23.   Teudulfus episcopus hos versus conposuit (Bishop Theodulf Composed These Verses)

This poem stands on the threshold between Theodulf's religious and secular poems inasmuch as it begins with a praise of Christ and ends with a praise of Charlemagne. It is a so-called *carmen figuratum*, an immensely strenuous exercise in which the hexameters can be read to make sense not only in the usual way but by tracing the evenly spaced letters from top to bottom on both sides and down the middle of the contrived square, as well as diagonally from the top center out to the middle edges and then diagonally back down to the bottom center (see the figure in Dümmler's edition 1881:482). This tour de force, recalling Hellenistic figured poems, originated in the West with Optatianus Porfyrius in the reign of Constantine and was imitated by Venantius Fortunatus and the Carolingian poets. Schaller 1960 made the case that the Carolingian practice originated with Alcuin and a student of his named Joseph (see also Bullough 2004:373; Godman 1987:56–59). Charlemagne then commissioned Theodulf to try his hand at the exercise, as the poet suggests in verse 40. As Schaller writes (1960:23): "The demands made on writers by this often extremely artful figural pattern were usually so difficult that the required form was destined to damage or even overwhelm the phrasing and content of the poems." The reader will see immediately that the form has robbed Theodulf of his usual energy. Schaller believes that the poem is relatively early, not later than the late 780s, since Theodulf still adverts to his status as an exile in verse 28. See also Sears 1990:607–10, 624.

---

[1] 1 Corinthians 9:22

Religious and Moral Poems 63

All-powerful Lord and perpetual grantor of peace
Thundering from the top of the world, giving the dew of kind benefaction,
For you are the source of light, O Creator, great Redeemer,
Exalted in all things, sower of supernal deeds,
You rule the regions sagaciously with heavenly virtue,
Creating all holy things, enricher of the frosty abyss.
For, as a beneficent Godhead enthroned on the heights,
Blessed peace, giving law and holy ascent,
Piety in person, virtue, brightness proceeding from light,
10 Sent here by the high honor of his father,
Freeing the miserable world from corruption, crime, and plague,
Instantly you confer the coveted crowns, which in this
Life purify us like the flaming sun.
Generously bestowing high gifts with sweet approbation,
Indeed, glorious one, you extend the breadth of the earth with your commands,
For your name is guide and lord amidst the stars.
Holiest salvation, path, and abundance of virtue,
You guide history with shining law, and therefore
With supreme approval you grant celestial judgment.
20 Brilliant light of the church, crowned with wisdom,
Make Charles prosper with felicitous fate, thou redeemer;
He, preeminent with the mark of clear faith,
Now is able to maintain the shores of a subdued land.
And make him, Christ, the partner of the highest leaders,
Whom the pleasing glory of station properly raised.
He reigns in the devoted world, a stream enriched by the stream,
Protected by the decrees of the Lord and the holy altars.
He granted me, who am banished by enormous misfortunes,
That I now may bring forth such poems on an extended field.
30 Powerfully creative, he lays out the church by supreme contract,
Where Christ pronounced words of good anointment
And by worshipful reciprocation receives pure service.
Now, with gracious king and admirable wife, immeasurable hope
Will increase endeavor and rewards for all who are holy
By providing income to country dwellers in due season.
Thus I wish you to accept my song, great offspring of David,
And my service rendered with a prostrate countenance.
For this page contains the prayers and praise
That I, Theodulf, have sung on behalf of the king,
40 A humble servant constrained by the master's command.
Noble reader, brilliant poet in all things,
Do not, though expert, reproach my little verses,
For I have issued them only now in their present form.

Secular and Historical Poems

The secular and historical poems begin in Dümmler's numbering with 24, a six-line epitaph for Charlemagne's queen Fastrada, who died in 794. The epitaph has been read differently. Baunard (1860:162–63) thought it positive and not in accord with the negative assessment of Fastrada given by Einhard, but Cuissard (1892:75) wrote that Theodulf limited himself to an "éloge vulgaire," designed to conceal Fastrada's true character. The fact that it is such a nominal obituary, and really more about Charlemagne than Fastrada, tends to favor the latter reading. Schaller (1962:22) questioned whether the attribution to Theodulf is authentic.

24. Epitaphium Fastradae Reginae
(Epitaph for Queen Fastrada)

Here lie the preeminent remains of Queen Fastrada,
  Whom cold death carried off in her flowering prime.
Noble herself, she was wed to a powerful monarch,
  But now, nobler still, she is joined to a heavenly groom.
The better part of her soul, King Charles himself, is still with us,
  To whom may merciful God grant a long life.

25. Ad Carolum regem
(To King Charles)

"Ad Carolum regem," dated to 796 because of Charlemagne's recent victory over the Avars, is surely the best known and most familiar of Theodulf's poems. It can be read in Latin with facing English translation in Peter Godman's excellent anthology of Carolingian poetry (1985:150–62). Godman also provides a keen reading of the poem (12–13). It stands out for its liveliness and great range of tonalities, from fulsome praise to satire, to arch banter, to merciless malice (see also Godman 1987:68–70; Godman 1990:579–81). These registers were not always appreciated; Baunard notes them with some disapproval (1860:233–35), and Cuissard (1892:77) focuses only on the celebration of Charlemagne's victory over the Avars and passes over the satirical effects in studied silence. Godman, on the other hand, appreciates the satirical inflections fully. He persuasively points out that even the overwrought praise of Charlemagne and the royal family with its escalating impossibilia borders on irony, not at the expense of the persons but rather at the expense of the overblown panegyric style practiced by Theodulf's contemporaries. The irony is hinted at in the comic alliteration of verse 8. It may be noted, however, that Theodulf's critique did nothing to curtail the panegyric tradition, which became ever more inflated throughout the ninth century.

Much of the delight afforded by this poem comes from the dramatic inter-action among the courtiers in Charlemagne's circle. Theodulf's mockery of such central figures as Alcuin and Einhard is within bounds, in the case of Wibod perhaps a little less so. But the animosity directed against an Irish member of the court circle, identified in a famous article by Bernhard Bischoff (1955; repr. 1967) as Cadac-Andreas, is as surprising as it is difficult to account for. The attack is launched in verses 160–74 and culminates in the charge that the Irishman cannot pronounce Latin because he mispronounces his own national identity as a "Scot-tus" so that it sounds like "sottus" (fool), thus specifying exactly what he is (cf. de Riquer 1992). (On the pronunciation problem see Sidwell 1992.) But the ridi-cule does not stop here. Theodulf returns to the attack in verses 213–234 with a veritable catalogue of invectives. It is as if the victim had counterattacked and inspired Theodulf to renew his vitriol. Even this assault did not satisfy Theo-dulf's antagonism, and he engages in a third round of vilification, including a repetition of the "sottus" joke, in a later poem addressed to Corvinianus (27.55–68 below). In this poem he actually refers to a response in distichs from the Irish-man so that we may detect a real literary feud, though at a rather low level. What could have provoked such an exchange will no doubt remain a mystery. It stands in vivid contrast to the moral concerns elsewhere in Theodulf's verse, but it also supplements them. What is missing in "Ad Carolum regem" is the kind of serious underpinning that we find in "Contra iudices," which is also rich in humor and irony but counterbalances these effects with a zeal for ethical and social reform.

The vitality of the poem has inspired a first attempt at a purely literary approach to Theodulf in a book by Alejandra de Riquer [Permanyer] from 1994. Up until this time the studies devoted to our poet had been predominantly philo-logical, but now we may perhaps look forward to a more literary orientation. De Riquer reviews the information on Theodulf and then provides a full hundred-page (139–238) study of the poem as poem, including such matters as structure, genre, and historical classification.

On one matter we depart from Schaller (1970:19), Alexandrenko (1971:130), Godman (1985:155n15), and Bullough (2004:439). In a detailed analysis of the poem (1970:14–36) Schaller assigned it to a subcategory, which he described as *Zirkulargedichte*. That is to say, such poems were circulated from hand to hand before being recited in public. The idea is justified in Schaller's reading of lines 9–13:

> Ludicris haec mixta iocis per ludicra currat,
> Saepeque tangatur qualibet illa manu.

Secular and Historical Poems   67

Laude iocoque simul hunc illitat carta revisat,
  Quem tribuente celer ipse videbo deo.

Schaller takes "haec" in line 9 to refer to the "laus" alluded to in line 5 and echoed in the "quam" in line 7 and the "tantam" in line 8, but he takes the "illa" in line 10 to anticipate "carta" in line 11. The written version is thus circulated and "touched" by one hand or another. But it also seems possible to read "haec" and "illa" as both referring to "laus": "let one praise run sportively, let it be struck up (sounded, performed, recited musically—on the musical image for reading cf. "Ad Gislam" 43.11–12) by any hand whatever." De Riquer also detected a problem in this passage (1994:149). Indeed, in another paper Schaller (1993:96) notes that an "ille" can be identical with a "hic" closely preceding it, and that possibility might apply in the present passage. On the use of musical imagery for poetic recitation one might compare Venantius Fortunatus book 2, carmen 9, 3–6:

Iamdudum obliti desueto carmine plectra
  Cogitis antiquam me renovare lyram.
En stupidis digitis stimulates tangere cordas,
  Cum mihi non solito currat in arte manus.

Here "tangere cordas" is equivalent to Theodulf's "tangere laudem." To circulate a poem so that it can be "touched" by hand seems like an odd locution. Furthermore, a prior circulation in written form would seem to take much of the sting out of the invective and spoil the effect of a public reading. Schaller counteracts this problem by suggesting that the prior circulation was only in the royal family and Theodulf's inner circle (1970:24), but once the joke began to circulate, especially such a malicious and potentially scandalous one, it would be difficult to keep under wraps. Consequently there may be some reservation about considering "Ad Carolum regem" as a *Zirkulargedicht*.

The whole world celebrates you and your praises, O sovereign;
  Although much it can say, it cannot say all.
If the Maas, the Rhine, the Saône, the Rhône, the Po, and the Tiber
  Can be measured, your praise is measurable too.
Quite immense is your praise, and immense it will be in the future,
  As long as the earth is pervaded by man and beast.
If I cannot do it justice with the resources of language,
  Still my insignificant self scorns to silence such salient fame.
Let praise, mixed with sportive banter, scamper lightly,
10 And let praise be struck up by whatever hand.
Let writing scribbled with pungence and praise visit his highness,
  Whom, God granting, I myself will soon see.

O countenance brighter than gold after triple refinement,
    Happy is he who may always be near
And view the figure worthy of bearing the scepter,
    Which has no equal throughout the whole earth:
The distinguished head, chin, and beautiful bearing,
    The golden hands that put poverty to flight.
Chest, legs, feet, there is nothing not to set store by,
20   Everything is alive with beauty, all shines with grace;
And to hear the beautiful pronouncements of your genius,
    By which you exceed all others and none exceeds you.
No one exceeds you, whose expert wisdom
    So greatly excels, and to which there is, I think, no end.
It is wider than the Nile, larger than the frosty Danube,
    Greater than the Euphrates, smaller than the Ganges by no means.
No wonder that the eternal Shepherd created
    Such a shepherd to pasture his flock.
Your grandfather revives in your name, Solomon in your heritage and wisdom,
30   David in your strength, in your beauty Joseph of old.
Guardian of wealth, avenger of crimes, dispenser of honors,
    All good things are given to you.
With a joyful heart accept bounteous treasures,
    Which God has sent you from the Pannonian land.
Therefore give devout thanks to God in heaven;
    To him may your hand be liberal, as it always is.
The peoples come forward, prepared to serve the Savior,
    Those you call to Christ with a beckoning hand.
Then the Hun comes to Christ with his hair braided,
40   Humble in faith, who was once a fierce foe;
Let the Arab join him, both with long hair styles;
    Let one proceed braided, the other with flowing locks.
O Cordoba, send treasures over long years collected
    With all speed to the king, for whom all noble things are meet.
As the Avars come, come too, O Arabs and nomads,
    Bend your necks and your knees before the feet of the king.
The Avars were no less than you ferocious and savage,
    But he who subdued them will subdue you as well,
God residing in heaven and ruling Tartarean regions,
50   He who rules sea, land, heaven, and stars.
Lo, a new spring is at hand, and in its train good fortune
    Attend you and your family, God granting, O king.
Gladly the year is renewed subject to eternal order,
    And now mother earth scatters her seeds.

Secular and Historical Poems 69

Woods grow green with leaves, fields are adorned with flowers;
    Thus the elements revolve each in turn.
Let the messengers come from all parts bearing good tidings,
    Let there be guerdons of peace with all anger gone.
Then with eyes, minds, and hands raised to heaven
60   He will give and renew thanks to God.
Let the honor of the assembly be pronounced, and in the hall prayers,
    Where beautiful architecture rises with marvelous domes.
From there let the heights of the palace be accessed,
    Let the people saunter back and forth through the halls.
Let the door open, and though many press, let few enter,
    Whom one rank or another has raised.
Let the dear children surround the fair sovereign,
    May he shine above all, as the sun is wont in the sky.
Let the boys attend on one side, the girls on the other,
70   And let the father be rejoiced by the new wine.
Let Charles and Louis stand together, one a youngster,
    While the face of the other already displays youthful grace.
In their strong bodies inheres the vigor of youth maturing,
    A heart eager to learn and firm in resolve.
They are vigorous of mind, outstanding in valor, with piety overflowing,
    Both an ornament of the people, both dear to their sire.
Now let the king turn his shining eyes on them,
    And alternately on the chorus of girls,
On the bevy of girls, than whom none is fairer,
80   In dress, manner, beauty, figure, heart, faith;
To wit on Berta, Chruodtrud, and let Gisla be with them,
    Their sister, and let the younger group of three beauties be there.
With them is Liutgard, a beautiful and powerful woman,
    Outstanding in intelligence and pious works,
Beautiful in elegance, more beautiful still in deeds that are worthy,
    When she alone favors all leaders and the crowd.
Generous in giving, kindly in spirit, most agreeable in conversation,
    She is ready to help all and oppose none.
She attends studiously to the business of learning
90   And absorbs noble arts in the vault of the mind.
Let the delightful children of the king be quick in service
    And compete with pious love to please more.
May Charles quickly provide the double tunic
    And the comfortable gloves, and Louis the sword.
While he is seated, let them give dutiful and welcome kisses,
    That is, the outstanding daughters, with affectionate love.

Berta gives roses, Chruodtrud violets, Gisla lilies;
    Let each bring also prizes of ambrosial draughts,
Rothaid apples, Hiltrud bread, Tetrada a new vintage;
100   Each has a different appearance, but all are a uniform joy to behold.
One girl shines with gems, another with gold and purple,
    One shines forth with a green gem, another with red.
A brooch secures one, a fringe ornaments another,
    Bracelets adorn one, another a torque.
A rust-colored gown suits one, a saffron gown suits another.
    One wears a milk-white bodice, another red.
Let one favor the king with sweet words, another with laughter;
    Let one beguile her father with delicate steps, another with wit.
If by chance the king's holy sister is in attendance,
110   Let her give her brother sweet kisses, and he in turn;
Let her moderate such joys with demure visage
    So that she may be agreeable to her eternal spouse.
Should she ask that the crossroads of Scripture be opened,
    Let the king be her teacher, whom God himself instructs.
Let the nobles advance and stand in a joyful circle,
    Let each strive to fulfill his role.
Let Thyrsis [Meginfred] always be quick to render his lord service,
    May he be active and nimble afoot, in heart and hand;
Let him listen here and there to words of petition.
120   Some let him neglect, and listen receptively to some.
Let him decide, bidding one enter and another be patient,
    One to be inside, another however to stay without.
Let him stand diligently with his bald pate in the royal presence,
    Let him attend to all things with wisdom and respect.
Let the cheerful bishop attend with benign countenance and spirit,
    Displaying kind features and a pious heart.
By sincere faith, such high rank, and innocent instincts
    He is recommended to you, Lord and Christ.
To bless the king's food and drink let him be ready,
130   Whenever the king wishes to take it, let him hasten too.
Let Flaccus [Alcuin] also be present, glory of our poets,
    Who is able to resound with lyrical verse.
He is a powerful scholar, no less a melodious poet,
    Powerful in intelligence, powerful in deed as well.
Let him issue pious teachings on holy Scripture
    And resolve numerical problems with a light heart.
Whether Flaccus's questions be easy or sometimes a puzzle,
    Sometimes rehearsing secular arts, sometimes heavenly ones,

Secular and Historical Poems

Though many are eager, let the king himself be beforehand,
140　　Who is able to solve Flaccidian tasks.
Powerful in voice, vigilant of mind, polished in language,
　　Let Riculf be present, noble in learning and faith.
Even if detained abroad in distant regions,
　　Still he does not return with empty hands.
A sweet tune I would sing you, were you not absent, sweet Homer [Angilbert]
　　But since you are, you fall silent, my Muse.
Let not the skilled presence of Ercambald be missing;
　　A double tablet arms his faithful hand,
Which, hanging by his side, let his fingers swiftly revisit
150　　And pick up the words that he may voicelessly troll.
May Lentulus join in, bringing sweet apples;
　　Let him bring them in baskets and faith in his heart.
He has a lively mind and is otherwise slow in his movements —
　　Be quicker, honest Lentulus, with words and feet.
Let Nardulus [Einhard] rush hither and thither in perpetual motion —
　　Your foot constantly comes and goes like an ant.
A great guest inhabits his little dwelling —
　　Great things too occupy the caves of an exiguous breast.
Now let him bear books, now painstaking drawings,
160　　Now let him prepare darts designed for the Irishman's death,
To whom, as long as he lives, I will give such kisses
　　As the fierce wolf gives you, O long-eared ass.
Sooner will the wicked wolf breed lambs, or the dog rabbits,
　　Or the cat flee the timid mouse
Than will the Goth make peace with the Irish,
　　A peace that, should he make it, will be void like the wind.
He will either pay the price or be fleeting like the south wind,
　　So that, if nothing else, he will be naught but a whistling gust.
If you delete the little letter third in alphabetical order
170　　That happens to be placed second in his name,
Which is pronounced first in "caelum" and second in "scando,"
　　Third in "ascensus," fourth in "amicitiis,"
Which he slurs badly, using you, O letter of "salvus,"
　　So that there is no doubt that, what he pronounces, that will he be.
Let the upright deacon Fredegis stand together with Osulf,
　　Both knowledgeable in letters and properly trained.
If Nardus and Ercambald are joined to Osulf,
　　Under a single table they will provide the three legs.
One is fatter than the other, and one thinner,
180　　But a higher measure put them all on a par.

Let skilled Menalcas come from his fruitful garden,
    Wiping the sweat from the stronghold of his brow with his hand.
How often entering, surrounded by battalions
    Of bakers and cooks, he bears in synodal soup.
Doing all things wisely, let him bring the dainties
    And delicacies before the honored throne of the king.
Let the powerful cellarer Eppinus step forward,
    Let him bring fair vessels and welcome wine in hand.
Let those invited sit around the regal bounty,
190   And let the gift of joy be given from the heavenly heights.
Let Father Albinus [Alcuin] be seated to speak pious phrases
    And eagerly attack the food with both hand and mouth.
Or if, O Bacchus or Ceres, he should chance to seize goblets,
    Of one of your liquids, or indeed both,
So that he may teach better or versify better
    When he moistens the caves of his garrulous breast,
Begone peas and sour milk pottage,
    But be close at hand, table of colorful food.
Let them share in the tables of plenty and the sweet portions,
200   Let them partake of the wine either sitting or standing up.
With this done and the tables and leftover dainties disposed of
    Let the people go out in a lighthearted mood.
For those remaining within let Theodulf's Muse re-echo,
    Let her support kings and mollify the elite.
Perchance the stout hero Wibod may hear her
    And bang his thick head three or four times.
Gazing sternly let him threaten with voice and visage;
    In my absence let him overwhelm me with threats.
If perhaps the pleasing kindness of the king should call him,
210   Let him approach with sidling and tottering gait.
Let his swollen belly precede the rest of his body,
    Let him copy Vulcan with his gait and Jove with his voice.
While this is done and our verses are recited,
    Let the Irish midget stand in a furious state,
An abomination, vicious foe, bitter plague, foolish outrage,
    Contentious infection, monstrous evil, wild thing,
Wild, foul, stupid, and execrable being,
    A peril to the pious and a foe to the good.
With crabbed hands and head bent back crooked,
220   With arms not straight from the vacuous chest.
Two-faced, gaping, quivering, raging, and puffing,
    Let him stand defective in hearing, touch, sight, mind, and foot.

Secular and Historical Poems

With a quick stroke let him assail now these, now others;
    Let him now emit groans, now fearsome words.
Let him now wheel on the reader, now on the listeners,
    The nobles in attendance, making no sense at all.
Let the fierce foe eagerly strive for disapprobation,
    He who is all aspiration and total inexpertise.
He learned this and that, but nothing fixed or certain,
230   He thinks he knows all but knows not a thing.
He did not learn in order to gain reputation for wisdom
    But to be quick with contentious arms.
You are stuffed with learning but, O fool, you know nothing.
    What is more to be said? You know and are without wit.
Let the king go to bed and each retire to his lodging;
    Let the king be of good cheer and the people well pleased.
And you, my flute, ask the pious king for leave to exit,
    And beg all for forgiveness whom this joke affects.
May it please the love of Christ that it offend no one,
240   The love that endures all and takes pleasure in all good things.[1]
The man who foregoes this help and is deprived of such great favor
    May well be enraged—that means nothing to me.
May he, O king, who raised you to the summit of earthly regions,
    Grant you the better rewards of the eternal realm.

26. Super sepulcrum Hadriani papae (Inscribed on the Tomb of Pope Hadrian)

Theodulf's epitaph for Pope Hadrian, who died in 795, is as engaging as his epitaph for Fastrada was pro forma. Charlemagne seems to have issued a general commission in order to elicit a worthy epitaph, and no fewer than three survive, an anonymous one, one by Alcuin, and Theodulf's submission (Alexandrenko 1971:145). Alexandrenko rightly prefers Theodulf's (see also Schaller 1970:28), though Alcuin's was in fact chosen. Alcuin's authorship was not always recognized, and the poem was therefore not included among Alcuin's works in Dümmler's edition. Instead it is found in a separate collection of epitaphs (Dümmler 1881:113–14). On the basis of many verbal reminiscences Luitpold Wallach (1951:128–44) established that it is very probably Alcuin's work. He also established very clearly the formulaic nature of the poem. By contrast, Theodulf's epitaph is highly personal. The poet transposes himself into Charlemagne's state of mind. He not only offers conventional praise of the pope but also conjures up the idea that Charlemagne experiences the loss of Hadrian as he did the loss of

---

[1] 1 Corinthians 13:7

his own father Pippin and mother Bertrada. The relationship is thus a familial one. We would like to know whether this idea originated in a conversation with Charlemagne or whether it was Theodulf's own creation. In the latter case it was perhaps a little too personal and induced Charlemagne to opt for a safer, though less imaginative, alternative. Either way, Theodulf uses a conventional form to cultivate, here as elsewhere, his interest in personal relationships. On the context of the dust-to-dust topos at the end of the poem (Genesis 3:19) see Willeumier-Schalij 1953:227–33. It is much more fully developed in the long *memento mori* passage of "Contra iudices" (28.509–550).

> This funeral dirge is inscribed in gold letters;
>> The golden color pronounces words of lament,
> Which my love and grief for you compel me, Charles, to utter,
>> O Bishop Hadrian, greatly beloved.
> Model of priests, light of the people, standard of salvation,
>> Pious man, wise man, man to be greatly revered,
> Brilliant in mind, handsome in appearance, bright with wisdom,
>> Outstanding in exalted love, eminent in hope and faith,
> You, ornament of the church, gleaming torch of world and city,
>   Distinguished father, you are dearer to me than light.
> When the dire day, not destined to allow another,
>> Carried you off from the living, and the matter was known to me,
> I recognized from afar the traces of former sadness
>> And the death of my parents was recalled to my eyes.
> I felt the misery coming on with the death of Pippin,
>> And this grief, alas, recalls Bertrada as well.
> When I recall your appearance, most holy father,
>> Nothing but grief grips my heart and my eyes.
> I was preparing to send gifts to you while you were living,
>   Now I prepare gifts from a mournful breast:
> Marble for garments and lachrymose verses for treasure,
>> Inscribed on your large urn, already your narrow home.
> When hastening from west or east you may see it,
>> O travelers, and have occasion to pay your respects.
> Both sexes, old, young, child, foreigner, or local,
>> Whoever you are, bid a pleasant rest for Hadrian, the pope.
> May you forever remember, O Rome, this bishop,
>> He who guarded your wealth and was your wall and defense;
> You too, O successor, occupying his holy station,
>   Remember him, I pray, if God should remember you.

Secular and Historical Poems 75

May he be given welcome rest by Peter and Paul's intercession,
　　And may the whole heavenly host take his part.
Give him holy light and grant him quiet,
　　God our King, and take pity on us whom you made.
Behold, he is what he was, from dust taken,[1]
　　But you are able to restore ashen decay.
I believe that, with death overcome, this dust will recover,
　　And will not succumb when buried and gone.
Whoever reads these letters, know that you will turn into
40　　That which is here, for all flesh passes this way.
Therefore, bending your mind to the untimely future,
　　With prayer and beseeching remember this man. Farewell.

27.　[To Corvinianus]

This poem is untitled but is referred to as "Ad Corvinianum" by Dümmler. It
is in the same, at once playful and caustic, vein as "Ad Carolum regem" and to
some extent has the same cast of characters, though a number of them cannot be
identified. Alcuin and Einhard are particularly prominent. Theodulf begins by
cataloguing an array of birds with notably disagreeable voices; these have been
understood as a group of poets, or would-be poets, on whom Theodulf wishes
to heap scorn (Schaller 1971:140). At line 27 he returns to the court characters,
first of all Charlemagne and then a certain Delia, taken to be the pseudonym
for one of Charlemagne's daughters, who is also referred to by Alcuin in two
small poems (39.11 and 40.9 in Dümmler 1881:253). There follow mocking ref-
erences to Alcuin, Bezaleel (Einhard), Thyrsis, an unidentified Lucius, Damaeta
(Riculf, archbishop of Mainz), Menalcas (Audulf, a steward), and, of course, the
unfortunate Irishman Cadac-Andreas. This last is preparing to deliver a blow
on the head of "Getulus." Dümmler originally understood "Getulus" to mean
"the Goth," referring to Theodulf himself, but Collins (1950:217) argued that it
should be understood as "Gaetulus" (the Gaetulian [from North Africa]).

　　This became the point of departure for Schaller's detailed resurrection of the
idea that the Gaetulian is not Theodulf at all but Hrabanus Maurus. He is the
Corvinianus (also titled "corvulus" [little crow] in line 56) whom the Irishman
is preparing to attack. Hrabanus is the Latinized form of the German word for
raven, and Schaller, on the basis of Isidore of Seville's *Etymologies* (14.5.8–10) and
other sources (1971:127), makes a strong case for believing that Gaetulian could
be equivalent to "Moor," that is, "Maurus." Hrabanus Maurus was a very prolific
scholar and poet in the next generation under Louis the Pious and later emperors,
thus acquiring the honorific title *primus praeceptor Germaniae* in modern times.

---

[1] Genesis 3:19

He was born ca. 780 and we know that he was a very precocious poet; he was a pupil of Alcuin's and could have been at the court in the late 790s. Schaller in fact calculates a surprisingly exact date of ca. June 798 for our poem (1971:133). Despite the customary title "Ad Corvinianum" and despite the concluding farewell to Corvinianus, Schaller proposes that the poem is not addressed to any particular person at court but to the court as a whole.

Theodulf avails himself of this new court portrait to heap more abuse on the Irishman. He renews the by now stale joke of Scottus/sottus by adding a third element "cottus." Alexandrenko (1971:153), following Bernhard Bischoff (1967:23), took this to be a Latinization of Cadac with perhaps a play on Middle Latin "cottarius" (Du Cange 2:599), meaning "peasant." But since "sottus" is a word from Romance vernacular, we could imagine that "cottus" might be from the German vernacular, OHG "quât" (ordure). There seems no limit to Theodulf's vilification.

In the last forty lines or so Theodulf runs through a few more characters, some transparent and others not, including three court eunuchs, who become the butt of Theodulf's only sexual joke (see Tougher 2004). He also mentions two giant figures, one named Nimrod and the other Polyphemus. Liersch (1880:53), who also provides a translation of the poem (1880:48–54), and Alexandrenko (1971:151) identified the first as the Wibod familiar from "Ad Carolum regem," but this is not certain. In line 106 Theodulf seems to suggest that he and two others should stick together. The other two could be Corvinianus and Menalcas (Audulf), with whom Theodulf listens to the Irishman's barbed poem in verse 66, but again there is no certainty. Helpful annotations may be found in Christopher John Blakeman's thesis (1990:202–36).

> What do swans do while crows caw out such medleys
>   And shriek many ditties in my house?
> Now the false magpie deceptively mimics human language;
>   Disdaining the birds, he sits by sacred plates.
> The parrot also imitates various songs with his clamor,
>   Disgracing, O Homer, my bard, your Muse.
> The black cormorant, in the waves of the Loire, a fisher,
>   Now is wont to dwell in the woods of Brie.
> And it thinks itself a lovely peacock with feathers,
> 10   Which, O Lemuel, has added to your praise,[1]
> His voice, I think, sounds the same, but the feathers fall short in color,
>   Nor does alternating beauty shine on the plumes.
> Now the cuckoo of spring announces the light of Phoebus,
>   His talkative voice echoing with a harsh guttural tone.

---

[1] Proverbs 31:1, 4

Secular and Historical Poems

Now the crow, hanging from branches, maliciously calls forth rainfall
     And deceptively boasts of having nine lives.
Let the voice of the blackbird be still, the goose in swamps make music
     Devouring foul stuff with his head submerged.
Let the vernal thrush silence his sweet singing,
20   And the unfriendly owl echo nocturnal sounds.
The ass of Balaam once more brays his verses
     And emits strange sounds with a strident voice.[1]
All efforts are suddenly turned upside down and inverted:
     Let Tityrus smile on golden-voiced Orpheus,
You, Orpheus, should pasture nasty goats in the forest;
     Tityrus devotes himself to courtly delights,
With a few maidens perhaps, David stays in the palace
     And pipes a few songs with a Pierian blare;
Delia at the forefront shows off Alcuinian verses,
30   Then others perform on sacred instruments instead;
Delia strums a Thracian chord with her fingers
     And adorns her holy temples with flowers;
A delicate flute explores mellifluous music,
     And runs through fifteen tones with its voice.
Alcuin leaves town as an elder, accompanied by youngsters;
     As full light returns, he himself returns home.
He is up in years, let him take care of his business;
     He will answer for himself and the boys.
Either he will have bidden that they blow light reed pipes
40   Or bind the wreaths of ancient Silenus on their heads.
The psalmist David sees these few verses
     As he already proclaims at the regal feast.
Adding threads to the warp, Virgilian Delia
     Also adds some feminine feet.
Einhard caught sight of Lupus [Theodulf?] in silence
     And therefore was silent himself, fearing sweet words;
As Lupus flees, sense returns to Einhard's spirit,
     And with song he fills rivers, fields, and homes.
On whatever day red curls grow on Thyrsis's bald spot,
50   To wit, shining red locks, then he too will sing.
While hoary Lupus seeks about in his cupboards for poems,
     He will find perchance that Virgil resounds.
Poems are composed in brief compass by Lucius,
     Such as perhaps the crow is unable to learn.

---

[1] Numbers 22:28

The Irish midget girt with sharp sword is on the lookout
    So that, Corvinianus, he can plunge it into your chest.
He does not fear crows, and would spare no feathered creature
    If only he may hope that Damoetas [Riculf] is far off.
He is not a pious poet, our Irishman, Damoetas,
60   The impudent fun from his mouth turns to grief.
Wielding arms the Irishman readies himself for battle,
    Wishing to strike the head of the Gaetulian with his sword.
He will have three appellations: "Scot," "sot," and "cottus,"
    And he himself rails with a hollow sound at Theodulf.
With a versified song in distichs, and a face all grimy,
    Lo, Menalcas [Audulf], he performed it for us two.
With a wicked grin the dead man struck down the living,
    But these battles are fit for boys.
Three boys rejoice around the table of Daniel,[1]
70   Three who overcome flames with nobility and faith.
Now Job shines with great multiplication of honor,
    And the psalter gleams with love to pious eyes.
In the center David rules all with his scepter,
    Distributing feasts in peaceable trim,
And pious Aaron [Hildebald] blesses all things in the palace,
    Blessing all the dishes with holy words.
Nemias [Nehemiah, Eppinus, Eberhard], who once restored Jerusalem's city,
    Powerful with drink, though bald, will bring sweet wines.
What place is there for a black crow in this party?
80   Let him stay in the woods, himself among wolves,
Unless Elijah cleanses the crimes of the crow
    And bids him again to his holy board.[2]
Hardberd, the stingy dispenser of Spanish potions,
    All loaded with beer in his hall,
Stirs with his ladle in the pot warm liquid in the kitchen
    So that what first he stirs hot, he can later drink cold.
The little Greek Potiphar, unpopular perhaps with the ladies,
    Armed to no purpose and waging no war,
Accompanied by his associates Bagao and Egeus,
90   Out of these three decrepits not one man is made.
I think they are not voluntarily faithful in chambers,
    But the fierce hand of the physician forces them to keep faith.

---

[1] Daniel 3:13–30
[2] 1 Kings 17:4–6

Secular and Historical Poems   79

The son of the widow, Hiram, constructed the temple[1]
  For God enthroned on high; may Christ assist in the work.
Among them the giant Nimrod brandishes weapons,[2]
  He who with darts prepares to strike the crow on the brow;
And huge Polyphemus, stirring up the sail-bearing waters,
  So that even the cormorant cannot escape from the sea.
  These two, different in size but equal in menace,
100   One will break the crow's feet, the other his head.
They are merely pygmies, wishing for a peaceful conciliation
  With you, little black crow, because of the wars of the cranes.
Let these words suffice on your arrival, just the threefold
  Phrase be enough: winter, hunger, and thirst.
Let us keep ourselves to ourselves in the palace,
  We three-footed brothers, a threesome, may our crowd be small.
May you, O sharp little crow, have only these verses,
  Reading them often, may you hold them in your heart.
When Alcuin comes in the company of boys and poems,
110   Then perhaps you can hope more for yourself.
Now may you have as many greetings as hairs turning
  White on your head; thus, Corvinianus, farewell.

28. Versus Teudulfi episcopi contra iudices (Bishop Theodulf's Verses against the Judges)

In 798 Theodulf was commissioned by Charlemagne as a *missus dominicus*, together with the bishop designate of Lyons, Laidradus, to carry out an inspection of the legal institutions in what is now southern France. This mission must have seemed to Theodulf not only important but exceptionally revealing because it inspired him to produce a long and passionate poem (956 verses). The observations he made seem to have engaged all his social and moral instincts in an unparalleled way. Manfred Fuhrmann (1980:72–77) argued that the poem not only echoes patristic and literary sources but also reinforces Charlemagne's legislation. It is therefore not surprising that it has received more attention than most of Theodulf's other poems. It was edited separately by Pierre Daniel as early as 1598, and again, at the same moment Dümmler was preparing his edition of the early Carolingian poets, by Hermann Hagen in 1882. But, apart from a few excerpts in Peter Godman's *Poets of the Carolingian Renasissance* (1985:162–67), there has been no published translation. See also Godman 1987:70–74.

Theodulf set out with Laidradus from Lyons and visited three towns along the Rhône River: Vienne, Valence, and Rochemaure. This part of the journey

---

[1] 1 Kings 7:13
[2] cf. Genesis 10:8–9

was presumably accomplished by boat since travel on waterways was the speediest and easiest option at the time. The voyage from Lyons to Avignon has been estimated to have taken two to five days (Ohlers 2004:84), but the stops along the way could have extended the schedule to two weeks or more. From Avignon he traveled west. For the stretch Avignon — Nîmes — Soutancion (now Castelnau-le-Lez) — Béziers — Narbonne he could have followed the old Roman Via Domitia, but from Soutancion he seems to have made an extended detour south to Maguelone and Agde. Once in Narbonne he would have proceeded along the Aude to Carcassonne; it seems unlikely that he would have traveled on the river going upstream.

Norbert Ohlers (204:108–11) has calculated average daily distances for travelers in the Middle Ages at 30 kilometers by foot or 40–50 kilometers on horseback. Most of the places mentioned by Theodulf are within an hour of each other on modern highways, and even in the Middle Ages the distances were not exorbitant. Modern roadways indicate the following approximations: Avignon to Nîmes (40 kilometers), Nîmes to Soutancion (52 kilometers), Soutancion to Maguelone (15–20) kilometers, Maguelone to Agde (60 kilometers), Agde to Béziers (30 kilometers), Béziers to Narbonne (35 kilometers), Narbonne to Carcassonne (50 kilometers). Theodulf also mentions the area southwest of Carcassonne called Razès or Le Razès, but it is unclear what his mission would have been since there appear not to have been any important centers in this region.

In some cases Theodulf could have managed the stages in a single day. He and his more distinguished companions, like Laidradus, would have been on horseback, but there would have been packhorses and perhaps followers on foot as well. What would they have have done when they could not reach their destination in a single day, for example between Maguelone and Agde (60 kilometers) or between Nîmes and Soutancion (52 kilometers)? To be sure, there were probably inns, perhaps especially along the old Via Domitia, but we do not know much about them (Ohlers 2004:149), and later indications suggest that they were by no means comfortable. The alternative for persons of high status like Theodulf and Laidradus would have been transportable tents, which are documented as early as Boniface's eighth-century travels (Ohlers 2004:233, 237). Servants and footmen would have slept in the open air.

Once Theodulf was back in Avignon, he seems to have gone to Arles, a long day's journey of 40 kilometers. It is the following stage that seems most demanding, a distance of 90 kilometers to Marseille with no obvious way stations to break the journey. One may wonder in fact whether Theodulf would not have accomplished this leg by boat, to the mouth of the Rhône and then along the coast to Marseille. From Marseille the itinerary would have become easier: 25 kilometers to Aix-en-Provence, 40–50 kilometers to Cavaillon, and 22 kilometers back to Avignon. Overall we might guess that Theodulf would have needed twenty to twenty-five days of travel time. If he spent four or five days at each of his destinations, a total of sixty to seventy-five days, the total length of

Secular and Historical Poems

81

the expedition may have been about three months. In other words, he could have accomplished the mission during the summer months when there was sufficient grass to allow the horses to graze. Assuming a departure in late May, Theodulf could have been back at Charlemagne's court to report in September.

What we miss in the poem is any allusion to the vicissitudes or hazards of such a journey, but our information may be supplemented by another poem (number 48). Here Theodulf describes a trip from Limoges to Périgueux and across the swollen Dordogne. In Limoges he gets a friendly reception but is attacked by a drunken crowd and narrowly escapes. At the Dordogne his horses become so frightened at the prospect of crossing that they scatter and must be reassembled "among fords, among cliffs, in woodland and caverns." They can be induced to cross over only when they are attached by their halters to the back of a boat. In the following poem (49) Theodulf refers to a less adventurous crossing of the Rhine. Poem 59 ("In xenodochio") concerns a simple inn for travelers constructed by Theodulf; we may wonder whether this project was inspired by Theodulf's discomforts on the road while traveling.

Because of its length and detail "Contra iudices" might appear to be a challenge, but it is in fact unusually well-articulated and lucidly phrased. It begins with an exhortation to the judges to be mindful of the trajectory toward heaven, and it places justice in the context of divine precedents. The catalogue of precedents begins with "the trumpet of the Gospels" (v. 19) but then proceeds to Old Testament figures (vv. 21–86). The emphasis on Old Testament precedent is interesting because it stands in contrast to a later emphasis on the transition from the Old Law to the New Law and the legal consequences of that transition. The prelude concludes with a special plea to the judges to avoid the temptation of bribery, a failing that Theodulf declares himself to be free of (vv. 93–96).

The poet now turns to his special commission. He outlines the extent of Charlemagne's authority with reference to twenty-four rivers and appends a eulogy of his companion Laidradus's virtues (vv. 103–114). There follows an itinerary of the trip touching on no fewer than eighteen towns or locations from Lyons to Cavaillon, both west and east of the Rhône (vv. 123–152). Of special moment is his reception by remnants of "the Gothic people and the Spanish population" in Narbonne, who recognize him as their countryman. The itinerary ends with a description of a few topographical features (vv. 155–162) that signal Theodulf's appreciation of landscape.

People flock to meet the inspectors general. They are by no means disinterested but offer an array of valuables in order to win their cases. Most notable is a fine silver vessel decorated with pictures of the destruction of Cacus and other adventures of Hercules (see Bretzigheimer 2004; Nees 1987 and 1991; Lendinara 1998:176). These pictures give Theodulf the opportunity for a long descriptive digression (vv. 179–202). The details of this description can be appreciated only against the background of the classical narrative in Virgil's *Aeneid* (8.184–275). The enumeration of bribes offered to Theodulf continues through verse 252, but he is proof against such inducements (vv. 269–270). Not wishing to appear sanctimonious, however, he does allow for small gifts such as fruit, eggs, wine, bread, and little birds (vv. 283–288). His denunciation of corruption goes on for another fifty lines (301–356) before he finally turns to the matters of judicial process.

The initiation of court proceedings should occur only after the consultation of relevant Scripture and appropriate prayers to God (vv. 359–360). In other words, Theodulf advises the same organizational principle that led him to begin his poem with references to the Old Testament. In this case, however, he advocates Christ, not the patriarchs, as the foundation of correct procedure (vv. 369–370). This refocusing becomes increasingly crucial later in the poem.

The next three hundred lines or so are given over to the details of propriety and procedure. The judge should be publicly accessible, attentive to the poor, orderly, and fully informed. He should not arrive late or leave early, and on no account should he show up tipsy or overfed so as to become an object of mockery (Monod 1887:5; Fuhrmann 1980:271). He should choose his associates carefully and not allow the doorkeeper to accept bribes. He should initiate the proceedings by addressing the court on "justice and the celestial commandments" (v. 449), and, most importantly, he should suppress any inclination to pride and remember the fall of Satan (vv. 465–490). Proper humility should teach a judge to bear his own transitory life in mind, and this leads to an extended *memento mori* (vv. 509–550). What is to be borne in mind are not the momentary delights of this world but rather the imperishable soul (vv. 556–588).

With the banishment of pride accomplished, the judge may proceed with attentiveness toward all, vigilance, and a pace that is neither too hasty nor too slow. In particular it is important to treat poor or disadvantaged people not only fairly but to give them extra help (vv. 629–632). The judge should keep order without offering violence and should moderate the passions of the litigants. Decisions should be taken with due consultation and thoroughness, and associates should not be subject to improper influence. In particular the judge should guard against the possibility that his wife may exercise her feminine wiles (vv. 691–714)—a counterimage to Matthew 27:19. Above all, a judge must resist bribes (vv. 719–734). He should also know how to evaluate witnesses (vv. 743–766), and the witnesses themselves should be truthful (vv. 767–780). At the same time testimony should not overshoot the mark and endanger the innocent or slander even the guilty.

Certainly the most curious item in Theodulf's admonition is the advice to litigants not to swear oaths (vv. 813–842; cf. Matthew 5:33–37). The argument is that if you do not swear an oath, you cannot perjure yourself; arguments can be used in lieu of oaths. If, however, a witness is forced to swear an oath, he should do so "with transparent words and a pious mind." He should engage in no verbal quibbles because God "does not heed the words that you swear but how the inquirer thought that you swore" (vv. 837–838). (This principle would of course disallow the famous ambiguous oaths of later medieval literature.) Theo-

Secular and Historical Poems

dulf concludes the argument up to this point with the sweeping summary (vv. 845–846):

> Let judgment come first, kindness come second, bribes come never
> In the judicial process, where Christ is also at hand.

The theme of kindness provides the point of departure for the final section of the poem. It begins with the cruel punishments prescribed by the law in the name of deterrence and denounces the loss of life or limb (see Geary 2008). The guilty should be treated "as you wish God to treat you" (v. 855). Theodulf then defends himself against those who might accuse him of excessive leniency; he urges moderation, but is adamant about capital punishment ("stain not your steel with wretched bloodletting" [v. 871]). Others may persist in their sanguinary ways, but Theodulf wants no part of it (vv. 881–882):

> May I be the one to redeem many crowds of wretches,
> May I deliver many from the cross and from death.

One may wonder to what extent this exhortation merely reflects the church's opposition to bloodshed ("ecclesia abhorret a sanguine") and to what extent it reflects Theodulf's personal commitment, but the strength of the language certainly suggests a personal investment. James Megivern's book *Capital Punishment* (1997) makes it clear that Catholic views on bloodshed were more mixed than we might imagine, but Theodulf appears to be perfectly firm. The final lines of the poem are an equally impassioned plea in favor of poor people who have been disadvantaged through no fault of their own and are victimized by rich people. Humans should not imitate the predatory customs of wild beasts but be compassionate, bearing in mind that everyone will ultimately be in need of mercy.

The distinction of this poem is not only its mounting eloquence on behalf of sinners and the dispossessed but also in its command of several registers, from the comedy of the bribery scenes and the behavior of intoxicated judges to the sober concern with the orderly administration of justice to the encompassing sympathy with human weakness and to the equality of all people before God. This range is not found in Theodulf's other poems and gives "Contra iudices" a special place in his repertory.

> Magistrates, choose the road of just judgment,
> And may your feet disdain crooked ways.
> One road leads to heaven, the latter runs down to the shadows,[1]
> Pious life follows the former, on the other gaping death waits.

---

[1] cf. Proverbs 7:25–27

Therefore, O men, avoid the seething waters of Acheron,
    Where Styx and all the fury of Cocytus flow.
But, O paradise, nothing is more agreeable than your mansions,
    Where no evil lives and all goodness dwells.
If I had a thousand tongues in a hundred inflections,
10   And a brazen voice to give iron words to all,
I would not be able, I own, to express all the rapture
    Of the pleasance that awaits those who observe the laws well.
Nor could I sum up in words the monstrous afflictions
    That the company of the friends of fraud undergoes.
Let pity be granted to the verdicts and to pity diligent devotion,
    So that cruel offices will find no place.
This the pages of the Old Law prescribe as a duty,
    And no blessed tongue of the prophets is mute.
This the trumpet of the Gospels proclaims through the crossroads
20   Of the world, this the words of the apostles thunder too.
This raises the names of the patriarchs to heaven,
    Where the holy order of prophets is enthroned.
Anyone among leaders and kings who followed the path of this holy
    Road gained the possession of all delight;
But those who were led by error along rough byways
    Have left this road and, at the same time, all that is good.
Moses, the most faithful spokesman of a kind Godhead,
    Enjoyed conversation with God, leaving the people in awe.
For forty years, through the paths of wilderness regions,
30   He guided the people with ample resources to the honor of God.
Always loving justice, always disdaining vulgar prizes,
    By example and word he showed the way to be saved.
Samuel, born by maternal faith and devotion[1]
    And by the gift of Him who creates all good,
Who before time created what with time he discloses,
    To whom what is present is at one with what was and will be,
Spurned all types of deception and opted for goodness,
    Nor made use of your means, lowly ass.[2]
What shall I say of the king who composed sonorous poems,
40   He who with all his spirit was zealous in the service of God,
Whom all things attend in the Thunderer's praises,
    Art, flesh, spirit, plectrum, lyre, strings, chorus, and voice.
With verse and deed and all due exertions
    He urges the avoidance of evil and teaches the maintenance of law.

---

[1] 1 Samuel 1:11
[2] 1 Samuel 9:20, 12:3

Secular and Historical Poems 85

That the just lord said, the lover of moderate guidance,
    Whose rejoicing countenance sees all just things,
  Thus admonishing wicked judges with these phrases,
    Articulating with such commands:
"Why do so many of you bear down with wicked judgments
50   And at once take up fierce words like those who sin?
Rush together for the case of a poor man or orphan,
    Let justice be done for the wretched and oppressed;
Release the poor from the dire hands of sinners."[1]
    More such eloquent things he set down with his pen.
His admirable power outgrows all limits,
    He who could be the happy ancestor of his Lord.[2]
He who was refined in many a furnace of his opponents
    Was thus exalted in strength and overcame what was wrong.
Because his famous son [Solomon] was lacking in these virtues,
60   With a foolish mind he left the right road.
The more the curved plowshare wounds the submissive furrows,
    The fewer the thorns, the more the welcome harvest abounds.
King Solomon was wise, just in law's administration,
    Except that he was caught in feminine snares.[3]
Alas, leaving such goodness behind, he turned to evil,
    Thus, sour wine, you lose your honeyed taste.
The glory of the reverend king Hezekiah grew greater
    By the merits of justice and the assistance of faith;
To him the Father of all wished to give fifteen years added,[4]
70   And pious life returned from the clutches of death.
He teaches the people to learn the laws of the fathers
    And flee the snares of wicked wrong.
He crushed on the mountaintop the coiled serpent,[5]
    First the cause of life and later of death.
Thus when someone is pierced by the physician's scalpel,
    To some comes health and to others dire ill.
You were given to worship, princely Josiah,
    And this raised your famous name to the heights.[6]
You who remove the remnants of ancient transgression
80   And do your best to renew ancestral laws,

---

[1] Psalm 82:2–4
[2] Luke 3:23–38
[3] 1 Kings 11:1–6
[4] 2 Kings 20:6
[5] 2 Kings 18:4
[6] 2 Kings 22–23

You were granted as a pious glory to a declining kingdom,
 You whom the due order of that twilight age installed.
Thus the fringe borders the robe, and wine concludes dinner,
 And after the fruits of the year the fat olive thrives.
There is a great crowd of fathers by whom the lesson is rendered,
 Whom pious law holds fast, and whom it would be long to list.
I often see judges abandoning the law for those who promise
 And follow gold with greedy mouths and words.
I often try to rein in the grasping lest they seize temptation;
90 There are more who covet and fewer inclined to refuse.
If someone diverts a broad river into streamlets,
 The smaller part goes to the brooks, the larger will stay in the main course.
On these matters I often remonstrate with the wicked,
 But they secretly say that I am the same.
Although I am not such as they say, I am often under suspicion,
 And though I am guilty of many, I will be free of this vice.
An ill man cannot be cured of all diseases;
 Among many, one at least can be healed.
A commission was given to me to manage,
100 A powerful office to accomplish great things.
Second to none in power, pious zeal, and weapons,
 King Charles, preeminent in excellence, assigned this task;
To him are subject Waal, Rhône, Maas, Rhine, the Inn River,
 Seine, Weser, Gard, Garonne, and Po,
Roer, Loire, Volturno, Marne, Lès, and Mosel,
 Danube, Aude, the Gave, the Lot, Elbe, and Saône,
So that the synod might rule the clergy and sweet law the people,
 And the leader may be a guide to all on his path,
So that the holy order of Mother Church might grow greater
110 And the pious customs and splendor in powerful sites,
Those washed by the Saône and the Gard and the Rhône swiftly flowing,
 The Allier or the Aude to be numbered as well,
Those that the Alps separate from Latium, and the sea from Libya,
 And those that the Pyrenees separate, O Ebro, from your land,
Or those that Lyons divides in northern and southern directions,
 And that beautiful Toulouse divides from your site, Aquitaine.
Our companion Laidradus accompanied us on this mission
 So that the great labor might be lightened by his aid.
Noricus bore him and you, Lyons, may look forward
120 To having him as a future bishop in support of our faith.
He stands out in art, stands high in intelligence, overflows with virtue;
 For him this life remains a trajectory to paradise.

Secular and Historical Poems 87

With your high walls, Lyons, left behind us
  We approach along the road prescribed by the task.
We seek the buildings of Vienne raised in a stony valley,
  Which the cliffs enclose on one side, the broad river to the east.
From there we headed for the city lying in the land of Valence,
  And from there to you, Rochemaure, on rocks.
Then we touch on the fields of Avignon and the land of Orange,
130   And we touch the territories that the Goths hold.
From there we gradually move on to Nîmes and her towers,
  Where a spacious town and active industry are found.
It has Maguelone on the left and Soutancion on the right side,
  On one side it is encircled by rough heights, on the other by the sea.
With these safely traversed we left Agde on the left hand
  And the roofs of Béziers welcome us in.
Then, Narbonne, we reach your site and beautiful city,
  Where a joyful crowd presses forward to me;
The remnants of the Gothic people and the Spanish population
140   Are overjoyed to see me as their countryman and chargé d'affaires.
From there we travel to see you, Carcasonne and Razès,
  And we approach your walls quickly, Narbonne.
From all sides crowds of people and clergy gather,
  The synod rules the clergy and kindly laws the courts.
With matters put in order the rich city of Arles received us,
  A city which its own citizens erected,
The city of Arles, the first among many a city,
  But second to you in rank, O Narbonne.
With the synod and the guidance of legislation
150   We subdue the hearts of the clergy and people with law and verbal art.
Marseille, founded by the people of Argos, received us,
  And your land, city of Aix, and Cavaillon.
But constraints prevent surveying the others in order,
  From which the people approach us, wherever we are:
Those whom the wildness of the nearby raging sea endangers,
  Or the foul odor fans with corrupt air,
Whom the hills lift high or the depths of the valley inhibit,
  Whom fierce winter beats, hail, frost, and snow.
There we continue the journey, avoiding brambles,
160   Thorny branches and abrupt caves.
Deep valleys plunge downward, mountains rise to the heavens,
  Steep streams rush from the crests of the hills.
Large crowds keep flocking to see us,
  All ages and sexes have something to say,

Infant, aged, youthful, father, bride, single,
　　Adult, young man, old woman, man, wife, and teen.
Why linger? People promise gifts with no hesitation;
　　What they want they think they can have if they give.
With this engine they compete to break down the wall of my spirit
170　　So that, battered by such a ram, my mind will succumb.
One promises crystal and Eastern jewels
　　If I help him gain someone else's fields.
Another brings a heavy weight of precious gold coinage
　　Inscribed in Arabic characters and tongue,
Or coins that the Latin stylus has impressed on bright silver,
　　If he can only acquire houses, lands, and estates.
One man in a secret whisper addresses my assistant
　　With words intended to be passed on to me:
"I own a certain vessel ornamented with ancient figures
180　　Made from a pure vein and of no inconsiderable weight,
On which are engraved the traces of Cacus's misdeeds:
　　The countenances of men all gory, impaled on stakes;
Jagged hills and signs of frequent plunder;
　　A field tinged with the blood of humans and beasts,
On which Herculean wrath crushes the bones of Vulcan's offspring
　　While he with grim visage belches ancestral fires;
On which he rips the belly with his knee or kicks open the stomach.
　　With his club he strikes smoke-breathing throat and mouth.
There you may see the bulls emerge from the recesses,
190　　Once more in dread of being dragged by their tails.
In the hollow part where there is a flat, circular surface
　　A small area displays lesser scenes.
How the infant from Tiryns crushes two serpents,
　　And in due order are inscribed his ten deeds.
But the exterior is rubbed smooth from much abrasion,
　　And an ancient image is almost erased,
Where Hercules, the River Calydon, and the half-beast Nessus
　　Do battle, O Deianira, by your beauty compelled.
The fatal garment is stained with the blood of Nessus,
200　　And the fearful fate of Lychas can be seen.
Antaeus too loses his life in a hard struggle,
　　Who is prevented from touching the earth, as is his wont.
"This shall I deliver to the lord ('lord' he happened to call me)
　　If only he will accede to my wish;
There are numerous people in my charge, both mothers and husbands,
　　Children, youths of both sexes all in a group,

Secular and Historical Poems 89

Whom father and mother, with the honor of exemption,
    Have left behind, thus a crowd of tax-free men remain.
If only I invalidate their charters, he will gain an ancient vessel,
210   I will gain what is mine and you will gain gifts."
Yet another said: "I have coverlets dyed in various colors,
    Robes that I think were sent by fierce Arab tribes,
On which a calf follows its mother or the bull leads the heifer,
    The heifer matches the calf in color, the ox matches the ox;
You may view the finery, and art fashioned in colors,
    Just as smaller wheels are joined to great ones with art.
I have a case at law with someone concerning beautiful cattle,
    For which I am ready to give these matching gifts.
For the calves I will offer a calf, for a bull a bull is awarded,
220   For the cow a cow, for the ox an ox."
One man promises to give beautiful goblets,
    If only I will give what he asks but should not have,
Decorated with gold inside and blackened outside,
    Since the color of silver tarnished by sulfur recedes.
"Fabrics which make couches and beautiful beds look splendid,"
    Says another, "we will give if you grant what I ask.
All adorned with vines and olive trees, with grasses and gardens,
    An irrigated field was left at my father's death.
My brothers and sister demand a portion,
230   But I wish to have it alone and not to share.
I will be satisfied if my wishes are looked on with favor,
    If you take what I offer, if you properly give what I ask."
One man wishes to acquire his companion's home, another fields that are
    fallow,
    Both covet what belongs to another — one has it, the other aspires.
One longs to acquire, another ardently hopes not to forfeit;
    One is prepared to give sword and helmet, the other shields;
One has a patrimony, his brother wishes to have it;
    One wants to give horses, the other mules.
One group has wealth in abundance, another is eager,
240   So that all may lay claim and have whatever they contest.
Nor is there a shortage of equivalent outlay;
    A common custom was pressed with varying force.
As the greater men offer great gifts, lesser men make more modest offers
    As long as they think they will get what they want in this way.
One has furs named after you, O Cordovan city;
    One unfolds snowy samples, another red counterparts.
He who is able gives linen gifts, if unable, woolen presents,
    A covering for the head, for the feet, or the hands.

One has a kerchief to give as a present,
250   With which we are wont to wipe moisture from hands and face.
Others make strongboxes as gifts, nor is any man missing
        Who cheerfully would give dark-dyed scrolls.
Who will tabulate the details? All were bent on giving,
        All thought, nothing given, nothing gained.
O criminal plague, widespread in every direction,
        O villainy, madness, too ferocious greed,
Which lays claim to whatever the earth has to offer.
        There is no lack of those who barter ill-gotten gains;
They rush to corrupt me, nor can they think that men like me are so easy
260   Unless such a one has been there before.
No one seeks boars in the waters or the scaly tribe in the forests,
        Water in torches, or pyres in the waves.
Araby has incense, the Ganges boasts ivoried giants,
        Hyrcania has griffins, Syria has balsamic scents.
Things have their own law and are sought by long-standing practice,
        And people believe that mortals will remain as they were.
But when they see that the barbs of their words are broken,
        And that the spikes of their promises are without worth,
They will see me stand firm like a strong fortress after battle
270   And know that I will not succumb to their arts,
That whatever each sought, each received justice,
        And that they cannot overcome me or their own by deceit.
Thus, everyone seeing the approach blocked by which he
        Was wont to defraud, must go on his way without hope.
Lest gentle prudence should be absent from our actions,
        And our affairs appear to be managed sanctimoniously,
And lest I should be known to many for sheer innovation,
        And that good be offended by the proximity of bad,
I have refused to spurn what was initially agreed on,
280   Which, to harmonize spirits, is cheerfully given and received,
And what good custom commonly sanctions,
        And though much is at stake, claims title to naught.
Considering this, I willingly accepted small trifles,
        Which not a greedy hand but a benevolent one gave:
To wit, tree-grown fruit from a verdant garden,
        Eggs, wine, bread, hay for the steeds.
We also accepted chicks and little songbirds,
        Tiny in body but very good to eat.

Secular and Historical Poems

Happy is every virtue if prudence, nurse of virtues,
290   Moderates, adorns, and nurtures your mind.
These matters have digressed somewhat on my adventures,
     But now let my Muse return to my original song.
Let the weights of a just scale, O judge, be equal,[1]
     So that, the scale granting, each may gladly receive his due.
Let the sickness of avarice, coveting, greed, and fear be absent,
     Lest they interfere, but let loftiness of mind stand fast.
Alas, the love of justice is quickly driven from these quarters,
     And fraud and trickery quickly take its place.
Four factors are guilty, one guiltier than the others:
300   That being fierce cupidity, the root of all sin.[2]
The acceptance of a gift is apt to turn fragile spirits
     From the true way, and put pious law to flight.
Not only by silver and gold is this promoted,
     But by the hoofs of swift horses pawing the earth,
Or purple dye, gems, or a beautiful garment,
     Or various things that a hand is accustomed to show.
By light words quite like the flitting breezes,
     And by the winds of flattery, the mind, thus driven, swells.
A robe is distinguished by color, purses delight in their heavy content,
310   But the breeze of favor wafts away like fickle winds.
In one is at least the glory of earthly accrual,
     But in the other, by contrast, there is nothing but empty air.
A rich man quickly vexes the mind of the judge with presents,
     The poor man trembles because he can give none.
Both one and the other promise to give often,
     But he who gives most gets what he wants.
There are people whom witnesses, law, and documents do not entitle,
     Thus they go to court deprived of all support.
He will carry the day if he just says "please be receptive";
320   He is supported by all if he can give more.
Refrain, O judges, from being annoyed at my efforts
     That aspire to suppress and not foster crime.
I do not bring criminal charges against all and sundry,
     Let praise and shame be allotted to each as deserved;
Lo, the crime for some is to abandon the true way for chattels,
     Or to sell what is proper for each to volunteer.
I do not wish you to be thought free of deceit or sharp practice
     If you carry off gifts even in a just case.

---

[1] Leviticus 19:36
[2] 1 Timothy 6:10

There are judges competing to sell both injustice and justice;
330   One is guilty of one crime, the other of two.
The first because he sells justice, which he should give freely;
     The other because he disdains the law and profits all the same.
He who seeks lawless rewards for just judgment,
     He carries out your deceit, O inimical fraud;
The pious gifts of law should be given without compensation,
     The greedy man reacts by taking an unworthy price.
If the infectious fury of greed should chance to beset you,
     May reason stand fast and speak with an amenable voice:
"Consider, for the Lord on high observes you from heaven,
340   And will note all you do with divine mind,
He who is judge and witness at once, and avenger of evil,
     Who rewards worthy action with good, and evil with ill."
If, however, a voice should say "Take a donation,
     Which you may now give to your associates (avoid being caught),"
Let victorious reason oppose it and say: "Unholy
     Corruption, begone," and let reason be at your command.
Let not the burning thirst by which you are harried be honored;
     The more you drink, the greater your thirst will grow.
The more the wood catches fire, the more it will kindle,
350   Thus the more a man has, the more he desires.
The bloodsucking leech grows fat from its feasting,
     The more it drinks, the more it thirsts.
Therefore take heed, I beg you, to banish the mad disorder,
     With me as your physic you will be healed of your vicious wound.
When my kind hand will have healed your illness,
     May it guide you, let your harsh condition pass away:
When the tumult of cases calls you to the flurry of court proceedings
     And the matter at hand is confided to your care,
First eagerly explore the relevant passages of Scripture,
360   Look them up, and while you do so, offer pious prayers to God;
As a suppliant ask that he direct your actions
     And let nothing be done not pleasing to him.
For this is the way to be followed in every action
     Whenever a matter is to be taken in hand.
The law and kingdom of God we are bound to consult in the first place
     So that all things be viewed by us with his help.
If with such help you cast the foundation in marble,
     All the more firmly will any pious work rise above.

Secular and Historical Poems

O once, O four times, O without number is blessèd
370   Whatever work adheres to you, Christ, our supreme rock.
Then make your way quickly and conspicuously to the court chambers
    So that for the contending crowd you may be on display.
As you stride back and forth, if a poor man cries out pleading,
    A man who may say that he must speak to you not later but now,
Though surrounded with people, exit the majestic portals;
    With the people gaping outside, you yourself will be embraced.
Let your just, pious, and faithful servant be your attendant
    So that the poor man can be introduced.
Say to him: "Bring the man into our presence,
380   The man who raised his voice in plaintive tones."
Taking your seat, first discuss the case duly,
    Let all the details follow each in turn.
Perchance you will ask the time and hour to appear at the hearing?
    Take my advice: come in the morning first thing.
Not for a whole day will this work be a burden;
    The more a man plows, the better his crop.
He who fasted greatly for his legal vocation
    Is said to have continued for days in this work.[1]
I have seen judges who are slow in legal service,
390   But I contend they are swift in grabbing up gifts.
They arrive at the fifth hour (11:00) and know to leave at the ninth hour (3:00);
    If the third hour (9:00) brings them in, the sixth (12:00) takes them out.
If they are to give, the ninth hour (3:00) is right, if to take, the first hour (6:00).
    They come, and he is quick who used to be slow.
Thus when a steed feels his mouth curbed by a sharp bridle,
    He will leap on his own and go for feed.
He who is always ready to injure and never ready to be of assistance,
    Is ready at hand when he ought not to be.
Drink should ever be shunned, all the more so
400   When the pious reins of justice are to be held.
For he who buries himself in excessive feasting and napping
    Reduces to dullness the strength of body and mind;
When he comes to law cases deprived of alertness,
    He sits there languid, distracted, and mentally slow.
When skill is needed in ambiguous cases, and the issue
    Is turned over at length this way and that,
He is inert, muddled, all hiccups, tipsy and breathless,
    He gapes, droops, is nauseous, anguished, and slow;

---

[1] Exodus 18:13

Now he says that his joints are affected, now his stomach,
410   And now that all his limbs feel heavy at once.
Sleep first infects him after eating and drinking,
      The next task for him will be wanton ways.
Therefore avoid too much food and the beakers of Bacchus,
      And sleep; these things one and all burden the mind.
Moderation favors digestion, while excess oppresses;
      Much water kills grain, a moderate amount makes it grow.
If drunk, you will be the secret object of laughter by the people;
      One winks at the other, and you are the mark.
If you speak soberly, all will respect you,
420   And will compete to do what you assign them to do.
Those whom honesty recommends, and just actions,
      Bring within, addressing each one by name.
May they manage with care and share your decisions,
      And tread the path that calls to better rewards.
In the meantime, let the doorkeeper hold the breathless crowd in abeyance
      So that the raging throng does not rush in pell-mell,
And so that the hall will not be overfilled with plaintive tumult;
      He who commands less attention shouts all the more.
The doorkeeper himself should be admonished to reject douceurs,
430   Which are often taken when people seek leave to come in.
It is a crime to hope for a bribe from suppliant people,
      And, sad to say, all doorkeepers are fond of this crime.
All doorkeepers love it, and the judge neglects to detest it;
      There is scarcely one in a thousand who holds it in contempt.
Powers to acquire are varied, but there is just one love of possessions,
      Which is rather to be called madness than love.
This pestilent plague encompasses the whole earthly circle
      And furiously consumes the greater number of men.
Our whole age and order is besieged by this infection,
440   Maiden, boy, old codger, and both sexes alike.
The great covet great things, lesser men are more modest;
      The mouser does to the mouse what the savage lion does to the sheep.
Therefore when all things are settled in detail,
      As your schedule and the order of your office require,
When the judicial body and the ranks of the people are seated,
      When you have occupied the presiding chair,
Looking about at the people, address them in the following language,
      And with pious affection of mind admonish them thus:

Secular and Historical Poems   95

"Be apprised of justice and the celestial commandments,[1]
450   Which the Father on high decreed from the vault of the sky.
Let God, the prophets, the laws, and also the monarch
      Review this justice, let their power rule our hearts.
If it rules us, then we will rule the people correctly;
      The mind rules all well that God himself rules."
Allow just a little time for these admonitions
      And you will give from the outset an excellent taste from the river of law.
But if perchance vacuous Pride with a light impulse
      Tries to attack you and wishes to wound,
With wild eyes, horrible hands, and foul visage,
460   With serpent-haired head and overgrown frame,
With its own mind swollen, its conduct fatuous, voice inflated,
      Whose food and drink are black bile,
Who leaps, not walks, has in place of feet avian feathers
      And with such oarsmen could plunge from the top of the sky,
And, mindful of the ancient crime committed in higher regions,
      Using the art by which it fell to the depths of Styx,
With which it might inwardly whisper that you are high and mighty,
      That you should think it disgraceful to mix with the crowd:
"Lo, you strive to be a humble part of the people,
470   In that you wish to be pious and merciful to all.
Your order and rank lift you higher;
      Why do you voluntarily lower yourself from sublime heights?
For, if you have a clear view, you are making no trivial error
      When you humble yourself like a fool,
When no one can oppose you, no one deny you,
      Why, madman, do you plunge head over heels?"
As an invisible wound begins to fester and infect you,
      Or, what is worse, to leak out,
Let the power of humility burst forth, for wisdom
480   Should be, for pious powers, a companion in arms.
Their shining countenance and bright clothing,
      An affable face and each fair detail will suffice.
The noble pair of virtues will arise against such a horrid opponent
      And will say: "Get thee far off, nasty corruption, begone."
They will say: "Go, abomination, and join the other shadows,
      Whose fate is conjoined with your own.
Go and seek Cocytus and sink in the depths of Phlegethon's chasm,
      Where your savage creator will suffer his woes,

---

[1] cf. Isaiah 1:17

He who wished to ascend to God's throne along with you,
490 Fallen from a heavenly throne, now lies in the pit.[1]
Where would he have fallen with you, or risen without you,
  While he was a servant in heaven's abode?
You are a heavy burden to the worthy, a vehicle to the wicked,
  A charioteer to those who are evil, a huge weight to the good.
Those whom you, O wretch, attack, those whom you seek to injure,
  Are not yours, but the obedient followers of Christ,
Who, coming from heaven, also opens the way to heaven,
  To which the road was long closed but now opens wide,
Who ever ascends from the earth to the heavens,
500 Though you always drag us down to the depths.
He places his own followers on heavenly couches,
  You plunge your adherents down deep below."
Let evil, caught by these darts, and driven off by this spear cast,
  Recede as the clouds recede with the sun in pursuit.
Let the wild tread of the injurious monster turn backward,
  Let a kind hand heal the wound inflicted by the foe;
Let it drive off the enemy with steel, and the illness with medication,
  And let the remedy be administered to you with these words:
"See to it that swollen pride not infect your natural instincts
510 When, raised aloft, you occupy greater heights.
While people favor you, you alone are circled by many,
  And you think yourself mantled in prosperous days.
Nor should you forget what you are in mindless oblivion,
  And let your last day be always in sight;
So that you may be free of all infection from vices,
  Heed what you are, but not what you have.
Perhaps you are seated adorned with gems and purple garments,
  But after the season of the flesh you will be moldy dust,
For the body now clothed in golden raiment,
520 Which a silken robe of various colors enfolds,
As an ill-smelling remnant of filth, cold and putrid,
  Alas, uncovered by clothing, will be pressed under the earth.
What sea, earth, and air provide you for eating,
  For which you have beautiful vessels in hand,
Alas, will be consumed by a mouth of rotten putrefaction;
  Thereafter, woe is you, it will be a sordid little heap of dust.
The flesh that glows with sweet-smelling musk and balsam,
  And the fragrance from the sack of the exotic four-footed beast,

---

[1] Isaiah 14:12–15

Secular and Historical Poems   *97*

When decayed, will emit a stench and be damp with corruption,
530   Having all that offends and nothing that is loved.
You who are housed in the paneled halls of soaring buildings
    And complain of a small house, though without cause,
You will be closed up in a tight little vessel,
    A home scarcely larger than your remains,
You, whom people in crowds from far and wide come to visit,
    You, whom one and all are prepared to obey,
You will be the sole occupant of a single burial;
    What reason will there be to visit you except to lament?
You will have no companions other than maggots,
540   For which such food is nurturing mother, without which life is short.
Though a thousand flocks are rendered to you, or herds by the thousand,
    No neighbor then will limit your land;
With everything gone, you will seek cover in an unlovely grave site;
    Deprived of property, you will seek out poorer things.
Not many bearers are needed to carry the lifeless person;
    An appropriate color is chosen, the body is decently clad,
Four shoulders are nonetheless needed to move you
    When your last mournful honor is paid.
An iron sleep will embrace your cold body
550   When, no more to return, you set out on your last road.
What more should I say? What is deemed proper for viewing
    In the sight of men, what is pleasing and readily embraced,
Is heir to the worm after death, and after the worm only ashes,
    When, according to the decree of the Lord, he returns whence he came.[1]
This is the law of the earthly body grown from his image;
    But a different power inhabits the soul, created in heaven above,
Which, though released from mortal bonds, is still of noble lineage,
    Which an earthly home limits and constrains.
These two elements the merciful Creator joined together
560   So that even moribund man stays alive.
Joined together they govern life, when severed death is their master;
    When present they constitute life, when absent, death.
With a differing course the things of this world remain earthbound,
    But heavenly origin restores themselves to themselves.
As air to the sky, mere earth yields to air that is higher;
    Thus the body yields to the soul in every respect.
Alas, what a crime it is to prefer body to spirit,
    And mortal things to you, O soul, ever alive;

---

[1] Genesis 3:19

To prefer servant to mistress, hemlock to pepper,
570   Lead to gold, lowly rocks to excellent gems.
May God govern the mind, and foresight the body,
     And may the flesh, with vital soul, live for God.
In this way may you in upright endeavor be drawn to heaven,
     Let your mind flee what is lowly and aspire to high things.
When the day comes that destroys only the bodies,
     Let the earth cover the body and the spirit rise to the stars.
Keep the last day in view, always pondering it in reflection.
     As a certain old king once wisely averred:
"Last things should be borne in mind to avoid ways that are sinful;
580   In all your actions bear this firmly in mind."[1]
For if careful meditation considers your future,
     You will be open to infrequent evil or none at all.
If you consider that death is followed by life eternal,
     You will live the better part of yourself.
When the loud blare of the trumpet shakes the earth's boundaries
     And you emerge from your grave as a new man,
And your mind returns to its former location,
     You will be numbered in the angelic hosts.
When humility and wisdom are achieved, prepare court procedure,
590   Ready to carry out their commands, eagerly relying on them.
May they join in, take their seats, advise, and bridle
     Any outburst inspired by your mind:
Armed with this help and in accord with such assistance,
     Let your quick steps run a faultless course.
Say: "Go quickly, boy, and from many choose a handful,
     Who live not too close to their friends,
Those who have come for their own cases, or choose others
     Who, though close at hand, are still an indigent group."
If one is mixed in with others, do not reject him;
600   Whoever is present, let his case be heard.
Nor, rejecting him, let a repeater precede a first-comer,
     And let not repeaters and newcomers get in each other's way.
Examine the cases of all with vigilant attention
     So that you can conclude each case one at a time.
Inform yourself well in advance as much as you are able,
     And let the words of Job be your example. He said:
"I was a light to the blind, a support to the crippled;[2]
     A poor man, deeming me a father, was safe.

---

[1] Ecclesiasticus 7:40
[2] Job 29:15–16

Secular and Historical Poems

I skillfully explored the twists and turns of unknown litigation
610   With all possible zeal, so that the case would be known to me."
Do not hasten to bring the case to conclusion,
     Nor, slow afoot, should you be inert.
Let not torpor find you slow, nor error compromise quickness;
     Let your course proceed safely between two extremes.
Be inventive when the case is unclear so that it will soon have plain contours,
     Be the first to apply wit lest you be wickedly deceived.
The threatened death of a child revealed the deceit of a false mother,
     And the true mother received the dear task.[1]
This matter raised aloft Solomon's reputation;
620   Fear is inspired in the people, the way is opened for his praise.
The great often and ever are wont to heap up their cases
     While the poor man is deprived of even his own.
Add the latter as your companion in the cases of the less lucky,
     Let every man lend you good help by deferring his case.
Those who suffer the loss of father or mother, or of a husband,
     Let it be your business to pursue his or her case.
For each of these be a spokesman and guardian;
     Some will acknowledge you as a mother, some as a spouse.
If, disabled or weak, a boy, a sick man, an aged man or woman
630   Come to you, take pity and give them kind help.
Allow those to sit who cannot stand, support those who cannot get their
       footing.
     Those whose heart or voice is atremble, or hand or foot, help them too.
With words relieve the dejected, calm the overexcited,
     Give strength to the fearful, fill with fear those who rage.
As for agitation and quarrels among many, contention of voices,
     Restrain them with sharp exclamations and a serious tone.
It is the custom of raucous geese and black ravens
     To screech in chorus all at once.
If the crowd is not silent, make threats, but not so far as
640   To exceed your harsh words by lifting a menacing fist.
Let your mind be even-tempered lest the body
     Of any man be struck by your raised staff.
Various crowds will assemble by custom in disparate numbers;
     One is unable, another is able, one is unwilling, another is keen.
Rule with skilled moderation the various passions,
     With foresight add what may be expedient each step of the way.

---

[1] 1 Kings 3:16–28

If a man is hasty, rein him in, if slower, urge the slacker
　　To be quicker, while the former should slow down his pace.
Instruct the man who is dull; if cunning, check his maneuvering
650　　So that one will not lose what is his and the other seek what is not.
Willingly prompt a man slow of speech, all the more a garrulous fellow,
　　And may an even hand bring help to them both,
Lest the dull man lose his case by silence
　　Or seek as his own more than is just,
Or the loquacious with a whirlwind of verbiage
　　Overwhelm the process and the matter in hand.
While you allow whole hours to pass with vacuous speeches,
　　Time and task will elapse to no end.
There are those who can never get beyond speaking,
660　　And an ignorant tongue can ruin the case.
It is as if someone with a bow drawn tightly
　　Wishes to strike the enemy but strikes only himself and his men.
When such a man utters words that turn against him,
　　The poor wretch is speared by his own cast,
Give a salutary turn to his phrases;
　　Support him lest he fall; if he falls all the same, raise him up.
When a knotty case echoes throughout the tribunal
　　So that it wearies you and the parties with doubts,
Impose silence on the pleaders, both defense and prosecution,
670　　Lest they injure the law, each yelping his case.
Once the crowd is silenced, with a few men take counsel,
　　Probe the case closely and consider it at length,
Until at last a path is found unaffected by falseness
　　To allay the fierce litigation so that each benefits from the law.
In addition be sure that whoever sits with you
　　May not through entreaty or gifts spoil the law;
Perhaps an ear may be caught by ever so little a whisper
　　Or a nod from a sly man here or a crafty man there,
Or a wink of the eye or a signaling gesture
680　　Or whatever art can be used to this end.
He may wish to favor one side, but, not wishing to reveal himself to you,
　　He will lean ambiguously, at once hopeful and in fear.
It is no different when an adulteress contemplates outrage:
　　On the one hand she covets a crime, on the other she fears blows.
Often the contact with a wicked companion injures his fellow,
　　Just as a beast is infected by the vicinity of other beasts.

Secular and Historical Poems

Disdain to consider as equal a man who is secretly wicked
    Lest he draw you, all unknowing, into his crimes.
Thus a thief may pretend to be a companion to gain entrance for evil;
690   Thus poisons are disguised when mixed with sweet wine.
Be on guard with respect to your helpmeet
    Lest she turn your mind with seductive ways.
She will bestow on your knees and hands sweet kisses,
    On neck and cheeks, and will mix them with soft words,
Accustomed to arm her own entreaties with such poison
    As the bowman tips his swift arrows with bane.
If your mind be furnished with a strong helmet,
    So that she can observe the missiles bouncing off,
Seeing that, she will depart heaving false sighs and groaning,
700   Lamenting that her pleas had no weight.
Then a boy or a nurse, or perhaps a lying maidservant,
    Will say, "Why do you flout my mistress's words?"
With face averted and a soft voice she will whisper:
    "The kind of honor now to be seen is what I get.
Whatever other women want, as they report, they are granted,
    Whether helpful or harmful, but I get no part of my wish."
They will say that she should renew her request and resort to kisses,
    And go on: "How can you bear to be so unkind?"
But your mind should resist as it would a recurrent foeman;
710   Fear lest you be overwhelmed by her repeated attacks.
Be vigilant and avoid with all the care you can muster
    That she should do ill and then say that it was at your command.
With the husband unknowing a queen once accomplished.
    That a hail of stones crushed an innocent man.[1]
No less caution should be taken with your own servants,
    With whom you consort and who are close at hand.
Let not the wild pestilence infect them, nor let them harm you
    And stain your inner being with their wasting plague.
Be on guard against those who would force you to be a taker
720   So that they may receive or accept if they can.
If something makes you stay away from the masses,
    Though others depart, one will always be closest to you.
Whoever is seen to be closer to you than the others
    Will utter these words by way of counseling you:
"Do not, I pray, spurn my requests, as much as I underplay them,
    For your devotion inspires me to be bold.

---

[1] 1 Kings 21:10

If you grant my wishes, compensation is in the offing;
    There are good things to be given if only a good man will give.
One man or another is ready to give you something or other
730   That you may take while incurring no sin."
In order to lure you, this sly one will add further cajoling,
    He whose hand is already jingling with coin.
Avoid this snake, this viper, this horned serpent,
    He will be a serpent, a snake, an inflaming adder to you.
A magistrate is wont to have fierce and threatening servants
    Though he is pious and has outstanding good will.
Thus they say that you, Scylla, have human features,
    But your savage groin bristles with fearsome dogs.
If a matter is unresolved, claimed by some, denied by others,
740   And they re-echo "'tis" and "'tisn't" when two are at odds,
From this the seeds and plentiful harvest of cases
    Arise, stirring contention and human cares.
Let witnesses be examined to dispel the clouds of litigation
    So that they can truly put any doubt to flight.
Take a careful look at reputations and family,
    Names and character, locations and trustworthiness.
Accept the man if he's honest, reject him forthwith if he's crooked,
    As you reject sour fruit as food and accept fruits that are good.
Do not allow suspicions or hearsay or money
750   To support them—they should report only what they have seen.
To test their trustworthiness, interview them singly,
    And take due note of what each individually says.
If there are two, separate each, if more, separate in proportion.
    If there are three, let the law treat them three different ways.
Suspecting a secret, the kindly confidant of a chaste man
    Accomplished this deed in the Persian land.[1]
There a hailstorm crushed reprehensible elders,
    Whom a cloud of black evil had burdened before.
Dismiss the wicked, strive to keep company with the virtuous
760   So that the former will not oppose, and the latter help all the more;
As evils are greater and more greatly impede, so good things prosper,
    As more sheep give milk, as more wolves cause loss.
Let not their premeditated lure be triumphant,
    See to it that false speech not stand unopposed.
You will understand them well, examining them over and over,
    If you draw them out with rephrasings and probes.

---

[1] Daniel 13:51–62

Secular and Historical Poems   *103*

Witnesses, disdain to say what is false or suppress what is truthful;
    Both habits are harmful, though in different ways.
To silence the truth or speak falsehoods is badly misleading,
770   The first because it offers no help, the latter because it wishes to block.
One is bad, the other, however, is less than useful,
    And, though in differing ways, error underlies both.
For though one is less criminal, and the other more so,
    There is not much difference in the degree of wrong.
One levels the man who stands upright, the other refuses to raise the recumbent,
    One explicitly suppresses, the other does damage without words.
Often for the sake of power justice is left to languish
    And favor or fear silently suppresses the truth.
But the wrath of the celestial Judge remains dreadful
780   When he sees human concerns overriding his own.
Be on guard in the meantime that, though you wish to be truthful,
    Another not be betrayed and succumb.
A guilty man may appear to be worthy of death, but do not slander the guilty,
    So that your voice opens the path to death.
Blessed is the man who could rescue the wretched from destruction,
    By word and deed render delivering aid,
But if an innocent man experiences evil, condemned be
    The credulous judge and the witness with a black heart.
To three persons is the wicked witness an execration,
790   The magistrate, the innocent man, and you, heavenly God,
Whom he scorns by bearing perjured witness,
    Whose lordly name he takes in vain.
This applies to the judge whom he deceives with falsehoods,
    And whom he binds in the knots of his lies.
Finally it applies to the innocent man whom he injures with wicked assertions,
    And for whom he plots fearful ills with wicked heart.
As a carnivorous kite is drawn to flesh, and a fish to the fishhook,
    A bear to honey or cattle to salt,
So the wicked witness rushes to profit
800   And, in return for great evil, gets welcome rewards.
If it is a crime to sell truth, why sell falsehood?
    Do you wish, vicious witness, to double your crime?
Though such you are, I pray you not to sell untruths,
    They will not be welcome, even if given for free.
What is good is not to be bought, nor to be offered for purchase,
    What was transacted for empty dust still remains dust.
Bribe, bribe, more harmful than any transaction,
    A single bribe that slays two, one who gives and the other who takes.

Thus the wicked pestilence of perjury is present
810   When someone wishes trust to credit lies.
Those who deceive by entreaty, by tears, or false whispers
     Are those to whom trust comes in this guise.
Whoever you are, swear no oaths, I urge you,
     For, believe me, oaths are a thing to be feared;
Not because they are bad in themselves or unlawful
     But because, when taken, they often merge with deep crime.
No one who does not speak will be perjured,
     You cannot experience dreams without sleep,
Only those who enter fierce battles fall in combat,
820   Only the hunter of a boar is torn by its tusk,
No one is shipwrecked unless plowing the waves on shipboard,
     No one succumbs to fire if far from the flames,
And no one commits perjury unless an oath binds him,
     For unless he fear it, he will succumb to this sin.
When an interrogator examines you, tough or undecided,
     "Yes, yes" and "no, no" should be your response.[1]
Let there be words to relieve the burden of swearing,
     Which perhaps you can use without guilt.
If someone doubtfully persists, use illustrations, logic,
830   And arguments attesting to your good faith.
If he does not believe it, if he still has a stony reaction,
     Leave him and go your own way in peace.
But if the case constrains and presses you, to the point of swearing,
     Do it with transparent words and a pious mind.
Do not think that you can trick God with verbal quibbles,
     For to him nothing is hidden and all things are clear.
He does not heed the words that you swear but how the inquirer
     Thought that you swore, and thus you are guilty in the eyes of both,
Guilty before God, by whose name you swear vainly,
840   And before your fellow litigant, whom you wish to deceive with black
       fraud.
If you swear, committing yourself to a crime, let your oaths be invalid:
     One is worse than the other, but both are wrong.
Small wounds are minor, great ones are greater;
     Happy is he who departs uninjured by wounds.
Let judgment come first, mercy come second, bribes come never
     In the judicial process, where Christ is also at hand.

---

[1] Matthew 5:37

Secular and Historical Poems

The law orders us to sever the criminal heads of the wicked,
    Feet, genital parts, eyes, skin off the back and the hands;
To cremate the members on pyres, pour lead by the mouthful,
850   Or whatever else is prescribed by human law.
The former is done to curb ignominious acts by deterrence,
    Mercy should temper the latter by moderate means,
So that on the one hand there be no allowance in criminal cases,
    And, on the other, no cruel hand remove life or limb.
Let the guilty be treated as you wish God to treat you,
    And be zealous to spare the guilty as far as you can.
Having read our poem, perhaps someone will venture:
    "That man tells us not to rein in any wrong."
May I be understood to counsel you in this poem
860   That your focused mind may avoid both ills.
May you not be remiss, nor threatening, nor hateful;
    Broad healing will serve for both extremes.
Let the law not animate cruel men, nor pity inspire hesitation,
    For the one who is more or less than just it does harm.
The evil of vice often hides in the appearance of virtue,
    And the more it does harm, the less it is seen,
For example, when someone is guilty of cruelty,
    Thinking that he has adhered to the path of the law.
Bind criminals in chains and apply scourging
870   So that the criminal people may know you are tough,
But stain not your steel with wretched bloodletting:
    Steel is for enemies; use the scourge to purge guilt.
If you wish to avoid being thought to favor criminal vices,
    Make use of arms so that you will be thought to be fierce.
Let others agree to be swift in defense of legal provisions
    And flay the guilty in various ways.
Let them say: "Not we but ancient law prescribes slaughter,
    And this death is useful because it prevents many ills.
Our ax should fulfill the service of legal tradition,
880   And that is obedience, not crime."
May I be the one to redeem many crowds of wretches,
    May I deliver many from the cross and from death.
Those whom the unhappy crowd may view with tears staining their faces,
    Whom the poor assemblage gasps and trembles to view;
Once they have seen it, let strength return to their half-dead bodies,
    Let both hope grow in their sight and warmth in their veins.
I was about to lower my sails and head for the harbor
    So that, weary vessel, you might have welcome rest.

But with the vast deep behind me there is a remnant,
890   A tiny distance of the great ocean still to be crossed.
It is proper to add, little book, a note of worry
        About the crowd of poor people oppressed by the rich.
For the last part should tell of the care to be taken of poor folk
        Since the first part of the poem was devoted to artful words.
You who are charged with the poor, be most gentle;
        You will know that you are their equal in kind.
Not their status but a wrong placed them in your tutelage,
        A wrong that brings about that a man is subjected to man.
Their sweat and their cares make you wealthy,
900   You are richer alone than all of them joined.
Great rivers grow from the confluence of small ones,
        The wealthy man profits and is enriched from the means of the poor.
Bodies grow fat, fed from the substance of other bodies,
        The flesh lives revived from another's death.
A big and powerful man squeezes his weak little companion,
        With the great growing greater and the small man reduced.
This is true of the falcon and hawk along sinuous coastlines,
        It is true of the wolf in the woods and fish in the stream.
Thus a fierce snake is often killed by a fierce serpent,
910   Thus an animal without tooth or claw is nothing but prey.
Humankind, you should flee the example of wild creatures,
        Humans should not be to humans as fierce beasts are to beasts.
The poor should not be stripped of resources, nor by false judgment
        Should a poor man surrender what is his.
How often does pestilent avarice masquerade as righteous action,
        How often does fury counterfeit the name of law!
Whatever a poor man loses, he is said to lose justly,
        Whatever a rich man seizes, he thinks he seizes by law.
"He's a thief, a fugitive, he has a mind bent on deception,
920   He is a wicked liar, he plunders and steals.
He was evilly intent on despising our service,
        He has long been fleeing our neighbor nearby.
Bind their feet, let chains grip their bodies;
        So that they confess their evil deeds, may they suffer the lash."
Thus do they rant when they wish to oppress the impoverished,
        When they wish to despoil them of possessions, not of vice.
More to be mourned is he who does evil than he who undergoes it,
        The culprit is condemned to perish, the sufferer to thrive.
Thus the cruel deeds of the wicked profit good people,
930   Thus a work of gold is polished with an iron file.

Secular and Historical Poems 107

For the more savage customs of the wicked are apt to further
 The just, who, when they suffer, mount to heaven above.
The more the Egyptians oppressed the Hebrew people,
 The more they guided them to the promised law.
Be not violent to the poor, but all the kinder,
 For their prayers are possibly better than yours.
Let no covert deceit nor open license harm them,
 Let them be safe and secure from both woes.
Impute no dire faults, but try to forgive them;
940 Without faults no one can live on this earth.
You who ask that debts be forgiven, do for the poor man
 What you yourself pray for from God,[1]
For if your mercy does not raise a poor man,
 When you ask for mercy yourself, help will be denied.
If a servant disdains to spare his fellow servant,[2]
 He will turn the wrath of the just Master on himself.
O mortal man, be prepared therefore to spare other mortals,
 With whom you share the same nature's law.
If the life of a prosperous man is different from your life,
950 The sun's rising and setting is the same for you as for them.[3]
The holy fount blesses them and the ointment of old anoints them,
 The body and blood of the Lamb is sufficient for them.
Just as for you, the Creator of life died also for others,
 He who calls you to his rewards for your deserts.
Here let the sails of the book brought to an end be lowered,
 Let the anchor cast overboard hold the ship on this shore.

Here end the verses of Bishop Theodulf against the judges.

29. [Comparatio legis antiquae et modernae (Comparison of the Old and New Law)]

In his "Contra iudices" Theodulf passes from the auspices of the Old Testament
at the beginning of the poem to the auspices of Christ in verses 369–370, but the
transition is so understated that it may well escape notice. In any case, Theodulf
seems to have felt that there was something unfinished about his treatment of
penal provisions, and he returns to them explicitly in this poem, not with a view
to reconciling the conflicting passages in Scripture but with a firm argument
that the New Law supersedes the Old (vv. 61–62):

---

[1] Matthew 6:12
[2] Matthew 18:23–35
[3] Matthew 5:45

But with limbs stretched on the wood of the cross, the Creator
    Drove out the old wrongs with new light.

As in "Contra iudices," Theodulf begins with Old Testament precedents, but he chooses his authority carefully. He selects Moses as God's representative, and on that basis he is able to advocate monetary compensation as the correct type of punishment for theft. That allows him to launch into an attack on execution and dismemberment as modern novelties. Only then does he cite the talionic language of Exodus 21:24, but he counteracts it with the compensatory provision of Exodus 22:4, which he espouses as "divine law." The contrast to this divine law is not so much located in other scriptural passages as in contemporary penal practice, which Theodulf condemns outright (v. 46):

I know not whether they [the provisions] are lawful or insane.

To underline the insanity, Theodulf contrasts the death penalty exacted for theft in contemporary law with the light penalties assessed for murder. He then enunciates the supreme value of human life and seals the argument with the "turn the other cheek" message in Luke 6:27–29 and Paul's admonition "never pay back evil with evil" (Romans 12:17). What Theodulf's case lacks in completeness it makes up for in directness and energy. See Godman 1987:73–74.

Legal authority shows by what law of the Lord crimes are uncovered,
    Closes off the wretched road to the lurking thief.
The excellent lover of law finally judged that the robbers
    Should be punished by fours in cases brought to light.
Although there are in the earliest time harsh provisions,
    Even crueler commands remain in our times.
When with close to forty days completed,[1]
    During which he had taken no food, he intones from on high:
"Whoever craftily steals an ox, relying on the help of concealment,[2]
10   Should restore five to the person whose property he seized;
He who deceitfully seizes a pretty lamb from the sheepfold
    Should return four to the person from whom he wickedly stole."[3]
Let him not receive the savage punishment of capital justice,
    Nor let the madman lose his eyes or his strength.
So that no cunning thief remain safe in our era,
    Lo, he is apprehended and delivered to the sentence of death,

---

[1] Exodus 34:28
[2] Exodus 22:1–4
[3] 2 Samuel 12:6

Nor can his life be spared by a payment of shining metal
    Or silver coins when he steals in this age,
Nor can golden gifts be offered as a delivery
20   From such a judgment when a man has now only stolen a sheep;
    Nor can a fragrant robe that shines on the back of the beaver,
        Or a brightly colored robe such as dark Arabs wear,
Nor can a shining crown for the head, set off by beautiful metals,
    Be the vehicle of reprieve;
Nor can a manor or estate, or an inherited servant
    After a father's death, save his life.
Nor let modern laws take the eyes or the source of
    Parents' beautiful offspring, nor feet nor hands.
They order mouths to be filled with lead, backs to be flayed by scourges,
30   Ears and noses to be severed, and all that sets beauty apart,
Swift feet to be chopped and chains loaded on the shoulders,
    The weight of a thief to be hanged from a high beam.
They echo the harsh laws of heaven: "The wicked taker of human existence
    Shall surrender his black life for a life.
Thus he shall give eyes for eyes, ears for ears in forfeit,
    Hands for hands, feet for feet.
If fire burns an innocent man, let it burn the guilty,
    Let a wound bring a wound on itself."[1]
Let rather four heifers for an ox be the forced compensation,
40   Or let only one be added if it is found with the thief;
If one removed sheep is found with the robber,
    He orders that two be returned so that evildoing is at an end.[2]
Thus sounds the blessed judgment that divine law has given;
    It orders that these things be observed and obeyed.
But all laws now run in a different direction,
    I know not whether they are lawful or insane.
Now the head is the price of the spilled blood of a farrow,
    And human blood is shed for the loss of a sheep.
If perchance someone seizes a hairy he-goat,
50   He dies tormented and hanged on high.
If a furious madman run wild should strike others,
    And faint warmth leaves the expiring limbs,
A low penalty is assessed for a crime of such importance,
    Either coin or cattle, or often cheap wine.
Although all created things remain dear to the Creator,
    .Dearer among all, believe me, is man.

---

[1] Exodus 21:24–25
[2] Exodus 22:4

He should not be considered equal to the low price of cattle,
   But rather he should be thought highest among all.
The Old Law of God, thus excising evil,
60   Instructed men, and devout order prevailed.
But with limbs stretched on the wood of the cross, the Creator
   Drove out the old wrongs with new light.
He judged kindly that the body of the robber should remain living[1]
   And that crime should pass away through remorse,
That dire crime should not avenge crime nor evil avenge evil,
   Nor does the Lord compel reciprocal wounds.[2]
Rather he bids us return kindnesses for injury,[3]
   He enjoins that this is better than vile words.
These things four masters echo eloquently throughout the crossroads,
70   Their voices sound a single tone.
The awesome voice emitted by Paul's great whirlwind
   Sounds down from heaven and crushes wrong.
Thus he spoke with his slight body lying prostrate:
   "I urge that no ill be returned for any ill,[4]
Let rather your skill be allotted to all men,
   Delights that abide, not breeding harm."
Thus shining with virtue, eloquent in the art of speaking,
   Thus he declares many mysteries with powerful words.
O, if only there were now the judgment of even-handed
80   Law, which God gave from aetherial heights,
So that wicked hands might return cattle deceitfully rustled,
   Cattle for cattle, or a proud robe.
That a robe be returned for a snow-white garment,
   Which a hand, savage and mad, took away.

---

[1] Luke 23:40–43
[2] Luke 6:27–29
[3] Matthew 5:44; Luke 6:27
[4] Romans 12:17

Poems Attached to Historical Events

30. Ad monachos Sancti Benedicti
(To the Monks of Saint Benedict)

It emerges from this poem, a personified letter to the abbot Benedict of Aniane in the style favored by Theodulf, that Benedict had provided Theodulf with two monks to aid in the reconstruction of the monastery at Micy. Theodulf now writes to implore additional help. Benedict of Aniane was an important monastic reformer in this period. He abandoned a military career at court at an early age and founded a monastery at Aniane, not far from Montpellier, in 779, eventually subscribing to the Benedictine Rule and taking the name of his predecessor Benedict of Nursia (ca. 480–547) in central Italy (hence the "Ausonian regions" of v. 23). This accounts for the play on the two Benedicts in Theodulf's poem. On the history of the foundation at Aniane see Barthès 1992.

There appears to have been another Theodulf in the monastery, and our poet plays on this double identity as well, seeking to enlist the intercession of his brother in name. Theodulf's connection with Aniane caught the imagination of Louis Baunard in particular. He surmised that Theodulf had spent time in Benedict's monastery and emphasized that it would have placed a large library at Theodulf's disposal (cf. Barthès 1992:27). Barthès (1992:28) referred to Theodulf without hesitation as "un ancien moine d'Aniane." More recently de Riquer (1994:31–32) returned to the idea without embracing it. The poem shows that Theodulf did indeed know a number of the monks by name. On the other hand, there is no suggestion of a personal connection in the poem, and there is no mention of Aniane during Theodulf's mission in the region in 798. Perhaps he simply thought of Aniane as the best source of devout monks.

> Go speedily, my letter, to the home of Benedict the blessed
>   And, having greeted him, revisit the fathers' retreat.
> Deliver my hail and farewell, reporting in detail
>   That all is well by the favor of God.
> Then return many thanks for the gift already given,
>   And eagerly pray that he be willing to send more,
> So that the pious work should arise from the initial foundation,
>   Which already delights me, which warms my heart.

May the roofing be better as the layout of the foundation is goodly,
10   Which the destiny and honor of two in number consecrate.
Lo, two monks are two precepts of salvation,[1]
      So that the love of a brother may join us to what is divine.
There is intellect to which is joined labor,
      Thus double talents enrich the good ward.[2]
There are two lives, which the double action of sisters[3]
      Approved, and in addition the New Law or Old.
Go to work eagerly, fear not for the foundations,
      What you will add will stand, made solid by God;
You can add more, the process of building
20   Will not fail, which this sacred number supports.
You sent little seeds to our meadows,
      Send more; there will be a great harvest for you.
What Benedict was as a guide in Ausonian regions,
      Such are you now, Benedict, in our tracts.
Be no less in merit than the one whose name you echo,
      May one fate bless two, both in name and fame,
As Pythagoras is thought to have been born from the brain of Euphorbus;
      Thus the work of the Nursian father is now reborn.
As through Theodulf you will fulfill the words of a beseeching
30   Theodulf when the name is the same in one prayer;
Thus may Benedict through you, Benedict, grant what he wishes,
      And may you proceed as the vehicle of his wish.
What this pious father once was to you, O Cassino,
      May he now be for your cell, Orléans,
Which antiquity rightly calls Mitiacus [Micy],
      Which of old was auspicious to the crowds of the meek.
There Maximinus presided over the blossoming circle
      Of brothers, together with them he rises to the stars.
Their bodies are interred in various grave sites,
40   But their spirits, O patriarch, rest in your embrace.
Fierce barbarousness, with the gift of peace cancelled,
      Overturned their dwellings and made desolate their abode,
Which held its own ashes, and, like the bird Phoenix,
      From the crumbling of ashes raised its head high.
This done, seek out and rouse the conclave of brothers
      And, viewing them, bow down, bending your knee.

---

[1] Mark 12:29–31
[2] Matthew 25:14–30
[3] Luke 10:38–42

Poems Attached to Historical Events

Pray in a few words to be blessed before you address them,
    Then, with due hesitation, raise the sound of your voice:
"Theodulf has sent me to you, O blessed assembly,
50   He who prayerfully asks to receive your help.
He asks that your land, with surrounding fields, flourish,
    From which may the fragrance of ambrosial nectar rise to the stars.
May the gentle stream of your prayer flow often
    Through which the root may extend strong arms."
When perchance you stop speaking, then visit the premises
    To report all the news of the fathers' house.
Observe where the pious group sleeps, where it takes refreshment,
    Where it reads and recites; go where work is performed.
Inspect the bakery and do not overlook the kitchen quarters,
60   Or where those strong of mind rest their limbs.
Then look at the guest quarters and who resides in them,
    Where a soldier just now has taken new arms.
Where you miss the presence of a desired brother,
    Grieve for him who has feared this fair road.
Then with devout greeting revisit the brother
    With whom I am joined in name, not in repute.
Seek the dwelling of venerable father Nebridius,
    And may then the home of Donatus be shown.
But do not pass over the quarters of saintly brother Atilus,
70   And reverently approach Anianus's home.
May Nampius observe you giving him gifts that are salutary,
    Let Atala see you and bid Olemundus good day.
Should you perchance be able to travel through worldly cities,
    Viewing individual towns, country places, and homes,
Convey our greetings in verse to the bishops
    And all the clergy, whom it would be long to list.
Attila, Clarinus, Teutfredus, Leubila, the whole assembly
    Of fathers—may they kindly accept our respects.
What more should I convey? Greet all of them from me,
80   And, having done so, return to me at once.

31. Ad reginam
(To the Queen [Liutgard])

The queen in question appears to be Liutgard, Charlemagne's fourth and last wife, who died in 800. That this is a correct identification is assured by the fact that the praise accorded the queen matches closely the description of Liutgard given in "Ad Carolum regem" (25.83–90) in terms of beauty, intelligence, learning, and goodness. In contrast to Fastrada, who earned a negative assessment from Einhard and only a tight-lipped epitaph from Theodulf (24 above), Liut-gard can be judged to have been a popular and admired queen.

> O powerful queen, glory of the great monarch,
>> Auspicious and beauteous light of the people and order of priests:
> May God in heaven preserve you for long ages,
>> May you profit the people and the church of God.
> You light and brightness, you distinguished adornment of the kingdom,
>> You are outstanding in beauty, enhanced by pious ways.
> Given by reason of merit and joined to the pious monarch,
>> Whom God exalts, on whom he confers all that is good,
> You labor day and night in his service
> And ever raise his name on high.
> Though beautiful in appearance, more beautiful still in spirit,
>> So that it remains in doubt which supersedes which.
> Beautiful in the command of words but more beautiful in action,
>> Only you are victorious in both.
> The Creator who allowed you to promote so much goodness,
>> May he grant you success and assist you without end.
> Grant me, O queen, a balsamic liquid
>> So that the ointment of chrism may suffuse the realm.
> Then may the harvest of supreme reward redound to you
> When the same baptismal balm will confer the name of worshipper of Christ.
> May the Almighty give you life and the rewards of salvation
>> So that you may bear us in mind forever: farewell.

32. Ad regem
(To the King [Charlemagne])

Theodulf addressed this relatively brief panegyric to Charlemagne probably between April of 799 and December of 800. It presupposes the events of April but not Charlemagne's imperial coronation in December a year and a half later. The events of April 799 involved an attack on Pope Leo III in Rome undertaken with the intention of blinding him and cutting out his tongue in order to make him unfit for office. For some reason that the sources do not make clear the plot failed and Pope Leo appealed to Charlemagne for help in gaining reinstatement. The upshot was the pope's arrival in Germany and a long conference held at Paderborn in the summer of 799; it resulted in Charlemagne's decision to support the pope.

This historical moment is a particularly well-studied phase of Charlemagne's reign because it became the subject of a substantial and vigorous poem (perhaps the fragment of an epic) known as *Karolus Magnus et Leo Papa*. The poem describes Charlemagne's reception of Pope Leo in Paderborn in 799. The 536 surviving hexameters have been attributed to various Carolingian poets (von Padberg 1999:68–69; Stella 2002:19–33) and have twice been printed with a facing German translation (see the bibliography under *Karolus Magnus et Leo Papa* and Hentze, Wilhelm). The monograph-length survey of the events and problems relative to the conference by von Padberg in Hentze's volume (11–104, esp. 42–104) provides a richly documented discussion of the material, including summaries of all the relevant sources (pp. 48–52). The beginning of the poem can be read in Peter Godman's facing translation in his *Poetry of the Carolingian Renaissance* (1985:197–207).

According to *Karolus Magnus et Leo Papa* the pope actually lost eyes and tongue (vv. 326–365), but they were miraculously restored by God (vv. 512–516). Theodulf modifies the miracle by leaving open the possibility that the pope's maiming was only an attempt, but he maintains that his rescue is a miracle either way (see Schieffer 2002:80–81).

> Blessed king, greetings, and may you fare well for years protracted,
> May his Goodness on high grant you a prosperous reign,
> For your prosperity is the glory and grace of the Christian
> People, whose protector and father you are.
> You are the protector of wealth, avenger of wrongs, bestower of honors,
> Whatever you do is done by the facilitation of God.
> You are the arms of bishops, the hope and defense of the clergy,
> Through you the priesthood maintains holy laws.
> I err if Pope Leo himself did not have this benefaction,
> 10 As our pipe will now rehearse in brief tones.
> His people wickedly ejected him from city and office,
> Whom they prepare for death rather than life,
> But your kind pity embraced him, O monarch,
> Who comforts, soothes, warms, nourishes, and adorns,
> A man whom a crazed hand deprived of tongue and vision,
> Of his sacred vestments and religious rank.
> Peter returned the things with which malicious Judas absconded,
> For one is a confessor, the other a traitor to God.
> A rebellious band followed with Judas as an example,[1]
> 20 One wishing the death of the Lord, the other the bishop's demise.
> The crowd denies they were taken, denies that there was restoration,
> But says that it wished that they be removed.
> A miracle that they were returned, or could not be stolen,
> A matter of doubt, however, which should be more admired.

---

[1] Matthew 26:47

For although Peter could have saved him in the Roman city
> From ferocious foes and savage attacks,

He sent him to be saved by you, most clement monarch,
> And he wishéd you to serve in his stead.

On his own he returned to him the fearful loss of organs,
30 > But by you the honor of office and see.

He possesses the keys of heaven, but he ordered that you should have others.
> He controls the keys of heaven while you control the keys of the church.[1]

You rule his estate, you govern clergy and people,
> And he will lead you to the heavenly hosts.

Thus, with seat secure, O priest, confer healing in safety,
> And for the king eagerly seek help from the Lord.

Let his realm always rise higher
> So that Christ may give him life and grant health.

May the Father enthroned on high, O king, long preserve you
40 > And give you life and help toward grace.

May the saints pray and petition the Lord in your favor,
> Whose spirits reside in heaven and whose bodies rest in the earth.

The people and clergy yearn to see you in this region,
> And may I too be granted this wish.

If only the Lord might lead you to this city
> So that the town of Orléans might see its lord.

May life, health, devotion, and Christ's blessing be bestowed on you,
> Pious king, wise king, king most given to God.

33. Ad Fardulfum abbatum Sancti Dionysii (To Abbot Fardulf of Saint-Denis)

There are four short verse pieces by Abbot Fardulf, in three of which he names himself. Dümmler published them in *PLAC* 1:352–54, together with a summary of what is known about him. He was a Langobard and was brought to Francia by Charlemagne at the same time as King Desiderius, after the capture of Pavia in 774. He apparently became a faithful adherent of the Frankish king and was rewarded with the abbacy of Saint-Denis. During his abbacy he made significant additions to the buildings of the monastery. He served as a *missus dominicus* in 802 and died in 806.

Theodulf's preface, which is no more than a note accompanying gifts, must therefore antedate 806. Or are the following poems themselves the gifts? In any case, two poems follow; Dümmler originally thought they belonged together with the preface, though he changed his mind in 1884 (*PLAC* 2:696 [525]). The

---

[1] Matthew 16:19

Poems Attached to Historical Events *117*

original numbering is retained here for ease of reference. Verse 5 of the poem is included among Andreas Fritsch's collection of formulaic good wishes (Fritsch 1990:141). Both appended poems are curious pieces and belong to a group that could merely be versified jokes or could in some way be allegorical; Baunard (1860:249) suggested, perhaps with a considerable stretch, that the first could be read to mean that one must commit fully to faith in God. In it a boy asks his mother to wake him early only so that he can fall asleep again. That behavior is then compared to a young man who goes hunting, catches nothing, and finally tries his luck in a small glade near his house, with an equal lack of success. Is the moral of the stories that one must be more enterprising, an elaboration of "nothing ventured, nothing gained"?

The second poem, "Delusa expectatio," is even shorter and more trivial. It tells of a boy who relates to his father a dream, in which an ox speaks to him in a human voice. The father naturally asks what it said, and the boy replies "nothing at all." Is this a reflection on meaning—in effect that only human speech, not animal speech, has meaning?

> Receive the little gifts that I have cheerfully provided,
>> Sweet friend, sweet and most fitted for me.
> Although they are small, great love transmits them,
>> Their value is not material but a labor of love.
> May life, health, and all happiness be granted to you,
>> And God the King lend you heaven's help.
> May he mercifully lead you through the blessings of this world,
>> So that you may tread a smooth path to the beyond.
> He who has granted you worthy honors in this life,
> 10   May he give you a place above the stars after death.

ii. Serio resipiscendum
(One Should Come to One's Senses in Earnest)

> What good is it for a time to abandon the masks of nonsense
>> If one madly seeks them out once again?
> What good is it to arise if you immediately stumble
>> And lie dully stretched on the earth?
> It is told that a small boy implored his old mother
>> And applied to her with the following request:
> "O mother, you for whom worry for me is always a torment,
>> Dearer than life you are to me, and I to you.
> Soon will the bird, harbinger of dawn, greet the morning.
> 10   Quickly endeavor to wake me up."
> She replied: "I will do what you wish, but tell me, son, to what purpose?"
>> "Perhaps," he said, "I will be able to fall asleep once again."

No less a madness had seized a man in the meantime
    Who brought nothing good from his hunt.
The hunt is ultimately carried out wisely
    If it is a matter of business or sport, or both at once.
The quarry, goats, deer, and elk, are wont to afford profit,
    Beaver, deer, bison, wild ox, bear, and boar;
To fix hares with darts, loose hounds for the capture,
20   Has been seen to be fun, but not much of a gain.
Dog and hare fly off with two different ambitions:
    One seeks prey, the other seeks to escape.
The dog seeks food with his paws, the hare seeks safety:
    With different desires the effort is the same.
Their desire and zeal possessed the madman,
    Who, having caught no game, spoke thus:
"I wandered through low valleys and broad meadows,
    But in them was found no hare for me.
Without the gain of the hunt I returned to my lodging;
30   Because I was able to catch nothing, I was sad.
There is a little glade, surrounded on all sides by open spaces,
    Isolated and not far distant from home.
Who would ever believe that wild game or a hare would be there
    When the place is so close to the house?
When, on that day, no hope of hares persisted,
    And I thought I would get no profit from them,
I view the place, loose dogs, and set out meshes;
    Having done this with zeal, I find nothing there."

iii.   Delusa expectatio
     (Deluded Expectation)

When trivial things are to be said, they have a grand preface,
    Then, great elephant, you give birth to a small mouse.
Thus a certain boy once told a dream to his father,
    Drawing forth frivolous words from his mind:
"Father, I will tell you what wonders I saw in my slumber,
    Such visions quite stirred me up:
During the night an ox spoke in speech that was human,
    He spoke and we were amazed," said he.
Then the astonished father inquires into the matter:
10   "Say what he said." The son answered: "nothing at all."

Poems Attached to Historical Events   *119*

34. Quod potestas impatiens consortis sit
(That Power Is Reluctantly Shared)

Political discussion is notably absent in Carolingian literature and must be read
from between the lines. The following poem, advocating unified kingship and
opposing shared thrones, is an exception. A divided kingdom is unflatteringly
compared to the three-headed monster Geryon killed by Hercules. The weight
of precedent is in favor of unification, which Theodulf casts in the catalogue
form to which he sometimes resorts. These precedents are far-flung, includ-
ing the remote Agareni, who may be found in Isidore of Seville's *Etymologies*
9.2.6 and are the Arabs called Hagareni in late antiquity. Baunard (1860:301–2)
placed this plea in the context of Bernard's conspiracy against Louis the Pious,
suggesting that it may have made Theodulf suspect and led to his exile, but this
seems unlikely since the poem is so clearly opposed to division and in favor of the
status quo. Dümmler (1881: 526n4) refers to earlier suggestions that the division
pertains to Charlemagne's "Divisio Regnorum" of 806, in which he established
how the realm was to be shared among his three sons (Barbero 2004:340–42).
The three-headed monster would seem to lend some credence to this view, and
Cuissard (1892:83) embraced it, but Godman (1987:97–100) finds it unlikely that
Theodulf would have voiced opposition to Charlemagne and more likely that the
poem voices support for Louis the Pious's "Ordinatio Imperii" of 817 in favor of
his eldest son Lothar. See also Greeley 2006.

> The legend relates that Geryon ruled in threefold head count,
>> That one heart could suffice for three brothers allied.
> The blessed page of Scripture relates with true wording,
>> Exceeding all fictions with the devout law,
> How certain kings, to gain the summit of earthly power,
>> Through cruel conspiracy surrendered their brothers to death.[1]
> This by all prayers and contrivance should be avoided
>> Lest in our age such a thing come to pass.
> Of old there was one usage among almost all peoples,
> 10   To wit, that one from a body of brothers should wear the crown.
> Let the remaining brothers be part of the high senate
>> So that the apex of kingdom may be unified.
> This was the custom among Assyrians, Egyptians, and Hebrews,
>> And the people once dwelling in Persian lands.
> The Parthians had this custom, the Greeks and the Romans,
>> The dark-skinned Indians and the Agareni [Arabs] as well.
> This was the custom of Getae, Huns, and swarthy Moorish people,
>> And I think the same custom applied to the foul Ethiopian throng,

---

[1] 1 Kings 2:13–25

To the Thracians and Phrygians and to you, Lacedemonian region,
20   To the people who now have kingship, or formerly had.

35.   Ad Carolum regem
(To King Charles [son of Charlemagne])

Here Theodulf addresses Charlemagne's oldest son Charles, who died in 811. Cuissard (1892:92) understood the poem as a special token of affection for Charles and seems to place it in the sequence of events that led to Theodulf's downfall under Louis. Godman (1987:96) also thought that the poem could have contributed to his estrangement from Louis. But Charles was the eldest, and it is not unnatural that Theodulf portrayed him as the heir apparent at the end of his poem. He was no less outspoken in his praise of Louis when the time came, as the reader will see below.

O great salvation of mine, O hope, O glory of the kingdom,
        Charles, hail to you with the favor of the celestial Lord.
You provide all splendor and multiply the pleasures
        Of your father and country and all the court.
Brighter than electrum, purer than thrice refined gilding,
        All metals defer to your brilliant gleam.
Lighter than birds, you are yourself stronger than the lion,
        Excelling in the arts, you are quick to take weapons in hand.
My two windows on the world long to observe you,
10   And the exalted love of my breast yearns for you.
For when you began to visit western regions,
        And I, your devoted servant, perceived my lord to be near,
Lighter than the south wind and swifter than the fleeting east wind,
        I wished to throw myself at your feet.
The orders of the king held me back from this longing
        And called me to follow the road of a different route.
Once more, forgivably held back, I was prevented,
        Twice preparing to come, twice was my journey denied.
When Gomis spoke your sweet message in my presence
20   And the humble servant heard his lord's words,
Then the tearful winter of my eyes flowed in a downpour
        And my alien brow's inundation wet my cheeks with a burst.
Thus joy is wont to produce such fountains,
        And, by a reversal, delight inspires tears.
I ask that you load your slave with double fetters;
        If you bind both arms, I will not be an absentee.
With these chains your great-grandfather, grandfather, and father,
        Binding the crowds, earned the throne of the realm.

Then they scattered more haughty battalions,
30   By battle they subdued more territory to their rule.
But to you, great youth, go greetings and wishes forever
      That the Lord of heaven nurture, protect, and adorn
You, that you may follow in brilliance the paternal succession
      And, with God's help, hold in your hand the scepter of rule,
And that you may leave the confines of the earthly kingdom
      Such that you may then share the heavenly heights.

36. [no title]

The contents make it clear that this untitled poem accompanied a treatise — almost a patristic florilegium — against the Adoptionist Heresy, *De spiritu sancto* (Migne, *PL* 105. 223–76), commissioned by Charlemagne. See Cavadini 1993. It is framed as yet another personified verse epistle.

Pursue, little book, swiftly the footsteps of Charles the exalted
      King, and say, "Pious emperor, hail."
Prostrate on the earth, bestow on his feet appropriate kisses,
      Then rising to your knees, make a respectful request.
Should he fix his bright eyes on your visage
      And his agreeable hand mercifully reach out,
Should he ask who you are, whence you come, your goal, your wishes,
      You will forthwith address him as a suppliant with such words:
"On Theodulf's orders I have hastened over many meadows,
10   And I am present, as you see, loaded down with flowers.
That the Holy Spirit proceeds from Father and Offspring
      I attempt to convey with the teachings of faith.
On that basis I come prepared to lend my support to the people
      Who proceed otherwise and flee this path."
If he piously asks you, "Can you indeed do this?"
      Say, "I can indeed do it, O king, with God lending help.
The high opinion of the holy prophets is with me,
      Whom the breath of this Spirit inspires.
You will put your hand to it, strengthened by the Spirit,
20   Whose case began to be moved in your time.
You are the adornment of the world, the light of the realm, the protector of
          justice,
      At once the wall and weapon of Catholic faith.
You promote justice, forbid injustice, are liberal with honors,
      You properly prepare nourishment to the liberal arts.
These you love, and bid others love them, you animate and foster,
      You drink large vessels from their stream.

What more should I say? You excel in virtue and overflow with religion.
 And I know that no one outdoes you in all that is good."
If Charles should say to you, "With your hand on your sword hilt,
30   Draw it now for the contest of courage if you have the heart,"
You should reply: "See the arms of the fathers drawn from the vast resource
 That the New Law or Old Law instructs.
Our battle line furnished with them knows no failing
 When you will conquer with truth, whose follower you are.
Shining victory will approach with bright-flowing garments,
 And, God-fearing, you will attain your holy wish."
Great king, following the commands of your rulings,
 I Theodulf eagerly dispatch these words,
By which, with the trumpet of law resounding, it is established
40   That the Holy Spirit proceeds from the Father and Son.
This the gospel, this the apostolic author announces,
 This the pious voices of the fathers proclaim with a uniform heart.

37. De adventu Hludowici augusti Aurelianos
(On the Arrival of Emperor Louis at Orléans)

Nikolai Alexandrenko did not translate this poem because, as he argues (1971:180), he did not think it was correctly attributed to Theodulf. He points out that a festive celebratory poem would not have been appropriate when Louis visited Orléans in 814 because Louis was on his way to his father's funeral. He connects the poem rather with another visit Louis made in Orléans in 818 (see the *Vita Hludowici Imperatoris*, chapter 53, [498]). At that time Theodulf was no longer bishop and had been replaced by Jonas. Alexandrenko therefore attributes the poem to Jonas (as one manuscript does), arguing furthermore that Sapphics were not a meter used by Theodulf and that two other Sapphic poems (70 and 77) attributed to him are equally suspect. We have elected to translate everything in Dümmler's edition for the sake of a complete picture.

1.   Caesar is at hand, pious and beneficent,
 Who shines brightly throughout the whole earth,
 And stands forth with goodness before all
   By the dispensation of Christ.

2.   Humble, wise, learned, modest,
 Gentle and clement, moderate in action,
 Temperate, strong, right-minded and honest,
   A just judge.

Poems Attached to Historical Events 123

3. He is the glory of Judah, and father of the church,
   He wisely adorns it, refreshes it, nurtures it,
   Instructs, supplies, cultivates, raises it
       With broad teaching.

4. He is powerful in arms, with the help of the Lord,
   He forcefully constrains arrogant peoples,
   As victor over these people he treads triumphantly
       On their necks.

5. His arrival, with Christ's mercy,
   And his radiant face, spreads great serenity
   And brightens you too, populous city
       Of Orléans.

6. Therefore inspire long-lasting praises to God,
   By whose leave he hastened to you,
   And whose visage he offered for viewing
       To you.

7. May the clergy and all people alike sing praises,
   Let the old and the young boy sing praises,
   With the poor and the rich echoing joy
       With a pure heart.

8. Let the chorus of clergy and the crowd of people,
   Singing this Sapphic song, pray that
   God grant Louis long
       Years to rule.

9. May He ever mercifully afford all prosperity,
   Drive off and repel adversity afar,
   Guard his life for all times
       Mercifully.

10. May for ages Caesar's noble wife
    Prosper as well as his brilliant offspring,
    May happy people and home be joyful
        In perpetual peace.

11. The faithful nobles guard the city
    By enduring the wars of the enemy,
    They who dedicated to loving Christ
        Their chaste bodies.

12. May these holy leaders return
    In order to favor you, Caesar,
    That with their help you may conquer by waging their battles
        We all entreat.

13. May you be pleasing to God in all deeds,
    And may you meditate on God's merciful laws,
    With which you may hold life's road
        On a straight path.

14. With the space of this life behind you,
    May you rise to the heights of heaven,
    May the kind host of angels greet you
        And take you to themselves.

15. O glory of the realm, progeny of the empire,
    May you, great Lothar, always thrive,
    And may you powerfully hold the throne of your father
        Over long ages.

16. Let there be to the Father and Son and Holy Spirit
    Eternal and perpetual splendor and honor
    Now in present days and alike in the future
        Ages and forever.

38. Versus scripti litteris aureis de Sancto Quintino (Verses Written with Gold Letters about Saint Quentin)

In these verses Theodulf writes on behalf of Abbot Fulrad, who shared a grand-father with Charlemagne, nàmely Charles Martel. The monastery at Saint-Quentin was founded in the seventh century and had fallen into disrepair when Fulrad undertook to renovate it. The first tablet dates the project to exactly 814, but at a time when Louis the Pious had already succeeded his father. Fulrad also served as Charlemagne's *missus dominicus*, and his commissioning provides an informative analogy to Theodulf's mission in southern France in 798 (Ohlers 2004:247–50).

Poems Attached to Historical Events

i. On the First Tablet

When for ten times five minus three years great
    Charles had continued his pious rule,
And, delivered from human concerns, had left the high office
    Of the great realm to you, King Louis,
And when the happy incarnation of Christ gave to the era
    Of eight hundred years an additional fourteen,
Abbot Fulrad, distinguished by noble forbears,
    Began to found the work of this worthy estate,
For Jerome was his father, and Charles his grandsire,
10   Who raised the model of his people aloft,
Fighting wars and guarding peace, who transmitted
    The summit of the realm to his son with God's help.

ii. On the Second Tablet

The limbs of the excellent martyr Saint Quentin rest here,
    Whose spirit belongs to Christ in the citadel of the sky.
In his honor and by ancient construction this temple
    Was built and has long been in place.
But, O wall, since you might show cracks, the wild signs of ruin,
    You gave reason for rising anew.
For with pious vows and God granting, I Fulrad
    Accomplished that this project would come to pass
So that larger and in every respect more elaborate
10   This dwelling would rise from foundations of old.
If anyone approach to address prayers to the Father,
    Include me, I pray, in your prayers and vows.

iii. On the Third Tablet

This sweet house of God is the path to the courtyards of heaven,
    Here is thrown open for the good the doorway of God.
This is the way, the life, and salvation, Christ has revisited his foundation,
    Accepting the gifts of the just, their vows and prayers.
Here lie at rest the bones of the blessed Saint Quentin,
    Who devoted himself to rightly pleasing his Lord,
Who with his own blood purchased the heavenly regions
    And acquired for himself a place in the heavenly home,
Whose burial site is sought out with devout spirit
10   By living people, pilgrims in search of help.

I, humble Fulrad, wish them to keep me in memory
    So that God himself will always bear you in mind.

39.   Eiusdem ad Hluduicum valedictio
(A Farewell from the Same [Theodulf] to Louis)

Alexandrenko (1971:230) connects this poem with Louis' designation as co-regent in 813 and his visit in Orléans in 814, sometimes also associated with 37 above. Alexandrenko may be consulted for further references. Liersch (1880:23) described the poem as "glänzend," perhaps with reference to the epanaleptic lines, a contrivance that has not pleased all readers (Baunard 1860:246). As a whole, the poem is peculiarly devoid of any real information or personal engagement.

May he who rules heaven and earth always, O king, be your helper,
    May he ever assist you, who rules heaven and earth.
May he who gave you rule give you long years in office,
    May he give you joy who gave you rule.
God subjected to your laws the regions of Europe,
    May God incline the whole earth to your laws.
As you conquer wild beasts, may you subdue barbarous peoples,
    Conquer Spain as you conquer wild beasts.
As the boar yields to you, may the Moor and Arab yield also,
10   May the Sarmatian succumb as the boar yields to you.
May you bruise proud necks as ducks are bruised by falcons,
    As a hawk bruises a goose may you bruise proud necks.
May eternal joys succeed these pastimes,
    Carry to immense heights both joys and sport.
May God's great grace bestow on you life's fortunes,
    May you be led and protected by God's great grace.
May you have long joys in constant delight, O monarch,
    With children and family may you have long joys.
You are honor abounding, and may you have health long-lasting
20   With clergy and people, you in whom all honor abounds.
For your welcome health is a light to their glances,
    For all good people wish for your welcome health.
Great honor of the people, great and powerful Caesar,
    Holding splendid rule, great honor of all.
Ever hail, emperor, with God granting,
    Cheerfully accept, O emperor, my greeting of "hail."

Poems Attached to Historical Events *127*

40. Epitaphium Helmengaldi (Epitaph for Helmengald)

Helmengaldus (Helmgoth) was a count in the service of Charlemagne. As Dümmler notes (1881:532), he and other nobles were entrusted with the prosecution of those who attacked Pope Leo III in 799 (referred to in 32 above). He carried out a number of other important missions as well. Theodulf calls him a prefect of the palace, but he is not mentioned in the court poems.

> In this soil resides noble Helmengald, the warrior,
> Who was the whole honor and glory of his land.
> Rich in wealth and intelligence and brilliant in breeding,
> By all good values richly adorned,
> Outstanding in counsel, strong in arms, enhanced in body,
> Imbued with the laws, potent in speech and arms.
> For he was prefect in the halls of the palace
> While pious Charles maintained serene rule.
> He endowed churches with many riches
> 10 And appointed them heirs to his wealth.
> He was a foot to the lame, the glory of sight to the sightless,
> All weakened men had him as support.
> He was accustomed to drive out hunger and thirst together,
> Or the dire cold from the limbs of the poor.
> This earthly Jerusalem holds the body,
> May his spirit seek out the blessed regions above.
> You who read this inscription or witness this burial,
> Say: "May Helmengald enjoy eternal rest."
> Let the holy community of monks speak the same message
> 20 When traveling back and forth they follow this road.
> May they be mindful of him through the ages.
> And may they pray that the heavenly realms be granted to him.

41. Versus Theodulfi (Theodulf's Verses)

Much of Theodulf's fame rests on his labor in establishing a better text of the Bible, a project that he shared with Alcuin but with differing results. (On Theodulf's use of the word *bibliotheca* for Bible see Meyvaert 1979:42–43.) Two "Theodulf Bibles" in elegant and nearly identical form, preserved in Paris and Le Puy, were known from the eighteenth century on, and both include the following verses. Cuissard (1892:174–96) wrote about them already at some length, and the very painstaking work of differentiating Theodulf's version from Alcuin's, identifying other Theodulf Bibles, establishing the dating and relationships, and exploring the paleographical and codicological peculiarities of each manuscript continues. Elisabeth Dahlhaus-Berg provided an able and detailed summary of what had been done up to her time of writing (1975:39–76). One thing that emerges from her overview is the importance of Spanish Bible redactions for Theodulf's decisions. She also emphasizes the text-critical innovations in Theodulf's work compared to Alcuin's. See now Chevalier-Royet 2007 for an update. For a general discussion of the poem see Stella 1993:54–68.

The following poem gives a summary, succinct to a degree, of the books of the Old and New Testaments, devoting two or three lines to each. It proceeds from the Pentateuch to the historical books, the greater prophets, the lesser prophets, the wisdom books, Daniel, Ezra, Esther, Wisdom, Sirach, Tobit, Judith, and the Maccabees, but in an order rather different from what we find in modern Bibles (Freeman 1957:692). In the New Testament, on the other hand, the order is the same as the one familiar to us, with the exception that the Acts of the Apostles are placed in penultimate position just before Revelation. The verses appended under ii, "Theodulfi Versus," provide a summary appreciation of the Bible and may have accompanied a volume of chronographical texts (see Dümmler's notes). Two final distichs under iii and iv bid the reader farewell. Poem 42 adds the whimsical note that, though small, the Bible is powerful; the comment on small compass is perhaps inspired by the fact that the writing in the surviving Paris and Le Puy codices is indeed very small. Theodulf also asks that he be remembered for the labor he has performed. On the placement of these inscriptions in the manuscripts see Delisle 1879:7–8.

i. [Praefatio bibliothecae
    (Preface to the Books of the Bible)]

Whatever the Greek or Latin pen took from the Hebrew,
   You, O reader, have it whole in this book.
In it Genesis holds first place, the world's beginnings,
   Relating the flood and the great deeds of the patriarchs.
Exodus despoils Egypt and cuts through the Red Sea,
   Opens the road in the desert, where water and law are supplied,
Then Leviticus adorns the rank of the priesthood
   And explains the types of offerings typologically.
The Book of Numbers describes wars, men, and exploits,
10   In which Moses destroyed idols, leaders, and sins.
Then it rehearses the law, blesses the people, frames legislation
   Kindly, and with the song ended the victor expires.[1]

---

[1] Deuteronomy 34:5–6

Poems Attached to Historical Events 129

Then the warrior, son of Nun, in his own book distributes
    The earth, having leveled cities and sites.
The order and acts once guided by judges
    Are related with a flowing pen by the following book.
Then come the deeds performed by Ruth, the Moabite woman,
    Famed for pious merits, famed for her pious heir.
The deeds of the psalmist and wicked Saul's transgressions
20   You take in turn, Samuel, books one and two.
The third and fourth books, to which the name of Malachim [kings] attaches,
    Tell in sequence the deeds of the Hebrew kings.
Then Isaiah tells how Christ was born to a virgin;[1]
    And calls the people to godly laws.
Next to him is Jeremiah, who has the rod and jar in keeping,
    Who in fourfold order covered the lamentable work,
Then Ezekiel, obscure on all levels, is often
    Called, in the way of the Lord, son of man.[2]
Then comes a godly order of twelve lesser prophets,
30   Giving a far different meaning from what their words state.
For Hosea often invokes the harlot and the offspring and that of Joseph,
    Samaria, Ephraim, and Gezdrahel bereft.[3]
Then Joel relates first the earth once overturned in dark destruction
    And then the arrival of the Holy Ghost.[4]
Amos thunders at the kingdoms for three and four transgressions,
    And proclaims that he has clearly seen mystical sights.
Obadiah skewers Edom with the prongs of his blessed phrases,
    And the envier of his brother succumbs to his words.[5]
The passion of Christ is conveyed by the shipwreck of Jonah,
40   And the world gains life by Nineveh's name.
The daughter of the robber is overwhelmed by the words of Micah
    Because she tore the cheeks of Israel's king.[6]
With his steady voice Nahum beats down the city running with bloodshed
    And loudly proclaims the feet of peace from the height of the cliff.[7]
Habakkuk with his inner eye sees Christ tormented;
    There is power in his horn, hidden it blares.[8]

---

[1] Isaiah 7:14
[2] Ezekiel 2:1
[3] Hosea 5.5
[4] Joel 2:28
[5] Obadiah 10
[6] cf. Micah 5:1
[7] Nahum 1:15; cf. Romans 10:15
[8] Habakkuk 3:4

Zephaniah pronounces what he hears from hill and gateway,
    And to your natives, O Pila, brings plaints.
Haggai erects a temple and relates that God in heaven
50   Will shake seas, lands, and sky.
After seeing many mystical things in their order Zechariah
    Says that the Lord will ride you, O ass.[1]
Malachi says that the gifts of the former people are cancelled,
    And that the crowds of nations with their families are loved by God.[2]
Then the little book containing Job's words and actions
    Is found; though small, it carries great weight.
Then the sweet song of the psalms professes
    Christ's sweetness, fashioned in lyrical feet.
Located next in order are found three books of Wisdom,
60   At one with the name Solomon or Cohelet [Ecclesiastes].
The first [Proverbs] addresses everyone with "son" as a title
    And corrects morals, O Ethics, by your law.
The second declares all things vanity under the sun's brightness,
    The material details of which are a labor to count.
The third [Song of Songs] adorns the nuptial chamber of Church and Savior
    And his work is devoted to logical themes.
Then the philo-historian of all the earth, to wit Daniel,
    Who relates that stone will shatter all realms.[3]
Then are placed two books, the words of the days by title;
70   Their labor is to relate the deeds and the lineage of kings.
Then comes Ezra reforming the law and the temple
    And relating the return of Israel to its land.
Then there is an account of Esther, the forerunner of Christian religion,
    Who was a glory and honor to the exiled race.
Next is the book to which is given the name of Wisdom
    Because the advent and death of Christ is revealed.[4]
Next to it is adjoined the book of Ecclesiasticus [Sirach],
    Where devout laws and the blessed praises of the fathers resound.
Then comes pious poverty, splendid devotion, O blessed
80   Tobit, duly set down in your book.
Then is found Judith inscribed, a woman with a great mission,
    By whose hand mad unchastity fell.
Then two books of the Maccabees follow,
    In which the cherished deeds of four brothers reside.

---

[1] Zechariah 9:9
[2] Malachi 1:10–11
[3] Daniel 2:45
[4] Wisdom 2:12–20

Poems Attached to Historical Events   131

From here on the trumpet of the New Law openly proclaims Christ's person,
    Whom the Old Law foretold under an allegorical veil.
Matthew, Mark, Luke, and holy John's gospel,
    One voice sounds his name, all four at once.
The first began with how he proceeded from human beings,
90   And therefore carries the form of human kin.
The second with a terrible voice denounces ways that are wayward,
    And therefore the appearance of a lion is ascribed to him.
To the third, because he began with priestly matters,
    Is properly ascribed the shape of a young bull.
The fourth flies over the skies with words elevated
    And therefore has the shape of an eagle flying aloft.
On the heels of these follow fourteen Pauline epistles,
    Sent to the world by the sheep that was once a wolf.
The first recalls the Romans from the weight of tradition
100   And judges that they should have the gospel faith of New Law.
The second calls the Corinthians, seduced by many an error,
    With kind written words to the true faith.
The third is pleased they repented and comforts them also;
    Praising, it exhorts to improvement at the same time.
The fourth leads the Galatians to the vigor of religion,
    Whom, with faith spurned, a great burden had overwhelmed.
The fifth lifts the people of Ephesus with laudable recognition
    Because not at all did they abandon holy faith.
The sixth consoles, praises, and commends the Philippians
110   Because they consistently maintained the honor of faith.
Then the seventh advises the Colossians in rejecting
    False prophets; it corrects and instructs.
The eighth favors the people born in Thessalonica
    Because they stood firm over time, however many the clouds.
To them also the ninth predicts the world ending
    And how dark pestilence should be overthrown.
But the text of the tenth informs Timothy and makes adjustments
    With respect to holy matters and ranks of the church.
In the eleventh the evils of the last time are related
120   And he is instructed in all goodly ways.
Then he instructs Titus in the twelfth subjoined letter
    How he is to avoid heresy and how to be a priest.
In the thirteenth he gives you, Philemon, pious counsel,
    Which the captive father sent from the city of Rome.
The last one through the prophecy of the law and the prophets
    Preaches to the Hebrews that Christ is the Son of God.

To these are added seven Catholic pages in order,
   Which the pen captures from the mouth of the apostles in turn;
That is to say, one of holy James, two of Peter,
130   There are three of John, and one is yours, O Jude.
They fill the whole church with general teaching,
   They instill faith and contain salvific law.
Then the pen passes to the Acts of the Apostles that Luke assembled;
   They declare the new deeds of the church.
The holy vision shown to Saint John closes
   The books and marks them with a veiled end.
The Old and New Testament in a single sequence
   Open a double path and leads to the heavenly heights.
This food satisfies hearts with eternal nurture
140   And feeds the hunger for justice the more one consumes.
This drink coming from the fountain of Eden,
   The more someone approaches, the more he thirsts for all good.
This terrible trumpet resounds through the worldly crossroads
   And sends the earthly race to heavenly realms.
This light dispels the horrid shadows of error
   By which light the feet of your mind hold you, O right path, fast.
Here are the laws of God stripping the world from shadows,
   More brilliant than the stars, whiter than snow.
They dictate justice, prohibit injustice, cut off all evils,
150   Engender virtues, drive off wicked sins.
The law of God is precious, for what is yet more precious?
   It is given by the fountain of life, light and the source of what is good.
It is a powerful teaching, a knowledge surpassing all others,
   To which none other can compare under the heavenly skies.
If you should wish to compare it by concept or contrivance,
   The other will yield to it as earth yields to heaven above.
Whatever of higher arts is learned with worldly cunning,
   Here it runs a freer course.
Whatever flourishes by reason or whatever is loved in artistic endeavor
160   Flows from this fountain and runs from this stream.
Just as it triumphs in all things, it rules in the art of speaking
   Because it teaches many remarkable things in a simple address.
It sounds a single body of words, not changing direction;
   Thus one locution rightly expresses many at once.
Thus, however, it recounts in order to reveal mysteries;
   While it tells of great things, it implies even more.
Thus it compares great things with small, and small with greater,
   So that you, Precious Lord, may speak through lowly deeds.

Poems Attached to Historical Events

With past history it shows future events by narration,
170 And by relating events, it forecasts by miraculous means.
Thus it describes acts in order to convey the right way of acting,
  And, with deeds past, it admonishes you on what is still to be done.
I am silent on the burden of these things; who could explain them in detail,
  How this honor abounds and thrives?
When closed, it inspires no fear, when open, no aversion.
  On the one hand it is not discouraging, on the other not cheap.
Here hope seeks it out, there a quick faculty grasps it.
  Where it lies hidden, it animates, where it is open, it sustains.
In obscure locutions it fights battles more bravely,
180 And you, modest crowd, it comforts with humble speech.
To the strong it is bread, to the weak a mild liquid,
  It nourishes the former with solids, the latter with milk.
It heals like pure wine and soothes like the oil of olives.
  Thus with various words overall health is secured.
With constant use it also diminishes aversion,
  The more it is read, the more it is sought.
Though things are wont to inspire fear with great meditation,
  The more one meditates on this book, the greater love for it grows.
It aids the mind of the reader with humble phrasing,
190 And with high aspirations lifts him aloft.
The crowd of rude readers think they know it fully,
  But there are always new things for the learned to learn.
What is it that summons the crowds to heavenly dwellings
  And assigns you to unending life?
By virtue of the book worldly love flees and divine love increases,
  Turning the heart of the reader to better work.
Add by what examples it instructs worldly actions,
  And with its assistance the way lies open to advice,
So that as each man learns the deeds of the ancients,
200 He may see what he should avoid and what he should do.
Thus it teaches us to model our deeds on outside examples
  And that we should not control words and deeds on our own.
Who can record the details? In number they surpass the sands of the seashore,
  And the high order of law exceeds drops of rain.
To whatever you devote your reading with maximum effort,
  Whoever you are, beg God insistently
That He mercifully visit your heart with this nectar
  And with it take possession of the caverns of your breast.
On its arrival, may the doorway of your mind be open,
210 So that, shining brightly, it may avoid any stain,

So that it may welcome him who was its Creator
　　And so that the Giver of law may enter the doorway with law.
May scorn not enter your mind, nor deceitful vainglory,
　　May you not love vain and empty praise.
May the Holy Spirit put to flight fierce falsehood;[1]
　　It does not inhabit bodies oppressed by sin.
May your mind be humble, your heart wise, your acts untainted,
　　May your studies flourish and your works be devout;
May your meditation regularly be on Holy Scripture,
220　　And may you heed its admonitions night and day.[2]
Bear it in heart and hand, and may it be present in your language;
　　May it correct your actions, and you others in turn.
May it share your couch, may your eyes scrutinize it closely,
　　May your neck, knees, and flexible arms convey its sense,[3]
May it be at your head when you sleep on a regular schedule,
　　When sleep eludes you, may it swiftly seek you out:
May you love it not just to be learned but so that you may be righteous:
　　One surpasses the other though both are good.
For the Almighty requires not your words but your actions,
230　　Though nonetheless you can please him with both.
Learn by reading, devote yourself often, teach by doing,
　　Let the book be your guide in the practice of holy law,
So that many a reading may lift your spirit
　　And lay out a fair path for your mind.
Let it not hastily falter, may it gather strength by practice.
　　Reading holds much of what a sharp mind reveals.
A path in the thorny forest, with the hard wood leveled,
　　When trodden by many feet, becomes a broad road.
May holy examples instill vigor with holy sayings;
240　　Do what you say, and relate what you yourself do.
Let your deeds not counter your words, nor words your actions,
　　Let each in parallel run nobly abreast.
What you grasp well in your mind, speak in humble language,
　　So that you may not lose by pride what you have studiously acquired.
It takes long to say more, compress much with economical wording,
　　O reader, in whom glowing penetration of mind is contained.
Thus from a little investment the reaper harvests
　　Great grain, enjoying a more productive return.

---

[1] Wisdom 1:5

[2] cf. Psalm 1:2

[3] Deuteronomy 6:6–9

Poems Attached to Historical Events

As you view this work and reread our verses,
250   Bear Theodulf in mind, I pray you, farewell!

<u>ii</u>.   **Theodulfi versus**
       (Theodulf's Verses)

Theodulf composed the work of this codex with affection
     For him whose blessed light is conveyed in this book.
On the outside the work gleams with gems, gold, and purple,
     But it shines within with a more splendid light;
After the esteemed volumes of Catholic religion,
     Observe, this little note takes up a small space.
Thus, departing from the very beginning,
     The work weaves the names of patriarchs and kings.
It takes note of the number of years, names reigns in order,
10   Down to your time, Prince Heraclius [7th century].
It brings many deeds to memory in limited wording;
     Thus with a brief nod a great work is implied.
Then are revealed the names in the Hebrew language,
     Which the noble custom of holy law maintains.
The Greek names then follow, which an early age gathered,
     By which the riches of the church are named.
A little cluster is gathered with Latin nomenclature
     That conveys the worthy burden of great fruit.
These matters retain great mysteries in a small body,
20   Matters that the threshold of this codex contains.
He will be able to survey the river of law with these lanterns,
     He who wishes to find fish in the stream of the law.
With nets the man will be able to gather a precious harvest,
     He who has the skill to find sustenance in holy law.
Do not disdain them, good reader, as trivial matters,
     For a lowly box can contain fair things.
An iron key fashioned from cheap metal
     Opens the way to the location of silver and gold.
Whatever is a small burden for keeper or bearer
30   Shows the way to where a weighty reward can be found.
Let them not displease you because they are of small compass;
     Great weights are concealed in little chests.
By small nails a great structure is held together,
     A small hammer polishes great metal sheets.
Thus great harvests are born from little seedlings,
     And a great weight of tree from a small seed.

They open up hidden things and reveal many secrets,
      A little touch lifts a great veil.
Whatever flowers the great fields of books exhibit,
40   This basket gives you all at once: pluck with your hand.
Use them happily so that you may become still happier
      When your life seizes on perpetual wealth.
I ask that you deign to remember me in all circumstances
      When you read and reread and approach this work.
As you approach it, which my effort effected,
      Grant me a reward for my zeal:
As my reward I ask you to pray to God in my favor,
      That he may grant me forgiveness and his kind help.
May he drive off evil things and grant a prosperous outcome,
50   And allow, blessed life, that I take part in you.
May he harmonize morals, confirm hope, correct actions
      So that by his leave salvation may embrace my soul.
Thus may he mercifully purge me of all sinful habits
      So that he may give me a place above the stars after death,
And join me to the angelic hosts, he by whose office
      The earthly progeny ascends to the heavenly stars.

<u>iii</u>.

Live happy in God for long years, O reader,
      And I pray you not to forget your Theodulf.

<u>iv</u>.   **Explicit liber**
       (Conclusion)

Here the work ends; to those by whose execution it was completed
      Peace, life, health, and to you, O reader, farewell.

42.   A foris in prima tabula bibliothecae
       (Outside on the First Tablet of the Bible Compilation)

Anyone wishing to know who I am, know that I am the Bible
      And convey the rules of the Old Law and New.
Do not spurn me, I pray, because I am small in body;
      I am small of body, but still ample in strength.
Whoever sees me, remember Theodulf I pray you,
      Whose efforts formed me, arranged me, and gave me love,
Who adorned my cover with gold, silver, and gemstones,
      And embellished me with refining file: farewell.

Poems Attached to Historical Events

In altera tabula
(On the Second Tablet)

He who wishes to be good, who seeks an honorable lifetime,
> Seek me out, I advise you: I am the holy law of God.

I am the path, the light, the teacher of true knowledge,
> He who obeys me has inextinguishable light.

I prepare the heavenly realms and reveal earthly reasoning,
> In all matters I stand out, am supreme.

Avail yourself of me, O reader, and locate me in your spirit.
> When you search out the book, may your hands be clean.

43. Ad Gislam
(To Gisla)

Some of the discussion on this poem has been about the identity of Gisla. In a helpful footnote Alexandrenko (1971:252n3) points out that Cuissard (1892:54–58), Fichtenau (1957:93), and Manitius (1911:539) thought that she was Theodulf's daughter by an otherwise unrecorded marriage; Hauréau (1861:47) suggested that she might be an illegitimate daughter; Tiraboschi (3[1823]:293), Liersch (1880:17), and Chiri (1954:53) opted for a spiritual daughter; and Rzehulka (1875:14) believed she was Charlemagne's third daughter. It may be added that Ledru (1926:60) thought that Gisla was Theodulf's daughter by an early marriage and that Baunard (1860:90–91) had anticipated the view that she was Charlemagne's daughter. Alejandra de Riquer (1994:38) leaned toward the spiritual alternative. The rather staid marriage counsel does in fact sound more appropriate for a princess than for a daughter. The psalter with facing translations of two of Jerome's three versions (Nowell 2003: vol. 11:794) may also seem more appropriate for a state occasion than for a family event. On Theodulf's personal knowledge of the psalms and his special dependence on the Mozarabic Psalter see Freeman 1987.

> Gisla, with the favor of God receive an honorable present,
> > Which your father Theodulf presents,
> For I ordered this psalter to be executed for you,
> > Which, as you see, gleams with silver and gold.
> In it the first page agrees with the true Hebrew version,
> > Then the next has the same as the old [Gallican] page.
> These Jerome translated well, transcribing the first and correcting the other;
> > Both, believe me, shine with excellent sense.
> Scan them with assiduous and studious spirit,
> > And vigorously apply your mind to their significance.

With this instrument in your lap, keep in mind the rhythms,
May your hand be full of this plectrum and the sound of the beat.
May the sweet melody refresh you, strum the music;
May the harp sing for you and the lyre resound.
Run over it, now singing, now reflecting,
So that divine love may grow greater in you.
Should you pray assiduously, and if your reading be frequent,
You yourself will address God, and God will speak to you.
Let your hand be generous, your morals becoming, your actions prudent,
20 So that on this basis you may rightly please God.
May you be devoted to spinning and the chores of the household
So that your mind may soothe your servants and spouse.
In all actions let discretion be the dominant factor,
Be eager to display it, your life remains under its lead.
Spurn evil, pursue good, be proper in all things,
So that your exalted salvation may progress.
Prosper as a chaste wife long years with a chaste husband,
And may the lives of your offspring be a delight.
O Gisla, may you live happily with Suavericus
30 And happily grow old, God granting, with him.
May you be grandparents and great-grandparents, with a crowd of descendants,
May God grant this to you, who gave this to your line.
Hope, honor, due order, faith, piety, harmony, virtue,
Grace, and peace of God be with you forever: farewell.

Personal and Miscellaneous Poems

44. Cur modo carmina non scribat
(Why He Should Not Now Write Poems)

Alexandrenko (1971:254) refers to Raby's view (1957:1:173) that this poem reflects "the disillusion of age," but he finds that understanding unlikely. The sentiments nonetheless suggest old age more than youth. The combination of tired encouragement of the youth and patronizing experience, the retrospective cast, the loss of future ambition, and the air of completion point in that direction. The Wulfinus whom Theodulf addresses in verse 27 has been variously identified. Karl Strecker (1922:487–90) argued for a Wulfinus who claimed Die as his birthplace and composed a metrical life of Marcellus (also from Die). The latter had been bishop of Avignon and died in 510. Strecker found telltale echoes of Theodulf in this poem, making it likely that this is the right Wulfinus.

> You have often brought me welcome poems, O brothers,
>   And those you bring now, believe me, are a delight.
> For I am pleased by them, and I praise your zealous
>   Labor and urge that you persist with even greater success.
> You grow better and better, therefore my joys grow also,
>   I love that you improve more and more.
> I who was formerly able with ease to produce verses
>   Burn to create song but cannot do as I wish.
> You ask when this new custom began to be followed,
> 10   Which causes my lyric Erato to be still.
> Now it is more incumbent to lament my sins with tears streaming
>   Than to utter poems set forth with lyrical feet.
> My love, Christ himself, will seek not my poems,
>   But rather the great rewards of the flock committed to me.
> For them and for my errors I wish intercession;
>   I do not sin as long as I do not make verse.
> Play the game, my boys, I have plied the metrical art amply;
>   The rewards you desire have already been granted to me.
> Thus learn, O brothers, that you may be held to be learned,
> 20   And become the companions of the heavenly host.

But the observances of so great a festival esteemed by the pious
　　Do not allow me now to versify much.
With this practice behind us, let us celebrate this feast with elation;
　　There will be a better time for the production of verse.
Let us reverently cultivate feasts in yearly sequence,
　　So that God will grant us feasts without end.
For, Wulfinus, to you are owed rewards for your praises,
　　From whose river flows good metrical art.
Therefore, dear one, I render manifold thanks to you,
30　　And God the King will give rewards for your deserts.

45. De libris quos legere solebam et qualiter fabulae poetarum a philosophis mystice pertractentur (On the Books That I Used to Read and How the Stories of Poets Should Be Interpreted Allegorically by Philosophers)

Theodulf here combines two different literary types, the catalogue poem surveying his reading and a sample of allegories, which at the same time touches on the problem of whether any truth can be extracted from pagan writers (see Dronke 1974). The former type may be compared to Alcuin's recollection of the library at York ("Versus de sanctis Euboricensis ecclesiae," vv. 1532–1561); both resort to the "too long to list" formula. Indeed, Theodulf passes over the list quickly and goes on to the problem of truth, assuring the reader that though there is much falsehood in the pagan writers, there is also some truth. Echoing Virgil (*Georgics* 4.387–414), he attributes truth to Proteus and the Sibyl and contrasts the strength of Hercules with the weakness of the robber Cacus (cf. Bretzigheimer 2004:201–3). The latter instance exemplifies that pagan poets have the valuable function of revealing evil. This function also underlies the detailed allegory of Cupid and his various properties — nakedness for the palpability of crime, a quiver for poisoned arrows, a torch for the heat of passion, and so forth. The passage is interesting not only for the negative parables but also because the portion of Theodulf's "Ad episcopos" on lust is missing so that the present poem partially fills the gap. It concludes with an interpretation of Virgil's gates of horn and ivory (*Aeneid* 6.893–896); the eyes are transparent horn and see clearly, whereas ivory pertains to the mouth, which tells lies. On Theodulf's use of Ovid see Lendinara 1998:175–76.

I had been accustomed to read these books often,
　　This labor was mine both day and night.
Often I read Pope Gregory the Great, and often Augustine,
　　The sayings of Saint Hilary, and, Pope Leo, yours as well,
Jerome, Ambrose, Isidore of Seville, and John Chrysostom
　　And, Cyprian, great martyr and father, you too,

Personal and Miscellaneous Poems 141

Or others, whose names it would take long to number,
    Whom the honor of teaching wafted on high.
I also frequently read the heathen writings of the philosophers,
10   Who were quite eminent on various themes.
A proper attention to the pious fathers was not far distant,
    Whose names you will see recorded below:
Sedulius the Red, Paulinus, Arator, Avitus,
    Venantius Fortunatus, and you, Juvencus with a thundering voice;
And you, wise in evoking many things in various meters,
    O Prudentius, my kinsman by blood.
Sometimes you, Pompeius, I read, and sometimes you, Donatus,
    Sometimes Virgil and, voluble Ovid, sometimes you.
Though there are many frivolous things in their poems,
20   Many truths are concealed under a false disguise.
The pens of poets often relate false things, the pens of the wise are truer;
    They are often wont to convert falsehood to truth.
Thus Proteus renders truth and the Virgin justice,
    Hercules strength and impoverished Cacus theft.
So that the truth may be concealed, a thousand lies lie open;
    With Proteus firmly bound, the original shape returns.
The uncompromised power of justice shines in the ways of the Virgin,
    Whom no stain of injustice can deform.
The madness of deceitful thieves goes with footsteps in reverse order,
30   By rejecting honest ways they foam at the mouth with foul smoke.
But strength of mind reveals them, destroys and shakes them,
    So that their wickedness lies open to see.
The boy Cupid is figured as winged and naked,
    As carrying bow and quiver, poisoned arrows, and a torch;
Winged because light, naked because crime is open,
    As a boy because he lacks mature mind.
An evil mind is symbolized in the quiver, deceits in the longbow,
    Arrows are your poison, O boy, the torch is your amorous heat.
For what can be more fickle and lighter than lovers,
40   In whom a changeable mind, an unstable body, inheres?
Who can conceal the evil that piercing Amor occasions,
    Whose wicked deeds will always be revealed?
Who will be able to bind him with the coils of reason
    Since he is an unbridled boy lacking sense?
Who will be able to penetrate the malignant recesses of the quiver,
    Knowing how many threatening arrows lie concealed in the wicked case?
Whither does the poisonous missile joined to the torch leap forward,
    Which flies, fatally wounds, strikes and burns?

For he is the fierce and criminal demon of adultery,
50   Luring to wretched abysses and savage excess.
He is swift to deceive, always ready to injure,
    For the power, work, and practice of the demon are his.
As poems relate, sleep has two portals,
    One admits truth, but the other gives access to lies.
The gate of horn bears truth, the gate of ivory breeds falsehood.
    Eyes see the truth, but falsehoods emanate from the mouth.
For smooth horn and the delicate eye are transparent,
    But the cavity of the mouth displays dull ivory teeth.
The poet does not mean brightness by eyes, or darkness by horny substance,
60   The strength and color is the same in ivory and tooth.
There is no single force in these two portals,
    The mouth utters falsehoods, the eye sees nothing but truth.
May it suffice to have set down as examples
    These few things bound with many short chains.

46. De septem liberalibus artibus in quadam pictura depictis (On the Seven Liberal Arts Shown in a Certain Picture)

Initially the poem pictures a tree with Grammatica at its root because grammar is fundamental to all arts, a concept ubiquitous in Carolingian thinking about education. Wisdom (Sophia) is further up to mark her exalted position. A branch on the right hand supports Rhetoric and Dialectic, with the four virtues on the left (Prudentia, Vis, Justitia, Moderatio). Rhetoric is depicted with the head of a lion (strength) and wings (eloquence), and she addresses a large crowd. Rhetoric stands, but Dialectic sits apart to avoid crowds, and she works with a pen. In her left hand she carries a serpent, but her right hand is free to use against any attacker. Its task is to distinguish truth from falsehood. On other branches sit Logica and Ethica, though subservient to Wisdom (Prudentia), who is accompanied by the most powerful of the virtues, the well-armed Vis. Nearby is Justitia, with crown and scales, and Moderatio, who urges a moderate pace, reminiscent of "Contra iudices" (vv. 611–612). Åslaug Ommundsen has also placed moderation at the center of her study of the *Libri Carolini* (2002:191–92). The trunk is grasped by Ars Numerorum (arithmetic), and above her in the branches can be seen Musica with lyre and pipe and Geometria with wheel and measuring rod. They measure out the climatic zones, over which the stars, constellations, and zodiac loom. Returning to the tree, the poet tells us that it bears both leaves (words) and fruit (meaning). As a whole the tree conveys how our understanding rises to higher things.

Mähl (1969:64–72) thought to identify the main source of this description in Isidore's *Etymologies* 2.24.1–7, but this is a partial model at best. The closest similarity is with Isidore's distinction between rhetoric and dialectic in 2.23.2,

Personal and Miscellaneous Poems 143

where we read: "While dialectic is indeed sharper for examining things, rhetoric is more fluent for those things it tries to teach. Dialectic sometimes appears in schools; rhetoric continually comes to the public forum. Dialectic reaches very few students; rhetoric often reaches the whole populace." Ank C. Esmeijer (1973) provided a much fuller accounting of both textual and art-historical parallels. She believed that the "discus" referred to in the first line was not a table or tray, as sometimes supposed, but a wall picture or mosaic. Her wide-ranging study shows that there are no similar pictures of figures in a naturalistic tree until much later; in the absence of similar pictures or any mention of materials we might be led to believe that the poem is based not on a real picture but perhaps on an imaginary one. Apparently without knowledge of Esmeijer (or Mähl) Alejandra de Riquer [Permanyer] (1990) provided a rather sketchier review of the echoes from such writers as Isidore, Cassiodorus, and Martianus Capella. See also Lewis 1964; and for Theodulf's use of Ovid see Lendinara 1998:176–77.

> There was a disc with the image of the round earth depicted,
>> Which the work of a single tree adorned.
> Grammatica sat at its root in huge measure
>> Urging us to copy and retain her art.
> The whole tree is seen to rise above her,
>> For, without her, no art can produce.
> Her left hand holds a whip, the right hand a saber,
>> The former to urge on the slow, the latter to uproot erroneous views.
> And since wisdom everywhere holds first position,
>> Therefore a diadem adorned her head.
> And because good intelligence or good opinion creates you,
>> Exalted Sophia, they are both close to you.
> From the straight trunk of this tree branches
>> Extend from all sides out from their source.
> The right branch holds Rhetoric, and you, Dialectic,
>> And the four virtues are borne by the left.
> Rhetoric sat, right hand stretched out to the people.
>> And the layout of a towered city was close at hand.
> She delivered civil laws with great skill in speaking,
>> For she is accustomed to rein in the disputes of the crowd.
> The head of the body bears wings, also the crown of a lion,
>> Which the well-skilled hand of the artisan had carried out.
> The lightness of winged words and the strength of the lion
>> Adorning the head provided symbols of eloquent speech.
> Thus Mercury, wearing wings on head and ankles,
>> Suggests that he has a light flow of speech.
> Not far away sits Dialectica, mother of meaning;
>> The previous woman was seen standing, this one sits.

Equal in mind in several respects, they differ in action.
30   The former declaims on her feet, the latter reads from a seat.
The former seeks bustling places, the latter remote isolation,
        The former always seeks crowds, the latter a pen.
The former expresses herself in words, the latter in concepts;
        The former is a fountain of words, the latter adheres to ideas.
The left hand shows the head of a serpent, but hides its body;
        Since her right hand holds nothing, she can attack if attacked.
What she proposes and reasons, she acutely meshes,
        So that with her serpent she can cleverly and quickly attack the
        unwary foe.
With great zeal she burns to distinguish what is truthful
40   From what is false and knows how to find the path of truth.
On one branch sat Logica, and Ethica on another,
        One is distinguished for reason, the other for honest norms.
Here Prudentia retains the leading location,
        She is unable to lose the way of holy life.
She stood there with pious earnest and held a volume
        So that her disciple could be instructed with it.
Next to her stood Vis [Fortitude], the strongest of virtues,
        Recognizable by her arms and her role.
One hand holds a shield, the other a dagger;
50   Her whole head was covered by a helmet's cone,
With which she may overcome the horrid specters of vicious behavior,
        So that godly freedom can be well secured.
Near her Justitia held a sword grasped in her fingers,
        And in her hand were scale and crown,
With which to bring rewards to the just and torments to the unjust.
        With just balancing may she test words and deeds.
Near her stood Moderatio, offering a temperate model,
        Bearing strong curbs or goads in her hand,
With which to urge on the sluggish and temper the swift, enabling
60   An even order to proceed with moderate pace.
A picture of the great tree rose in elevation,
        The trunk, perfectly straight, rose high,
Which Ars Numerorum held embraced with arms extended,
        And her feet were seen to stand on both branches for support.
One hand held the numbers, the other a volume,
        In which it is clear that your mother, O Physica, is found.
Above her two maidens are seen to emerge from the branches,
        From the same place and in appearance alike.
In part of one melodious Musica was seated
70   And was seen artfully to move the strings of a lyre.

Personal and Miscellaneous Poems 145

There is a pipe with dissimilar reeds, seven in number,
    A famed number bearing much mystical lore.
On the left hand lay leaning Geometria,
    Her right hand bearing the measuring rod, her left hand the wheel.
The ruler measures from close at hand the rounded circle,
    But the wheel has five heavenly zones.
Of these the two farthest are oppressed by cold weather,
    In between a hot one moderates the two zones.
Between these a central trunk rises upward
80   And the art cultivated by astronomers holds it fast.
Her head rising aloft was weighted with a huge circlet,
    Which extended arms hold with both hands:
A crown formed in the image of the star-studded heavens,
    Which a beautiful flaming order of constellations fills.
Twelve signs and seven wandering bodies
    Adorn it by law, alternately by courses, orbits, and sites.
Here the Ram, the Bull, the Twins, the Crab, and the Lion,
    The Virgo with chariot, the Scale, the Scorpion too,
The Archer, Capricorn, Aquarius, and two Fishes
90   Encircle the orb of the sky with their signs.
Sun, Moon, and Mars, Mercury, Jupiter, and Venus,
    And ponderous Saturn, you go in the diurnal orb.
Let not the pagan names displease you, O reader:
    This custom is assigned by the fathers of ancient times.
By these seven stars and twelve signs of the zodiac
    Month, year, and day are controlled.
Some are adjusted to days, others to monthly cycles,
    Weeks serve for some, for others a year.
These things the tree held, leaves and fruit hanging,
100   Thus it shed beauty and provided much mystical sense.
In the leaves, understand words, in the fruits, meaning;
    The former grow often, the latter, used well, nurture us.
In this spreading tree our life is instructed
    So that with modest beginnings it can soar aloft.
Let human understanding gradually rise higher,
    And may it long be reluctant to tarry below.
Let Ethica be joined to Grammatica, and Logica joined in addition;
    Physica also consorts with companionable arts.
Of these the highest art takes a seat in the heavens,
    Which embrace the law of the stars and the sky.
110 Let eloquence follow morals, and sweet Logica follow both in succession,
    So that one may know well the natural scheme;

And let song proceed through the earth and vaults of heaven,
From the things of this world may it seek aetherial heights.

47. Alia pictura, in qua erat imago terrae in modum orbis comprehensa
(Another Picture in Which There Was an Image of the Earth Formed as a Circle)

That in this case we are dealing with a real artifact is indicated in verse 41, where Theodulf claims to have commissioned the piece: "I, Bishop Theodulf, caused the work to be fashioned . . . ." Prominent is the figure of a woman personifying the earth, "nursing a boy and filling a basket with food." She is equipped with an array of allegorical attributes; she carries a serpent, her head is bedecked with towers, and in her hands she holds a key, cymbals, and arms. She is surrounded by roosters, livestock, and lions. She herself stands, but next to her is an empty seat. She is conveyed by a chariot, which is propelled by rounded wheels. All of these properties are duly allegorized: the serpent represents the intelligence of the farmer, the basket represents harvests, the towers great cities, the key her opening of a new springtime, the cymbals the sounds of farm equipment, the arms a readiness to fight for the land, the chariot wheels the cyclical renewal of the earth, the roosters the seeds of procreation, the livestock the nurturing of the earth, and the submissive lions the transcendent power of the earth over all things. The empty seat is rather more elaborate, suggesting the sequence of worldly governance, while the chariot wheels convey the revolving earth. The personification of a woman appears to be seen as an extension of the earth (v. 39), although her chariot is described as being airborne (v. 31); it is after all the earth that she cultivates.

Having laid claim to the artifact, Theodulf passes on to the larger allegory, which interprets the picture in terms of body and spirit. The earth nurtures the body, which, however, is no more than dull flesh; to be preferred is the life of the mind, a concept represented by the very allegory of the picture.

The archivist and paleographer A. Vidier (1911) provided the fullest treatment of these verses, which are found (in a slightly different order and with two lines added) in two penned boxes on a mappa mundi in a manuscript once in the possession of Queen Christina of Sweden and now housed in the Vatican (Bibl. Vatic. Reg. 123, fols. 143v-144r). The manuscript originated in Ripoll in northern Catalonia in 1055. It shows a map of Europe, Asia, and Africa with the Theodulfian verses reproduced below. Between the boxed texts is a female figure with a serpent encircling her right arm and an unclear object in her left hand. There is no sign of a chariot. Beneath is the inscription "terra." Vidier showed that communications between Orléans and Ripoll were quite plausible in the ninth century. He believed that Theodulf created the picture as a fresco and in manuscript form, but Schaller (1962:84) thought that he might have taken the

Personal and Miscellaneous Poems 147

word "pictura" in the title too literally; the title could after all be the work of the editor Sirmond. Schaller inclined more to a mappa mundi inscribed on a table, not necessarily with the earth allegory. Indeed, he suggested that a new edition might have to separate the text into two poems, vv. 1–40 and 41–54. This separation would, however, break the continuity and the progression of the allegory, which proceeds logically from individual allegories to an encompassing allegory. Since there is really no indication of the mappa mundi in the poem as a whole, one could imagine that the mapmaker simply took over the verses of Theodulf to illustrate a mappa mundi of an entirely different origin. The only bridge between the poem and the mappa mundi is the verse: "Totius orbis adest breviter depicta figura." What Theodulf had in mind with this verse was a metaphorical understanding of "totius orbis figura" (a picture of the functioning of the whole earth), but the mapmaker took "totus orbis" literally to apply to the whole extent of his mappa mundi.

> In it a beautiful woman stood in the earth's image
>> Nursing a boy and filling a basket with food,
> Bearing a serpent with great coils and a head with towers,
>> In her hand a key, cymbals, and arms.
> By her stood roosters, livestock, and fierce lions
>> Submissively, and alongside an empty seat.
> Beneath her was the conveyance of a great moving chariot
>> Propelled by a rotation of rounded wheels.
> She nurses a boy, for she nurses newly-born creatures
> 10   And, at the same time, fosters all things born on earth.
> She signifies harvests with baskets, and great cities with towers,
>> The cunning mind of the farmer she signifies with the snake.
> It is shown in summer, for in winter the year comes to conclusion,
>> Therefore she carries the adornment of a key in her hand.
> The cymbals are the sounds made by agricultural equipment,
>> Or some worker manufacturing them with his craft.
> And because all should fight for their country,
>> Thus the image, O earth, conveys your arms.
> The wheels signified the procreation of earth, seeds were signified by roosters;
> 20   With the seed implanted, the world will return much.
> The livestock obey her because she gives them nurture,
>> Without her they can have no support.
> That the hostile fury of lions submits to her orders
>> Signifies that Earth tames all earthly things.
> Although all things are in motion, the chariot cannot move unaided;
>> Thus a perpetual seat was fashioned for her.
> By seats are signified worldly honors,
>> For no one is destined to have them without end.

Some delight to sit in the seat of another,
30   One sits, another one sat, one goes, another returns.
Thus earth was conveyed in a chariot that is airborne;
      Let it be sustained by a smooth watery flow.
Thus the true reading of the Lord informs us,
      Striving to multiply his praises,
The Lord who reaches over the empty vastness of northern stretches,
      And, O earth, hangs nothing higher than you.
That the chariot moves on wheels implies the earth turning,
      Which revolves swiftly and on a swift course.
The image was seen to stand in terms of the earth's extension,
40   For it always has earth to cultivate.
I, Bishop Theodulf, caused the work to be fashioned,
      And I properly made it function in two different modes.
To wit, that bodies should be fed with ample nurture,
      And that the image observed would nourish the mind.
O observer, love the food of the spirit more than the body;
      With the former the mind is illumined, with the latter dull flesh wins out.
Let heavenly words sound, let the table abound with food aplenty,
      Let no envious words hold sway.
The shape of the whole earth is briefly described in the image
50   And will reveal in small compass a great theme.
Here Amphitrite, the sea, along the long earthly seashore
      Extends her arms, absorbing all streams.
With cheeks full of food, differing brothers from every region
      Tread the earth with places assigned to each.

48. [Itinerarium]

As Dümmler suggests, this poem of thirty hexameters describes a journey that took Theodulf to Limoges, then to Périgord to the southwest, then apparently south across the Dordogne into an area that he addresses as "Populana Gallia" (v. 27). Alexandrenko (1971:273) translated "O populous France," but we are unable to find an adjective "populanus" in the dictionaries. "Populana Gallia" is more likely to refer to the place name Novempopulania, a region in Aquitaine (see Caro Baroja 1985:132). It might also mean "France full of poplar trees," from *populus* poplar.

In any event, the trip was an adventurous one. Theodulf and his companion Auredus were well received in Limoges by abbots and clergy but were attacked by a drunken crowd and might have fared ill if they had not been rescued by a certain Ephraim and a certain Mancio. A Mancio is mentioned in his later poem to Modoin (72.188 below) as bishop of Toulouse and could be the same person. Baunard (1860:283–84) speculated that Theodulf may have been engaged

Personal and Miscellaneous Poems 149

in another mission as *missus dominicus* and might therefore have been exposed to resentment and danger. That would account for his companion Auredus (otherwise unknown), his substantial following, and his critique of Gallic greed, but there is insufficient detail to allow for any certainty.

> From there my route was directed to the peaceful city
> Of Limoges, a people ready to serve all and sundry.
> Their prosperous city was richly hospitable to me until the moment
> When nine times the sun had put the stars to flight from human transactions,
> And Auredus had joined my waiting assemblage.
> There the crowd of abbots, clergy, and others
> Refreshed us with delights and ample kindness
> When a people lubricated with wine attacked us
> And our people attempt to put up resistance.
> 10 An impious sword would have destroyed the old city,
> Alas, and a terrible disaster come upon us,
> Had not Ephraim and Mancio the priest come to the rescue,
> With whose intervention the fury of death on both sides receded.
> Finally, with the customary pack-saddles loaded,
> We departed from there, and the land of Périgord received us.
> From there we sought out your flowing banks, Dordogne,
> Where, with the horses turned aside by the masses
> Of flowing water, the far shores lay open.
> We urged them three times swiftly into the river,
> 20 Loudly urging them on, even with stone casts,
> Three times, though weak and tossed by the weight of the water.
> Among fords, among cliffs, in woodland and caverns
> A worried group of searchers found them trembling.
> I think an evil omen made them tremble
> At the sight of the shore, and fear the low-lying stretches,
> For the pale hunger for coin, perhaps overflowing,
> O poplar-bearing Gaul (?), was wasting your region.
> After this we crossed the raging river with an oared conveyance
> And dragged the horses behind by tying wet halters;
> 30 The opposite shore offers itself to our eyesight.

49. In sepulcro Sancti Nazarii
(On the Headstone of Saint Nazarius)

There is a Saint Nazarius who was abbot in Lérins in the late sixth and early seventh century, but no indication that he was martyred in Rome and interred on the Rhine. The idea that "nazar" means flower in the Hebrew tongue can be traced to an etymology of Nazareth in Saint Jerome's letters (ep. 46, *PL* 22,

491; Liebeschütz 1957:87). Cuissard (1892:59, 272) speculated that Theodulf was present at the translation of Saint Nazarius's relics to Lorsch in 774, but that seems very early. He suggested further that Theodulf's verses were to be inscribed on the saint's tomb, but the verses seem to be more in the style of a travelogue, like the previous poem, than an epitaph.

> Christ interred your limbs here, dear martyr,
>> And your spirit in flight ascends to the heights.
> With your deeds you purified the banks of the Tiber,
>> And now you bless the Rhinelanders with the honor of your bones.
> O Rome, with God's grace you saw the marks of the martyr,
>> Now, German people, you see the burial site.
> You placed the courtly shrine in a forested landscape,
>> O martyr, and the chamber shines in deserted sands.
> The whole nation calls this flower the Nazarius,
> 10   For flower is called "nazar" in the Hebrew tongue.
> When I was hastily seeking it out while traveling
>> From Worms, I saw snow fallen from the clouds.
> I traversed the banks of the Rhine, rich in fish, on a ferry
>> So that I could more quickly approach the place.

50. De vulpecula involante gallinam (On a Vixen Attacking a Hen)

Schaller (1962:22) declared this poem to be genuine on stylistic grounds, but it is difficult to make sense of. Since it tells the adventure of a predatory fox that steals a hen from a monastery at Charroux (equidistant between Poitiers to the north, Limoges to the east, and Angoulême to the south), it has a certain similarity to an animal fable and was included in Jan Ziolkowski's *Talking Animals* (1993:53–54; translation 268). It has been compared to Alcuin 49 (ed. Dümmler 1881:262), in which a rooster is caught by a wolf and saves itself with the dying wish to hear the wolf's far-famed voice. This is in the tradition of the crow that drops a piece of cheese when asked by a fox to sing; it is a pure animal fable and ends with the moral that we should not be distracted from the work of salvation by deception and false words. Theodulf's poem does not fit this pattern and seems in some oblique way to be about the monastery, its founders, and its donors. The fox has the further anomaly of being arboreal (Ziolkowski 1993:53); with the hen in its mouth it climbs an elder bush and gets stuck. Here it is observed (and presumably dispatched?) by the monastic brethren. The reader is left with the impression that this uncharacteristically clumsy fox represents some real threat to the monastery, perhaps a criminal invasion of its assets (cf. Baunard 1860:256–57; Liebeschütz 1957:82–83).

Personal and Miscellaneous Poems

There is a place to which the French give the name Charroux,
    In which the gates of heaven are open to the elect.
There a residence shines under the name of the Savior,
    Where the beautiful walls of a monastery are found.
Here it shines under the bright auspices of saintly sponsors,
    And the faithful community lives there in excellent style.
In a word, Rotharius, an outstanding count and great warrior,
    With his wife Eufrasia founded this house.
He adorns it with tawny gold, gems, and silver,
10   It abounds in books and sacred garb.
He gave it manors, fields, houses, forests, vineyards, and tillers,
    Cattle and livestock and all that is good,
With which dire poverty may be driven away by generous donors,
    With the heavenly storehouse granting fruits,
So that exalted God may purge the donor of all sinful habits
    And kindly join him to the heavenly hosts above.
Christ is intent on barring him from black recesses,
    For him let Christ dedicate a place of worship of his own.
A vixen was accustomed to seize with inimical plunderings
20   Whatever was to be prepared as food for men.
The bird that, spreading its wings, produces a thousand colors,
    This too she craftily devours with her jaws.
The worthy community of monks remained unknowing
    As to what pest brought upon them such a loss.
The luring of the vixen took the winged hen to a distance,
    Thus the manner of the deception remained sealed.
The barbarous predator, along with the burden of booty,
    Hung by choice, but foolishly, on the branch of a shrub.
On purpose the foolish one hung, deprived of her crooked endeavors,
30   And this was altogether the end of her various crimes.
She gobbled the head of the bird with her mouth gaping open,
    But at the same time the other members remained untouched,
For the elder bush was smaller than a tree but higher than the bushes
    By which you, O foot of the trickster, were to be held,
Higher than the right hand of a man can reach lifting
    Rocks, with which a wall may quickly rise high.
From here the nasty predator hung, and from it the marauder
    Twisted this way and that with trembling head and neck.
Seeing this, the faithful crowd of monks is delighted,
40   Seeing the admirable signs given by God's grace.
Be far off, profane thief, away from here altogether,
    The crime of the devil begone; approach, O angel divine.

May peace prevail with the weapons of envy divested,
     And in this place may hope and faith reign.
Granting prosperity, may God drive off adverse conditions,
     And may minds, O Christ, sip your immortal draught.

51. De equo perdito
(Concerning a Lost Horse)

Unlike the previous poem, this one would appear to be purely anecdotal, perhaps
from an oral source. Alexandrenko (1971:277) pointed out a close analogue in
a one-page Chekhov story, "The Threat" in *The Image of Chekhov: Forty Stories
by Anton Chekhov in the Order in Which They Were Written* (New York: Alfred A.
Knopf, 1967, p. 71). Chekhov's version is so close that Alexandrenko's surmise
that it might be indirectly derivative from Theodulf's poem is not unreasonable,
though the poem is more humorously told.

Native wit often provides what strength has not granted,
     A man has a knack when muscle power fails.
Hear now with what craft a soldier recovered a charger
     That had been stolen in the turbulence of life in camp.
Deprived of his horse, he beseeches aloud in public:
     "Whoever has my horse, let him strive to give it back.
Otherwise, forced by such cause, I must take as an example
     What my father did in the city of Rome."
This trick moved all, and the thief relented,
10   For he fears terrible loss to himself or his own.
When the owner finds the horse, he happily retrieves it,
     And those who were fearful before are overjoyed.
Then they ask what he would have done if the horse had been forfeit,
     Or what it was his father had done in Rome:
"With the bit attached to the saddle," he said, "and his neck as a bearer,
     Loaded down with little saddlebags, the poor fellow went off.
The former cavalryman went back to his house as a pedestrian,
     Carrying his spurs on his heels, having nothing to spur.
Sadly I would have followed his example
20   If, believe me, this horse had not been found."

Personal and Miscellaneous Poems 153

52–57. De bilingue
Ad quendam de muneribus
De passione Domini
In die resurrectionis
De tabella
De talamanca

These poems were found to be inauthentic or of doubtful authenticity by Schaller (1962:28–29) and were not translated by Alexandrenko. They are included here for the sake of completeness. The first one is aimed at the chatterer without substance, like crickets or birds. How the glutton (*elluo, helluo*) in line nine is to be understood is unclear, unless it is being used metaphorically for a consumer of empty words. The "ortivagus" in line four is in Dümmler's "Index Vocum Rariorum" (649) but is not explained. If there is an underlying theme, it is perhaps meaninglessness.

"Ad quendam de muneribus" is a somewhat sour solicitation of gifts from an unspecified addressee of high status. The reception given the addressee will depend on the quality of the gifts and will be either warm thanks or harsh dismissal. This rude alternative seems not at all in Theodulf's epistolary style, though his register is so variable that hardly anything can be excluded.

"De passione Domini" is a very brief statement on Christ's suffering on behalf of humankind. What speaks against Theodulf's authorship is the absence of any development in the thought.

"In die resurrectionis" is an epanaleptic celebration of Christ's resurrection. Though Theodulf makes use of the epanaleptic mode elsewhere, Schaller (1962:29) is doubtful about its authenticity.

"De tabella" describes the decorative exterior and meaningful interior of a writing tablet. The conceit is reminiscent of Theodulf's lines in 39 <u>ii</u> (vv. 4–5):

> On the outside the work gleams with gems, gold, and purple,
>> But it shines within with a more splendid light.

"De talamasca" pictures a boy covering the face of a dead man in fear and trembling. It might be pressing a point, but the four lines could be understood to mean that we are never too young to begin reflecting in fear and trembling on the next life.

52. De bilingue
(Concerning the Chatterer)

> Lo, a frivolous man, whispering this and that in mutters,
>> Now jokes, now laments, and sometimes utters indecent talk.

He trills sweet nothings, then flits like a cricket,
    Repeats to ears those nothings that rumor (?) seeks out.
Just as a crow strikes its tough breast with its beak pointed
    When it calls down showers of rain with its caws.
Or the swallow tries with beating wings to sweep over
    The waters, chirping sweet nothings in a loud voice.
Hardly otherwise does an inimical glutton survey the unstable
10   Minds of youths, whom a light wind drives.

53.   Ad quendam de muneribus
(To an Unidentified Man Concerning Gifts)

Alas, do not turn my song from my custom;
    As is your wont, prevent it from returning with naught.
Let the impatient hoofs of your foaming horse echo
    On the tracks back bringing gifts.
Or let the robe, which the fathers of Rome refer to
    With the name of bright purple, press your neck.
Should you happily come bearing beautiful presents,
    May you sweetly accept a thousand thanks from me.
But if perchance you come empty-handed to my address,
10   Cut with a thousand lashes you, useless man, will go out.

54.   De passione Domini
(On the Passion of the Lord)

That the holy crowd give voice to the holy work of the Almighty,
    That is entirely proper to express with praise.
That the Creator of the great earth deigned humbly
    To suffer, it is proper to praise.
Christ the Son endured in human body
    All things for the salvation of man.

55.   In die resurrectionis
(On the Day of Christ's Resurrection)

O Muse, I ask that you recite songs freely.
    Now sing, I ask, the melody freely, O Muse.
Lovely feasts you should strive to stage with me,
    So that you may then receive very lovely feasts.
He is worthy of song, let us all perform cantatas,
    This bright day is worthy of song.

Personal and Miscellaneous Poems   155

Death lies overcome, undone when Christ arises,
    Let us all rejoice, for death lies overcome.
Hell lies overcome with Christ viewing the blessed,
10   With the demon prince conquered, hell lies overcome.
He drove the guiltless from there, and left the guilty abiding.
    With the enemy trampled he rescued the guiltless from there.
The blessed rise to heavenly realms saved from the shadows,
    Snatched from the shades, they rise to heavenly realms.
Turn your step, O Muse, inflict no woe on the brethren.
    Here I ask you, O Muse, turn your step.
Say "Greetings, O bishop" with neck and knee bended,
    Here and forever say "Bishop, hail."

56.   De tabella
     (On a Tablet)

In brief, I, a little tablet, make use and avail myself
    Of a double office, with an appropriate appearance inside and out.
Outside I give the bearer an adornment of appearance,
    And within I preserve words bound with signs.

57.   De talamasca
     (On a Mask)

When a boy covers the face of a dead man,
    What makes him tremble frightens him off; he flees, let him flee.
I believe he lay prostrate and extended his fingers
    Before the Savior, shaking with his little limbs.

58–68. Versus in altari
In xenodochio
In fronte domus
In fronte domus
In faldaone episcopi
Super ianuam
Super propinatorium
In altare Aniani
In obitu Damasi
Quod deus non loco quaerendus sit, sed pietate colendus
De sollemni anniversario

This cluster of eleven poems is largely made up of short inscriptions, some of them quite fine, and one of them definitely not by Theodulf (66). The first (58) is inscribed on an altar, the location of which is not specified. It is addressed to the worshippers who are sustained by Christ. The next three (59–61) are secular in nature, one inscribed in an inn and the others on dwellings. The inn is of particular interest because, as the last lines reveal, it was constructed by Theodulf. The twenty verses lay out the mission of the inn, care for the hungry and thirsty, the poor, the traveler, the weary, the sick, the depressed (cf. Brommer 1974:70, 76–77), according to the corporal works of mercy (Matthew 25:35–40). Baunard (1860:201) located the inn in Orléans, and that seems as likely as not. The two residence inscriptions seem to be addressed to visitors rather than inhabitants. The first bids them do no evil that would be visible from the house, all the more so because God in heaven sees all things. The second bids all those who have a pleasant perspective from the house bear in mind that everything they see was created by God.

Poem 62 offers a different perspective from the bishop's throne. The first line describes the throne as "sessio Teudulfi," and that would seem to justify Baunard (1860:193–94) in believing that the poet is addressing his own situation. He addresses a prayer to God that he may do good and deal with all appropriately. In the third stanza he echoes Saint Augustine in forbidding the slandering of any persons not present (Baunard 1860:196n1). Poem 63 seems to supplement the counsel on episcopal behavior by urging provision for the poor, while 64 calls down a blessing on a drinking hall from Him "who caused water to have the appearance of wine" (John 2:1–11). Poem 65 is another altar inscription, this time specified as being dedicated to Saint Anianus, presumably of Orléans (died 453).

Poem 66 was shown to be an epitaph for Pope Damasus (died 384) composed by himself, not Theodulf (see Schaller 1962:16). Poem 67 neatly makes the small point that salvation depends on a moral life, not on pilgrimages, and 68 marks the celebration of a church festival not otherwise identified.

Personal and Miscellaneous Poems 157

58. Versus in altari
(Verses on an Altar)

This altar, Creator of heaven and earth, I, Theodulf,
    Adorn for you humbly with a wish.
I ask that whoever approaches bringing holy gifts and prayers,
    May you remember me if God is mindful of you.
Shepherd, nourish the sheep of the Lord with heavenly sustenance,[1]
    To whom a pious life is given, to whom the hall of God opens wide.
Above the stars dwells a devout shepherd, by whom we all are nourished.
    Whom you love, O shepherd, is part of the flock.
Do you see the crowd breathlessly nearing the sheepfold?
10   Thus it takes sustenance from the blood and the flesh of the Lamb,
Whom you fear, savage serpent, and who conquered you, faithless lion,[2]
    Who bore the inveterate crimes of the world
And assigned us holy drink and heavenly nurture
    And granted us to sit at his board.[3]
He is the way, the life, the salvation by which and to which the road is more
        safely trodden;[4]
    With whom it is given to the pious to reign without end.

59. In xenodochio
(In an Inn)

Look, the house is open, laid out with modest adornment
    But nonetheless appropriate for human use.
May God visit it from the height of heaven, taking pity on his servants;
    Let him expel all adversity and grant all things prosperous instead.
Here let modesty and truth, piety and honesty be abundant,
    Let sweet faith be present, all evil far off.
May the hungry find food, the thirsty drink, the visitor find honor,
    May the unclothed be able to find attire.
May the weary find help, the languishing healing, the sad comfort,
10   And may this house have concern for all.
May the Father on high give this house to the dwellers
    Such that it is open to citizens and, O traveler, to you;

---

[1] John 21:16–17
[2] Psalm 91:13
[3] Revelation 3:20
[4] John 14:6

So that the love of brethren and of God reign forever,
    And under its leadership all virtues combine.[1]
With God's mercy may all proper things follow these virtues,
    So that there is no access to envy's savage deceits.
May law rule the minds here, and resources be in abundance,
    And far, far off remain hunger and thirst.
Whoever comes to this house I ask to be mindful of Theodulf,
20   Who constructed the house with God's grace.

60. In fronte domus
(On the Front of a House)

You who stand or sit, who wander through towns and country,
    You who devote your time to various pursuits,
Do no evil that any can see from this high dwelling.
    There is another thing that you may fear more:
God dwells above the stars beholding whatever the human race ventures,
    And he will make sure that your scale has a just weight.[2]

61. In fronte domus
(On the Front of a House)

Whoever wishes to see the crowds bound for Rome or returning,
    Or to Tours or from Tours, come up here and watch.
From here you will see crops, vines, and dens that beasts inhabit,
    Rivers, fields, roads, and groves bearing fruit.
While you observe these things, the more pleasant things you witness,
    Be mindful yourself of God, the Creator of these.

62. In faldaone episcopi
(On the Bishop's Throne)

May Theodulf's seat and all his actions, I pray, be pleasing
    To you, blessed God and King, whom all good things please,
Without whom nothing good can be done and with whom all good prospers.
    May you grant me, I ask, to wish and to do good.

When a superior approaches, let the people stand or a youth attend you,
    Address those standing about with kindly speech.

---

[1] Matthew 22:37–40
[2] Leviticus 19:36

Personal and Miscellaneous Poems

May your spirit be humble, your heart wise, and your action unblemished,
    And may the occupant devoutly contemplate God with his mind.

Whoever stands here, do not detract from any;
    It is a crime if slander is heaped on absent men.
You who stand by, avoid the use of vacuous language
    Lest he who is seated condemn you to depart.

63. Super ianuam
(Above the Doorway)

May your door always be open to the wretched, O bishop,
    And Christ himself will enter at the same time as the poor.
May the poor in want be fed with your provisions
    So that you may be chosen to be a guest in the presence of God.

64. Super propinatorium
(Over a Drinking Hall)

He who once was able to draw wine from liquid
    And caused water to have the appearance of wine,[1]
May he bless our cups with a beneficent gesture
    And cause us to have a cheerful day.

65. In altare Sancti Aniani
(On the Altar of Saint Anianus)

I, Theodulf, adorn this altar for you, God in heaven,
    And may you, God and King, favor my prayers.
Whoever is viewing this altar and you, most holy Bishop
    Anianus, be mindful, I pray, of my humble self.

---

[1] John 2:1–11

66. In obitu Damasi
(On the Death of Damasus)

He who trod the bitter waves of the ocean,[1]
He who brings the dying seeds of the earth to prosper,
He who was able to loose the law-given chains of mortals,
Who after death, after the third light of the sun, was able
To grant to the brother of Martha a return again to the living,[2]
I believe that he will cause Damasus after death to be resurrected.

67. Quod deus non loco quaerendus sit, sed pietate colendus
(That God Should Not Be Sought Out in a Place but Should Be Worshipped Piously)

It is not so helpful to have gone to Rome as to live justly,
    Either in Rome or wherever man's life is lived.
I do not believe that the path of feet, but of morals, leads starwards;
    God sees from above who does what and where.

68. Die sollemni anniversario
(On a Solemn Festival Day)

Here for our people, the clergy, and holy servants
The annual joys of the solemn feast are reinstated.
For who does not rightly rejoice at the treasure of such wisdom
And pay respect with ample praises and prayers,
From which the times are adorned with perpetual treasures
And golden spirit shines with heavenly teaching?
Words exceed the brightness of light or silver,
All gems are obscured by the light of virtues,
With which the confines of Libya and realms of Francia are illumined,
10 With which the people of Spain flourish, and the people of Britain,
And the pure capital of the world, holy Rome, is brilliant,
And with which the famous and faithful people of all the earth are resplendent.

---

[1] Matthew 14:25
[2] John 11:1–44

Personal and Miscellaneous Poems 161

69. [Versus facti ut a pueris in die palmarum cantarentur (Verses to Be Sung by Boys on Palm Sunday)]

Although "Contra iudices" and "Ad Carolum regem" have been singled out as Theodulf's most remarkable creations, it could be argued that his Palm Sunday hymn is the best known and most discussed of his poems by virtue of its place in hymnology. It was reedited in Dreves and Blume's *Analecta Hymnica Medii Aevi* (vol. 50 [1907], 160–63), and the first twelve verses survive to this day in the Anglican *Hymnal* (no. 62). It therefore figures in general discussions of medieval hymns such as Josef Szövérffy's *Die Annalen der lateinischen hymnendichtung* (1964:202–4). There has been much debate about whether Theodulf actually composed the poem (e.g., Cuissard:134–48). An intermediate position was taken by Ledru (1926), who thought that the first thirty-six lines to the glory of Christ were genuine, but that the last forty-four lines, which recount the celebration of Palm Sunday in Angers and enumerate the city's churches, were added by someone else. This view was connected with Ledru's opinion that Theodulf's part of the poem was composed in Le Mans, not Angers. More recently see Adamik 2001.

Of particular interest is a story attached to the hymn and preserved in Hugh of Fleury's *Historia ecclesiastica* (pp. 363–64) from the early twelfth century in the following form:

> When he was being held in custody, it happened that there on Palm Sunday the aforementioned very pious emperor arrived, and when the procession passed by the residence in which Bishop Theodulf was being held, and silence fell in the presence of the emperor, he sang through the window the very beautiful verses composed by himself, which on this solemn occasion are intoned throughout France:
>
> > Gloria, laus et honor tibi sit rex Christe redemptor,
> >   Cui puerile decus prompsit osanna pium,
>
> and hearing them the emperor was softened and ordered that he be released from his chains and he restored him to his previous favor.

The story found its way into Guillaume Durand's *Rationale divinorum officiorum* (ca. 1286) and was reprinted by Ledru (1926:60–61):

> Note that Theodulf, Bishop of Orléans under Emperor Louis, the son of Charlemagne, was falsely accused by some of his rivals and was ordered by Louis to be imprisoned in Angers. When, on Palm Sunday, the procession passed by his residence, he, with an open window and in a moment of silence, sang these most beautiful verses, which he himself had written, in the presence of the emperor: "Gloria, laus, etc." The verses so pleased the emperor that he then freed him of his chains and restored him to his bishopric, arranging that the verses should be sung at the end of the procession.

This story has, more often than not, been considered legendary, but it has not failed to delight even the authorities. Baunard (1860:317–21) did not reject it outright, and Cuissard (1892:146–48) also found it hard to resist.

Glory, praise, and honor to you, Christ, King, and Redeemer,
        To whom an array of boys sings devout praise.
You are King of Israel, the exalted descendant of David,
        You, blessed King, who come in the name of the Lord. [1]
The heavenly host all praise you in the highest,
        And at the same time mortal man and all created things.
The Hebrew people approached you with palm branches,
        Lo, with prayer, vows, and hymns we are present for you.
To you, about to suffer, they rendered services of adoration,
10   We render song to you who rule over us.
They pleased you, may our devotion please you in addition,
        Good King, merciful King, to whom all good things are a joy.
The glory of lofty descent made them Hebrews
        Lo, the godly transition makes us Hebrews too.
With earthly things overcome, there is a transition to exalted heaven,
        Sweet virtue snatches us away from foul sins.
Let us be boys in evil and old men in virtue; [2]
        The road followed by our fathers, let us retain.
So that we depart not from our fathers nor from the ways of the pious,
20   May your holy grace carry us in their tracks.
May you be our godly rider and may we be your little donkey
        So that the holy city of God may include us with you.
May we be covered with the bright effulgence of apostolic raiment,
        And may you be conveyed by our worthily-clad crowd.
May we strew our clothes, spirits, and bodies
        So that by our service your way will be always secure.
May we be victorious with branches of palm trees
        So that we may sing for you with victory in turn.
May our hearts be pure for the branches of willow,
30   May the greening of our works bring us to pleasant fields.
With branches of olive may piety, light, and the teaching of the Holy Spirit
        In ourselves be rightly pleasing to you.
Let us yield certain teachings to the tree of religion,
        With which the way of your coming to us may be kept safe.
May our devotion celebrate the occasion before us
        So that annual feasts can follow in due course.

---

[1] Matthew 21:9
[2] 1 Corinthians 14.20

Personal and Miscellaneous Poems 163

As we go to this city with praise and branches,
    Let us likewise approach with devout merit the heavenly heights.
Look upon this people assembled in your loving devotion,
40   And gladly accept their prayers and vows.
Lo, the crowds of priests and the body of people,
    Both men and women, sing your praise.
Those whom the confines of the venerable city of Angers encompass,
    They sing with a devout spirit pious songs.
The city that the slow-flowing Mayenne nurtures, the golden Loire washes,
    Which the lovely Sarthe beautifies on its left bank,
Abounding with produce, wealth, markets, and beautiful objects,
    The whole is well sprinkled with holy sites.
The people come from the holy seat of Albinus,
50   Performing worthy songs with prayers and fronds.
The people stream together from the vault of John the Baptist,
    Joining sonorous words with their palms.
Nor, good Martin, does your group gather more slowly,
    They carry branches in their hands, song in mind and mouth.
The crowd of blessed Saturninus comes joined in this company,
    Whom cross and branches and exultant praises adorn.
And, Peter, your cell, called after the name of your patron,
    Wishes to send to this work of praise as many as it can.
The martyr Sergius, worthy of veneration, sends his own charges
60   To the blessed service of this devout time.
To these your crowd is joined, devoted Maurilius,
    And sings pious wishes with prayers, music, and praise.
Not more slowly assembles the crowd of blessed Anianus
    In order to sing these praises to you, Christ the King.
The people run up from the building of Mary, who performs wonders,
    Whom, O Mayenne, your bridge conveys.
People come from the blessed Germanus,
    The people of its exalted bishop and priest.
We ascend the holy hill to the halls of Michael,
70   Where your sweet love joins us, O Christ.
So that the crowd may be joined to its kindly bishop,
    Let praise sound to God from throat and limbs.
From there let us come to the pious halls of Saint Mauricius
    So that this voice of prayer and praise may sound all at once.
There let one mother collect us in order,
    She who holds the head and the ideal of this town,
Where the prayer and benediction of the bishop may adorn us.
    May he send one and all with praise each to his home.

70.   [untitled poem to Emperor Louis]

Ebert (1880:2:84) and Liersch (1880:56) surmised that this poem in Sapphics marked a visit to Orléans in 818 when Theodulf was already in exile. Dümmler (1881:560n1) agreed, noting that Theodulf was perhaps trying to moderate Louis' sentence. Alexandrenko (1971:293) thought it unlikely that Theodulf was the author of the poem, but Schaller (1962:28) thought that he probably was. Other writers (e.g., Cuissard 1892:91) had associated the poem with an earlier visit to Orléans by Louis, a visit noted by Ermoldus Nigellus (*PLAC* 2:28, vv. 139–140).

1. O father of the clergy and ornament of the people,
    Emperor outstanding with great piety,
    That you may eagerly approach our gates,
        We all request.

2. O venerator of God, and sustainer of the poor,
    O guardian of children and widows,
    Great merciful king, we ask that you incline,
        To our prayers.

3. Therefore, finally moved by our prayers,
    Come to our expectant houses
    And enjoy cheerful days within them,
        Blessed king.

4. You a chorus of priests and clergy
    And a great crowd of all the people,
    Old and young alike,
        Desire to see.

5. Hail, wise king, owed veneration, hail!
    Accept, O king, our greeting, we beg,
    We ask Christ to grant you health
        On bended knee.

6. May Christ with prayers of blessed Albinus
    Preserve you, your children, and life's companion,
    Confided to you by happy good fortune,
        Christ all-present.

Personal and Miscellaneous Poems

7.   After the days of this life may you enter God's
     Realm in bliss, may you have rest
     Among the elect, Christ granting,
          In time without end.

The Exile Poems

71. Ad Aiulfum episcopum
(To Bishop Aiulf)

The exile poems proper begin with an epistle addressed to Bishop Aiulf in Bourges (see Godman 1987:100–1). It emerges from the poem that Aiulf had been a particularly promising student of Theodulf's and had duly risen on the ecclesiastical ladder. Theodulf congratulates him and flatters him a bit cloyingly, passing along the alleged praise of another protégé, Sintegaudus, as well. Sintegaudus had also risen to the episcopal dignity under Theodulf's auspices before being removed from his office under unknown circumstances. It is sad to see Theodulf calling in past favors and cajoling a junior in the hope that he might intercede with the emperor. The circumstances of Theodulf's exile are reviewed in the "General Introduction." See also Greeley 2006 and Meens 2007.

> To you, Aiulf, most holy bishop, I, Theodulf,
>   An exile, send you this poem from afar.
> Formerly you were a boy with a noble and lovely nature,
>   Now you are a man adorned with noble qualities intact.
> What was an apt skill in a small youngster
>   Now remains, God granting, in a grown man.
> You had always as a boy the promise of great virtue,
>   Indicating that you would turn out a great man.
> Thus the seeds promise the rewards of an abundant harvest,
> 10   Thus the shape of the bull is revealed in a tender calf.
> Your study was able to teach you noble learning,
>   And your heart, cultivated by these, is sufficiently full.
> Now your task is to transmit holy teaching
>   And to inculcate in the people heavenly laws.
> You who once sipped cups from the grammatical fountain
>   Now excellently moisten minds with ambrosial dew.
> Rumor widely reports that your life is holy,
>   Your great reputation is widely proclaimed by word of mouth.
> Who can aptly convey all your laudations,
> 20   Which Sintegaudus is wont to report?

Sintegaudus in whom probity, truth, and faithful nature,
　　And all good qualities remain tightly joined.
Him God and an honest life and the election of brothers,
　　With my mediation, put in charge of the holy flock.
But gnawing envy and deceit and snares laid with malice
　　Removed him from his own episcopal seat.
God in heaven will restore him to his own sheepfold
　　So that he may care for his own flock as he did before.
It was he who brought your kind words to my attention
30　　And transmitted your presence to me by his own mouth.
When he tells me good things about you, it warms me in my suffering,
　　And my mind cheers up hearing of your deeds.
In return he is eager to learn certain things about us
　　And has a reply that he may bring to you.
He conveyed to me the zeal, the honor, the manner
　　With which you discharge the worthy weight of your task;
How you do not cease with word and example
　　To lead the people to the godly realms above.
Though you do many great things, I pray you do even greater,
40　　We ask that Christ may give you the desired help.
The examples of earlier fathers you should follow
　　So that you may be instructed by their examples and words,
And that your teaching will grow in the future,
　　So that from you at the head it may flow to all the pious limbs.
You were raised to the patriarchal honor of leader,
　　And the sweet crowd of fathers is subject to you.
Thus wise skill should be allotted to your position,
　　So that you may be the model, honor, standard, and example to all.
No matter how high you are, remember to be correspondingly humble,
50　　So that by the sweet grace of exalted God you may be enriched.
Be a lamb to the good, a fierce lion to the wicked,
　　May one part love God and the other inspire fear in the proud,
So you may be pious to the pious and severe to the haughty.
　　May one part reflect the mother, the other the sire.
May your hand be liberal, your heart peaceful, your words kindly;
　　May you be honest and skilled, prompt to do all good.
But what should I do, or where should my shepherd's pipe lead me?
　　I have now become like a teacher in school.
I beg you in the meantime to be mindful of my ruin;
60　　Perhaps with beseeching and prayer you can lighten my plight.
Perhaps with your prayers and the aid of the company of brothers
　　The Almighty may give me, in pity, a reprieve

The Exile Poems

And mercifully relieve me of this exile,
    He who released Joseph and Peter from chains.[1]
I admit to God that I myself am guilty of many transgressions,
    Which exceed you in number, sands of the sea,
Exceed the drops of rain, the waves of the sea, the stars of the heavens,
    The sprouts of the grasses, all seeds of the soil.
They explain why I have been sent to these tribulations;
70   I suffer as my acts have not been as they should.
But against the king or his children, or, believe me, his lady
    I have not sinned, that I should deserve to suffer such woe.
Believe my words, most holy brother, believe me:
    That I am not guilty of the crime charged to me.
That he should lose scepter, life, and his own nephew,
    To these three things I never agreed.
I add a fourth: it was not with my wishes
    That such terrible things should come to pass.
This I averred, aver, and will aver forever,
80   As long as blood enlivens my limbs.
He who does not believe now, will be constrained to believe later
    When it comes before the throne of the Great Judge,
Who will be my kind witness and most just avenger,
    To whom all things are naked and clear.[2]
He does not regard persons or remunerations,[3]
    Who is just and loves justice, loves all that is good.
Before his countenance all false matters will perish,
    Here my testimony will not be alone.
Your compassion, dear brother, nurtures me sweetly,
90   A great part of my sadness stays with you.
May the Father enthroned governing earth and heaven
    Grant that you may later share my joy.
I know you to be adorned with the flower of all goodness,
    And to glow brightly with virtue's light.
May you have life, health, and the grace of Christ the Ruler,
    And may the Almighty protect you wherever you are.
Live happy in God for long years, O prelate,
    And from good rise justly to better: farewell.

---

[1] Genesis 41:14; Acts 12:7
[2] Hebrews 4:13
[3] Deuteronomy 10:17

72. Incipit epistola Theodulfi episcopi ad Modoinum episcopum scribens ei de exilio: Theodulfus Modoino suo salutem (Here Begins the Epistle of Bishop Theodulf to Bishop Modoin, Writing Him about Exile: Theodulf Greets His Modoin)

The text of the poem to Modoin was reedited by Schaller (1962:43–51). Schaller made thirty-one, mostly small, changes in Dümmler's text, but only three affect the translation (vv. 19, 75, 122). In these cases we follow Schaller. It has most frequently been assumed that Theodulf was exiled to and died in Angers. We might therefore suppose that it was from Angers that Theodulf addressed his letter to Modoin, but in a later paper (1992:91–101) Schaller argued that the topographic indications in the poem suggest Le Mans rather than Angers as the point of origin. The poet identified his perspective in verses 121–122:

> They asserted that you, River Huisne, underwent the same fortune
> And that flowing close by this city the Sarthe drinks you up.

Schaller (anticipated by Ledru 1926:63–67) argues that "this city" can only be Le Mans, where indeed Huisne and Sarthe meet. He then reinforces the point by locating echoes of Theodulf's verse in the so-called "Carmina Cenomanensia" composed in Le Mans in the ninth century. He theorizes that by that time Theodulf had attained the status of a local celebrity and was therefore readily available for quotation.

After the wheedling tone of the poem to Aiulf Theodulf seems to have regained his footing; the verses addressed to Modoin are both humorous and intriguing (see Fried 1990:253). This may be explained perhaps to some extent by the fact that Modoin was an old acquaintance from their court years, an equal, and a fellow poet. Theodulf begins with the most elaborate, and therefore perhaps most ironical, version of his favorite conceit, the personified epistle (in the person of the Muses Thalia and Erato) making its way reverently to its recipient. The appeal itself is more indignant than cajoling and culminates in the claim that the only competent judge of the case is the pope, according to Cuissard (1892:95–96) the first such appeal recorded.

The plea is then immediately mitigated by the addition of three tall tales for the reader's entertainment, one on the sudden drying up of a stretch of the River Sarthe (dated in Dümmler's notes to 8 February 820) and two mock-heroic bird battles. Schaller (1970:104–5 [repr., 71–73]) argued that these seemingly detached poems are not humorous (cf. Ross 1954:276). The first appended poem ends with the poet's profession that he does not know what the event signifies, but Schaller interprets the desiccation and the battles as dire prodigies of future misfortunes not yet revealed. On the other hand, we could assume that the undeniable humor is not gratuitous but psychologically calculated to lighten the appeal and perhaps the burden imposed on Modoin. That would allow us

The Exile Poems 171

to reconcile the main message with the fanciful anecdotes. See also Godman 1987:101–2; Dutton 1994:83–86. A daring combination of contrasting tonalities is not the least of Theodulf's poetic feats, as is demonstrated in "Ad episcopos," "Ad Carolum regem," and "Contra iudices." For a thorough recent analysis see Greeley 2006:51–66.

i. De suo exilio
(On His Exile)

Lo, between priests, great Modoin, Theodulf
    Humbly sends you from his exile these lines.
Go swiftly, quick Muse, run with rapid footsteps;
    With no delay, let there be no pause on your way
Until you arrive at the house of blessed Modoin,
    The excellent bishop and devout man of God.
Arriving before him, you will prostrate yourself on your
    Knees, and if he should bid you arise, jump to.
You will forthwith bestow kisses on his amiable fingers
10   And, fatigued, you will be silent, focusing on the broad earth.
Should he ask who you are and from where you departed,
    Speak and give shape to the details with your mind:
"I am Theodulf's lyric   , come from the recess of his prison,
    Where great love of you kindles his heart.
There he is exiled, deprived, poor, sad, anxious, and suffering,
    Scorned and rejected and grieved."[4]
Perhaps he will ask what I do: Tell him that I suffer
    A life that is hardly better than a good death.
"He barely reads or teaches or performs offices of celebration
20   For the Lord and Father of all who rules heaven and earth.
He prays to him on his own behalf and yours, and for the clergy,
    For the salvation of leaders, of people and king.
He has sent me to you, and I give you his greetings,
    Subjoined are his words to be delivered to you."
I pray you, dear brother, be mindful of my condition,
    My brother, great part of my soul.
Your mind will always pity my trouble,
    The cause of my state is well known to you.
The better the matter is known, the more you should devote yourself to it.
30   Thus when a physician sees illness, by his science he puts it to flight.

---

[4] cf. Isaiah 53:3

You know that, like smoke, the joys of this world vanish,
But sweet brotherly love never dies.
You love me more now, although you already loved me greatly:
A mother loves a sick child more than the rest.
Strive, I pray, to assist my reduced circumstances,
And you should arouse the devout minds of our friends.
Although I myself am just one, the matter is not limited to one only.
What has happened to me can be other mens' fate.
Evil is common to all, and a common cure should be attempted;
40 What affects me today, tomorrow will strike someone else.
A prudent brother should fear infection,
Lest the same plague steal on him as on me.
A wound festers from a wound, fever escalates with fever;
Thus many waterways flow from a single source.
If my wound should yield to pleasant healing,
With the disease gone, my old strength will be restored;
The enemy camp will no longer be able
To assail me, and a heavy crime will not persist.
False servant and lying servant girl are subject to legal provisions,
50 The shepherd, baker, sailor, swineherd, and plowman too.
Alas, only the episcopal order has no legal recourse
And now totters without its own law.
The group intended to promote proper laws for others
Foregoes rights without its own cognizant law.
Confessed guilt causes the savage thief to perish;
The bishop has not confessed, but, lo, he succumbs.
Although worldly business may lack the resources
With which a case can be justly resolved,
My case lacked any just weight of reason,
60 And, savagery aside, it has no measure at all.
No witness is involved, no suitable judge is present,
I had confessed to no crime.
So be it: If I had confessed, whose court would have been able
To provide restraints proper to my case?
That office belongs only to the Roman Bishop,
From whose hand I accepted my holy charge.

It pleased me to send, dear one, some poems,
Which my jocund Muse lightly contrived.
At this time a few additional wonders that were witnessed
70 Will be told, which I will briefly recite.

The Exile Poems

ii. De siccitate cuiusdam fluvii
(On the Drying Up of a Certain River)

There is a river, given the name of Sarthe by earlier Frenchmen;
  Originating in Le Perche, it feeds the Mayenne.
It flows into the fields of Le Mans
  And branches off because of the walls of the town.
Because the inhabitants are wont to guide their boats on the water,
  A not inconsiderable wonder happened to them there.
When the dawn finally dispersed the dewy shadows
  And men took to the waters as they were wont,
There was found a place without its own water
80   That had been accessible to boat and oars before.
The people were dumbstruck at the vanished current;
  The open channel beckoned them to approach.
Nobody asks for a boat, no one calls for you, sailor;
  The way stands open for people amazed.
At first fear and novelty inspire hesitation
  In entering, but fear gradually began to recede;
The novelty began to grow old, and the people begin to enter
  On both banks, and the cattle as well.
Their feet are dry or damp only slightly
90   As the people repeatedly go back and forth on foot.
If in days of yore the youth Leander had had such a passage,
  You would not have had such cause, O Hero, for tears.
No one seeks out hook or line for fishing;
  He who wishes, does it by hand in the woods.
A man was to be buried in a field on the opposite shoreline;
  He is brought among mourners over dry land.
The citizens were rather afraid lest the swelling waves set upon them
  And overwhelm all at once crossroads, fields, and homes.
Unrevealed stones lie open to the sky, which too is open
100   To the rocks, when the water retreated from its earth.
Where, O Sarthe, you offered no path for the walkers,
  You suddenly opened a ford when your rocks were surprised by boots.
At two other times the Sarthe suffered a similar occurrence,
  Not at this time, but not far distant in time and space.
Who will deny that the Lord remembered the ancient victory,
  At which time he divided the river and tumbled Jericho?[5]
This state lasted from the first to the fourth hour in duration;
  Then the swift waves returned to their watery paths.

---

[5] Joshua 3:13–16

I have not recorded the names of the informants
110 Because there are many who told me the tale.
But, reader, if you wish to know the time of occurrence,
  Hear it as I will briefly relate.
Now the fleeting seventh year expires in passing
  Since, O Louis, the paternal realms have been yours;
The fourth year of my undeserved exile, in addition,
  Has passed, unhappy as I am and sick at heart.
Perhaps you wish to know the day, that too is part of my story,
  So that the matter cannot be in doubt.
The whole of the sun of Aquarius had reached twice eleven
120 And the moon was in the sixth part of the Fish.
They asserted that you, River Huisne, underwent the same fortune,
  And that flowing close by this city the Sarthe drinks you up.
Ask the location from others, I will tell you the time scheme;
  It happened the day after the aforementioned event.
They say that Angers suffered the same deprivation,
  But place and day are not known to me.
I do not inquire into these matters with great zeal for the reason
  That those who tell wish to know the future from me.
My poem does not reveal it, but my voice will not always
130 Conceal, for these things remain to be told in due course.
We are able to know some things well by signs and examples
  Although I do not divine or know how this will turn out.

iii. De pugna avium
  (On the Battle of the Birds)

Although many miraculous things are seen as time passes,
  This too, as I am about to relate, has been seen.
What Gairardus told me, and Pascasius had told him,
  One told the story to me, the other told what he had seen.
At a place called Toulouse at the furthest reaches of Cahors—
  In both regions the district is edged—
There is located a field with the outer limits surrounded
140 By woods; men live not too far from there.
Many birds fill the field with great hubbub,
  And on its surface sits many a bird:
Those found in the river, those in the grove and muddy stretches,
  Those that are wont to build nests on the cliffs.
They have different food, different songs, different colors and maneuvers,
  Different feathers, claws, beaks, customs, places, and lives,

The Exile Poems

The path of the west wind brought some, the path of the north wind others;
    You may believe that one part or another has its marks.
The flocks sat apart on these meadows,
150   And some space separated them both.
You might imagine that messengers were flying from one to the other,
    Who are ready to carry terms of war and peace.
In the meantime a few flew from one side or the other,
    Some fulfilling their missions, others theirs.
It is clear that one legation had no peace to offer;
    After that they provoke major war.
Just as for a long time messengers run between Carthaginians
    And the Roman people until they fall on each other with arms,
In quite the same way, after flying back and forth on one side and the other,
160   With whatever vigor they can muster, they attack with might and main.
The companies of birds are burning for battle in both directions;
    One wing clashes with another, one cohort with its counterpart.
Their military resources diverge, but they are equally eager;
    Whatever the big warrior wishes, the small warrior wishes the same.
They have no aid from chariots, nor use of horses,
    No steel is in use, no throwing spears fly.
Their tufts serve as helmets, beaks and claws serve as spearpoints,
    In place of trumpets they all sing their songs.
A light wing bears a shield, the bird's feathers a dagger,
170   Tiny feathers make do as a coat of mail.
Already the sixth day of the encounter had ended,
    They attack on both sides in warlike ire;
They tear at each other, on one side with bites, on the other with wings beating,
    A war with overpowering spirit rages on both sides.
On one side you can see the Rutulians rise up, on the other the Teucri,
    You can see fierce Mars flare up on both sides.
As the acorn falls from the oak tree in autumn
    And the withering leaf at the first sign of frost,
Not otherwise did the expiring army of avian creatures
180   Fall and cover the earth with great gore.
For as the smooth threshing floor is filled with summer produce,
    So the field was full of dead birds.
A small number coming from the north returns northward,
    But a whole battalion lies dead on both sides.
Word gets around, people assemble, they are dumbstruck at what they witness;
    They are astonished at the remains of various birds.
Even the bishop comes from the city of Toulouse,
    Mantio by name; the people ask if the birds can serve as food.

"Leave those not allowed and take those that are licit,"
190   He said; they load the carts with birds and each returns home.

iv.   [no title]

A rumor flying about from mouth to mouth reported
    That this occurred at the time.
Those who wander to and fro from Rome say as follows:
    Among them a good woman attests.
She left from Tours to Rome to pray, then retraced her footsteps;
    She told the priest Arbaldus what happened, and he told me.
Near the slow-moving Saône and the swift-flowing Rhône River,
    As noted above, the great battle of birds took place,
Where among sharp crags and dense marshes
200   Few cultivated fields lie open on level ground.
There, they say, come all manner of bird species,
    Which, O Europe, your excellent acreage breeds.
Some live on cliffs, some on open spaces,
    And many sit on the branches of trees.
The youth is divided into two groups of soldiery,
    Both groups are eager for war.
Four hawks come from one side, four from another,
    Four falcons, as many from either side.
In the first encounter they destroy each other in mutual aggression,
210   A falcon kills a falcon, a hawk kills a hawk.
Beaks clash with beaks, claws clash together,
    The more the arms are equal, the more they slay.
The Roman people carried this out in the Emathian expanses
    When they waged fierce war, son-in-law against father-in-law,
When friend kills friend and brother kills brother,
    When equal weapons arm equal foes.
Two great birds are reported to have escaped to a distance
    And did not fight; the remaining multitude lies dead.
Both sides conquer, but victory gladdens neither,
220   On both sides it left the earth piled high with the dead.
As the fury of Hannibal filled Cannae with victims,
    Thus the fields are covered with the death of birds.
Who will relate what, where, why, when or from what region?
    These demonstrable signs often serve to reveal.

When will come the day when you will enter our garden
    And pluck our roses with eager hands?

The Exile Poems

Your great thirst grows greater and greater
  When you will overflow with verse, which you always love.
If there are faults in these verses, as surely there will be,
230   I pray you to forgive; I have no skilled writer at hand.
I ask that you send a faithful servant to meet me
  To bring me welcome news of yourself: farewell.

73. Incipit rescriptum Modoini episcopi ad Theodulfum episcopum. Modoinus indignus episcopus Theodulfo suo. (Here Begins the Reply of Bishop Modoin to Bishop Theodulf. Modoin, the Unworthy Bishop, to His Theodulf.)

Dümmler included Modoin's reply to Theodulf, presumably to complete the story. Alexandrenko did not include it among his translations because it is after all not by Theodulf, but it sheds interesting light on the case. Early receptions were critical. Baunard (1860:311–15) characterized it as a combination of genuine emotion and declamations in poor taste. He writes that what Theodulf needed was not sterile consolation but real help, and he imagines Theodulf's outrage at being urged to make an admission of guilt. Cuissard (1892:97) is no less critical, repeating the charge of poor taste and condemning the "timides conseils qu'une amitié mondaine dictait à Modoin." Godman (1987:102–4) stresses the writer's use of Ovid to nuance the contemporary political themes.

Schaller (1962:26n38) objected to Cuissard's characterization, but it is difficult not to share the early criticisms, which are only exacerbated by the inferior verse, mechanical down to the imitation of some of Theodulf's own wording. Modoin begins with a declaration of his own poor ability compared with Theodulf's talent, a humility only too justified. He then dispassionately catalogues other cases of undeserved exile, Ovid, Boethius, Virgil, Seneca, John the Baptist, Hilary of Poitiers, Peter, and Paul. One might even suspect that this roll call of precedents, alleged to be a comfort, is borrowed from Theodulf's own poem 21 "Consolation of a Certain Brother" above. Modoin then lapses into a rather inapposite few lines on the history of church organization before declaring what appears to be full support and the prospect of restoration. But this reveals itself to be an illusion when Modoin turns to the prerequisite of an admission of guilt (vv. 90–104). This sudden break in tone causes Modoin's poem to appear more in the light of a careful ménagement of court opinion than a letter of condolence. We can even imagine Modoin's consulting with emperor or court with a view to determining what it might be permissible to say to Theodulf. The disingenuousness is only confirmed when Modoin expresses surprise (vv. 115–116) that Theodulf has asked for no service — as if he had not written specifically (vv. 35–36):

Strive, I pray, to assist my reduced circumstances,
  And you should arouse the devout minds of our friends.

Modoin states that he "will eagerly do whatever you command" (v. 118), but that clearly stopped short of an intervention on Theodulf's behalf. For recent comments see Greeley 2006:71–72.

No one can toy with polished verse without training
>Nor speak correctly without art.
Nor will a hawk attempt to bear arms if not
>Instructed by a parent in this skill.
A boy does not usefully wage war in early childhood,
>But once trained, he earns prizes as a young warrior at arms.
For a sailor does not go on board without tackle,
>Attempting, like a Tiphys unarmed, to cross navigable seas.
Since I am unlearned in art, I declare myself unable
10 >To reply to your excellent verse.
For my Muse is lowly among learned poets;
>For this reason I will not strive to create a great work of art.
But, hesitant as I am, your letter requires me
>To write a poem in uneven feet [distichs];
Now I am forced to inscribe soft wax with iron
>And weave words in an unaccustomed way.
Indeed, the work that your messenger brought me
>Should rather be called an oversized little book.
You have heard the ancients play with friendly locutions,
20 >And this is what I have often learned from you.
Since the unskilled poet does not know the haunts of the Muses,
>That can rightly be said also of me.
Some people affirm that poets are also quite given to madness,
>That when they write poems they are out of their minds,
But my mind remains quite intact and dares not
>Venture any farther, with its order disturbed.
Nor does it aspire high, for it wishes to avoid scandal;
>It is content to be governed at a moderate pitch.
Do, O Theodulf, receive kindly my verses,
30 >And may you not look down on my words.
I should not wish you, with poisoned tooth, ever to shred my verses;
>In your estimation may they be safe.
If there are errors in my poems, as there will be,
>I humbly request that you view them with tolerant eyes.
I often lament with tears the fall of an innocent companion,
>The tears flow from my eyes like a stream.
Often have I mourned, weeping and groaning, your ruin;
>Alas, deprived of your honor, you are banished and succumb.

The Exile Poems

An outstanding priest, you innocently suffer sad exile,
40   A bishop, suffering extraordinary woe.
Great wisdom is apt to avail for many,
     But you, good father, have been injured by your very skill.
Not least, your great wisdom brought evil profits
     And brought about the heavy burden you have incurred.
Gnawing envy rises raging, attempting to topple
     That which a crowd with honest heart delights to revere.
Should you fail to remember, Ovid endured long suffering,
     Being in innocence made an exile by spite.
Boethius himself was cast down by a great city,
50   A famous consul sent far from Rome.
Vexed by a hostile soldier, the great poet
     Virgil was despoiled of his own estate.
Seneca is said to have suffered dire wounds at the hands of a tyrant,
     An outstanding man, who succumbed to Nero's homicide.
Why mention that many of our believers suffered
     Outrageous exile for our goodly faith?
The pious man, revered more by the great Master,
     John [the Baptist], endured hard exile alone.
You too, Hilary, experienced a cruel prison,
60   Sent off to an unknown place at the king's behest.
The key-bearer Peter himself, and Paul also,
     Teacher of the people, was held in the confinement of jail.
This resulted from the wild and contrary fierceness
     Of the pagans, hostile as they were to godly faith.
Add to that that the as yet uncouth church organization
     Was unshaped, inactive, and lacking in laws.
With persecution at an end it was destined to prosper
     In serene peace, and govern itself with law.
It is the fault of the clergy that the great order
70   Of holy service is poorly maintained.
Among them there is not one found faithful,
     Whom gratitude approves for holy sites.
No one takes pity on the discomforts of another
     Striving for his own advantage over that of his friend.
Everyone sets his mind on earthly advancement
     And, given to luxury, seeks empty wealth.
In this number, you may believe I do not wish to be counted,
     Among those who say counterfeit words with a frivolous heart.
But I will never cease to strive with prayer
80   For your return, and will eagerly work to that end.

Thus I always enlist your old companions
    And will be solicitous in the light of your loss,
(I think that you know this, for rumor spreads quickly
    Throughout all the world, bearing the talk of the court),
That you may finally be removed from that inimical region
    To return to the shining threshold of the emperor's house,
That, coming before his eyes, you will see his genial countenance
    Forthwith, he who was grieved on your account
And prefers to forgive you any misdeed committed,
90   If, however, you will recall that you sinned.
For a clean confession can be to your profit,
    If only you will admit aloud to the guilt of a crime.
But if you pretend not to know of what crime I am speaking,
    At least know on what grounds you would be brought here.
Choose what to do when it seems to you proper;
    I pray that you keep better counsel in mind.
It has seemed better to me that it be voluntarily stated,
    That which cannot be denied with any good sense.
By no other means, I think, can you overcome the wrath of the monarch,
100   Unless you admit that you are guilty of a crime.
The emperor promises, if you will admit that you have been sinful,
    That he himself will be willing to hear your case.
For he promises you that you will return to your former power
    So that you may reacquire your lost rank once again.
I know not, dear brother, what more I can write you,
    Since all these matters are no less known to yourself.
You are dearer to me than the great brightness of sunshine;
    I can say that the whole world holds nothing that is dearer to me.
A letter worded at length appeals to Mahtfrid,
110   May your words often be read by him.
He is able to apply the desired cure to the fallen
    And bring kind help to the ship that is wrecked.
With the poem at an end the tearful Muse falls silent,
    She has no more that she can say.
But I was surprised that your letter hesitated
    To ask me for a service to you.
For, believe me, I will never deny you any favor
    But will eagerly do whatever you command.
Therefore I dispatched this my messenger to your dwelling
120   So that he will report to me whatever you bid.
He, as I believe, is without doubt sufficiently faithful,
    From whose mouth you see my words flow.

The Exile Poems

He will recount to you whatever you ask, without deception,
    And without deceit in turn will convey everything about me.
As many liquid drops as a shower, as many fish as in the river,
    As many fronds as the verdant grove shoots up,
As much grain as the threshing floor exhibits in summer:
    So many greetings I send you, father; as always and everywhere farewell.
May you always be the worthy servant of the most high Father.
    Forever, I ask you, dear brother, to keep me in mind.
For now I beg you at the end of this poem
    That I may be carried safely in your prayers.

Here ends the reply of Bishop Modoin to Bishop Theodulf dwelling in exile.

POEMS OF DOUBTFUL ATTRIBUTION

Poems 74–75

"De paradiso," not found in Sirmond's edition, was added in by Dümmler from B.L. MS. Harley 3685. Schaller (1962:78) did not render a judgment, but Alexandrenko (1971:21; 311) did not believe it was correctly attributed to Theodulf. Nothing in it seems to echo Theodulfian habits, but it does have a minor place in the history of the pleasance and may reflect visual art of the period. "De resurrectione carnis," also from Harley 3685, is in one respect a twin of the preceding poem since it deals not with the lost paradise but the promise of a future (though there is a short description of the heavenly paradise). It shares some of Theodulf's capital themes, the ubiquitous concern with the importance of the permanent soul over the transitory body (20, 26.35–42, 28.556–588), the *memento mori* passage in "Contra iudices" (28.513–554), the rise to heaven (28.7–26), and eternity in the presence of Christ (also 28.7–26). Perhaps it was on the strength of these similarities that Dümmler attributed the poem to Theodulf. Schaller (1962:28) did not hazard an opinion, but Alexandrenko (1971:311) thought it was not by Theodulf. Yet in view of Theodulf's connection (through the *Libri Carolini*) with the iconclast/iconodule controversy, the subjects of paradise and the reality of bodily resurrection (compare poem 11 above) can be seen to have a connection with the debate over the nature of matter.

74.   [De paradiso (On Paradise)]

The first well-fashioned man, holding the pleasant spaces
    Of Elysium from the exalted Creator as a gift,
Led his life in meadows and among shade-giving flowers,
    Where your agreeable acreage, O paradise, thrives,
Enclosing flowering sites, banks with a pleasing murmur,
    Bordered on all sides with roses and blooms.
Fruits of trees hang from various branches,
    Never does one fail in its perpetual growth.
There all sorts of flowers come to life on the green expanses,
    The fostering earth is fertile with the fruit of apple trees;

Where the yellow pear reddens rustling in the branches,
     Where the bursting fig tree full of fragrant flowers turns green.
The earth becomes colored with apples red on the surface,
     And the laurel is scented, the dark myrtle as well;
Heavy and sticky to the touch, they swell with differing berries.
     There the olive tree filling baskets stands.
The tree of life, so-called, spreads hugely,[1]
     Rising aloft from the center of the Elysian park.
The beauteous field gives birth to a thousand fragrant
20   Herbs unheard of, which the pleasing ground yields.

75. [De resurrectione carnis (On the Resurrection of the Flesh)]

Since present life is filled with various perils,
     It is incumbent on us to live it well.
Nor should our provident minds be eager to pursue temporal matters,
     But they should ardently seize on what endures.
Let the excellent mind repel foul worldly temptations,
     The evils that entice the spirit with every kind of sin.
Nor should the mind be addicted to earthly preoccupations,
     But rather it should strive to ascend the heavenly heights,
Where, living forever, it will happily rule through the ages
10   And long enjoy manifold feasts.
More care should always be given to the soul than the body,
     The soul destined to live in a shining place above the stars.
For although the body can be adorned with gems and golden metal,
     Cut off by death, it will then turn to dust.
Let this frail flesh be mixed with earth and water,
     Then it turns rapid steps to the world below.
It flows with foul putrefaction and spreading corruption,
     And from it a rotten smell arises at the same time.
Let our mind be busy accumulating beautiful treasures
20   In heaven that will belong to it throughout all time,
Where gnawing worms with a harmful bite do not destroy valued possessions
     Nor voracious rust defile riches there,[2]
Where an undermined house or a faithless antagonist
     Or a wild, wanton thief lays waste the base.
These things, after cold death, will the blessed inherit,
     These things will the soul long have when the flesh is dissolved.

---

[1] Genesis 2:9
[2] Matthew 6:20

Poems of Doubtful Attribution

With the prison overcome the soul will be joined with snow-white-clad beings[3]
    And the beautiful treasure of Elysium will always be theirs.
When the divine power of the Creator moves heaven
30   And all that the earth itself conceals,
The body once utterly consumed by dust and worms will surface,[4]
    The body will rise and the flesh never die.
This will be the last road of the wanderer through earth's dissolution;
    The shape of the earth rejected by fire will fall.[5]
The sun will withdraw its rays, the sky will tumble,
    The moon likewise will forego its light.
The twinkling stars shining with great brilliance
    Will then be without imperishable light,
40 And in their multitudes will fall from the highest point of heaven
    And will perish with the thrust of a whirlwind from heaven's vault.
I do not think that nature will change its direction,
    But the shape of the earth will improve.
The holy Scripture of the four evangelists announces
    That the shape of the world destined to perish shall remain.
Christ teaches this in a few words, speaking wonders:
    "Sky and earth will perish, but my words remain."[6]
Likewise, that the resurrection of the flesh will remain then
    He contends with his own great love.
He attests that not a single hair will be missing,
50   But rather the numbers will survive in full.[7]
That this flesh destined to die, when revived, will then duly
    Be infused with life, Paul also proclaims.[8]
The last day deferred for many ages
    Will come for all, yet all fear will be shed.
For a trumpet will give a last blast from heaven,
    At which signal the earth will shake from its very base.
First will come quickly, but not ahead of those dead and buried,
    Those who are animated by vital spirit and heat.
Thus, bright with virtue, eloquent in the art of speaking,
60   Powerful in words, Paul celebrates many mysterious things.
Thus there is care with great zeal for the no longer living;
    You may believe that the spirit relinquished will not die.

---

[3] Revelation 7:13–15
[4] Job 19:26
[5] Matthew 24:29
[6] Matthew 24:35; Mark 13:31
[7] Matthew 10:30
[8] 1 Corinthians 15:52–53

When man resurrected and brightly appareled
        Stands shining in the splendid attire of his flesh,
Then, O paradise, the just will forever be recipients
        Of your riches, with the host of the Lord round about,
Where the rose-bearing field blooms with an assortment
        Of flowers, and the sweet fragrance of wafted scents.
There is one home for all, where the top is not weighed down by roof beams
70   But groans only under the weight of the radiant sphere,
Widely borne up by rotundas and divided into various recesses,
        A single structure houses many in its embrace.[9]
For their merits a brilliant residence is conferred on the blessed
        Dwellers in heaven where double honor obtains,
Where in holy office He himself shines brightly,
        And, in resplendent glory, is a friend to those above.[10]
He shines with such great brilliance of amity in these regions,
        Sweet virtue and love of piety at once.
That there remains to each what he possesses singly,
80   And whatever each individual has is common to all.
Where the earth is dried by the overheated radiation
        Of the sun, it will not retain these rays;
Nor with the darkness of the globe of the cold moon exhausted
        Will the star-bearing tracts cast rays,
Where the brightness of the true sun illumines
        Its crests and fills it with endless light.
It will never lack light; light there is, great and unsullied,
        In which Christ is ever and everywhere good.
Christ is present to all, a support and eternal garment,
90   A sweetly glowing libation, light, and food all at once,
Christ, beautiful life, adorned with snowy triumphs,
        Ever shining bright, that for the good will not go out.[11]
Christ, flowering peace, virtue and beauty of the spirit,
        Immortal goodness and perpetual at the same time,
Christ, a sun shining brightly for all righteous men forever,
        Inexhaustible fountain and monument of good,
Christ shining in the crown and brightness of a martyr,
        A palm tree flowering with his holy warrior throng,
Christ great brightness of virginity forever,
100   Purity of spirit and beauty of frame.

---

[9] John 14:2
[10] Revelation 21:23, 22:5
[11] Wisdom 7:10

Poems of Doubtful Attribution 187

Christ is also the Father's holy reward to widows,
    An undying honor to unmarried and wed.
Christ, virtue, Christ, rule, Christ the glory,
    Christ is all beauty and all things to all men.
They say you measure golden realms without holy limit,
    You whose blessed light shines without end,
Whose realms do not catch the heat of the sun from the axis of heaven
    When the day declines toward night.
Shadowy night does not wrap darkness in its shadows,
110   Nor does the greatest heavenly body shine at its crest.
Let Christ the Light illuminate shadows, whom none can
    Attain and whose company none can approach.
Dying for all as a gift of holy compassion
    He smote the maw of the black foe in hell.
Here the Victor carried off the spoils from the savage jaws of Orcus
    And lodged them in his own home.
By the suasion and tongue of the foe's serpent
    The first parent of men with her condemned mate succumbed,
But, powerfully good, the Lover of genuine concord,
120   Christ, in dying, washed away all evil ways.
May the true sun shine here for all, the eternal moon in addition,
    Undiminished light and love of good.
Here Easter Lamb, here virtue, here brimming libation,
    And beauty forever are here for the good.

Poems 76–78

Schaller (1962:27–28) thought that 76 was of doubtful authenticity (though Dümmler's notes give parallels to Theodulf's phrases in othr poems) but that 78 was properly attributed to Theodulf. He does not comment on 77. Alexandrenko (1971:311) excluded 76 and 77 but did translate 78. Poem 76 is a straightforward and uninspired eulogy of Louis the Pious with no personal touch. It dwells chiefly on the emperor's preference for spiritual nurture over material sustenance. Poem 77 is an equally unremarkable Sapphic celebration of Louis on behalf of the city of Tours, Alcuin's city, not Theodulf's. For that reason alone Theodulf's authorship seems unlikely. Poem 78 refers to an Albinus, whom Dümmler identified as the patron saint of a monastery in Angers. It addresses Louis along with his queen Ermengarde and brother Lothar. The indices are confusing, and the fragment is so short that not much can be said about it.

76.

Hail, great emperor, serene Louis, greetings.
    May the kindly Almighty grant you all good things.
The whole earth praises you, venerates, and loves you,
    And is concerned to obey your commands.
You are of the first radiance on earth, second to none in virtue,
    Powerful in arms, no one precedes you, I know.
You are the arms of the clergy, the summit of law to be respected,
    May you constantly and vigorously inspire to a higher plane.
You are the ornament of the clergy, the people's model of goodness;
10   As a just arbiter you love the path of the just.
You do and counsel what gives access to heaven,
    You keenly avoid what plunges us below.
You love peace, you are wise by Solomon's example,
    Handsome as Joseph, equal to David in might.
You have a wide command of divine Scripture,
    The reading of which often feeds and nourishes you.
You sparingly nourish your body with material dishes,
    But your mind thirsts for divine sustenance.
For a little ingested food satisfies your body,
20   But heavenly food sustains spirit and mind.
You yourself love the food of the mind more than the food of the body;
    One you take on schedule, the other you crave without end.
You are also much to be praised for your actions;
    You spare what the flesh craves, but love what the mind desires.
You flee what is evil and eagerly embrace all goodness;
    That is why, blessed king, God is with you.
You are the beloved son of holy religion,
    Which the only Son of the Father committed to you.
You constantly imbue it with good teachings;
30   You abide in it, instruct, and build it up.
No one is more outstanding in the faith of Christ than you are,
    No one is more correct in belief than you.
No one is above you, equal in piety and achievements;
    Your accomplishments show that I speak the truth.
You use the riches of the world with limited affection,
    With them you constantly ready the blessed realms for yourself.
Golden fringes do not exalt you, my ruler,
    Nor does a shining crown rest on the vault of your mind.
To these things regal pride aspires, not your devotion,
40   In which the sweet glory of Christ ever inheres.

Poems of Doubtful Attribution   189

You shine with high morals, are bright with goodness,
  You always desire to cling to God.
No voice can clearly express your praises,
  And my Muse will now also fall mute.

77.

1. Honored victor on land and sea,
    Majestic emperor, Louis,
    Famed in the teaching of Christ, ornament of our age,
      Hope too for the realm.

2. Though your arrival should everywhere
    Be properly celebrated with continual praise,
    To whom the whole earth with devotion
      And good faith prays,

3. This city [Tours] nonetheless surpasses in prayers
    The other cities of Transalpine Gaul;
    That you may live long years
      It ever beseeches.

4. Raised by the merits of Saint Martin
    By your gift, famed in the world,
    Our city excels others in
      Aforementioned Gaul.

5. May you shine throughout the nation with famous triumphs,
    In good fortune trampling wicked people
    Under foot, those that resist bending
      Their necks before you.

6. While the inimical foe tries to damage
    The bonds of law by winning over minds,
    It ever favors your prosperity,
      Great prince.

7. You will be able to go by any chosen road
    Safely by the gift of the Lord.
    Good king, Martin will fight on your behalf,
      The strong champion.

8. We desire that an angel directed from heaven
   With favor should guide your steps
   Through lands, forests, strongholds, villages
       As you ever progress.

9. Hail, Ermengarde, majestic queen and empress,
   And together with you, your children;
   For this reason we will always hold you
       In sweet affection.

10. With godly clemency you grant
    To your humble servants readily your solace

78.

    May Albinus himself ask with his prayers
That you may live happily in the whirlwind of the present world.
    This your submissive company asks the Father:
After the time of this life, at home in the seat of heaven,
    May you receive rewards that remain without end.
May you, Ermengarde, lovable wife, joined to your husband,
    Be queen, prospering all of your days.
May you happily live with your husband long years in the future
10   So that you may see your children's heirs.
You, adornment of the realm, most faithful hope of the empire,
    Fair youth, O Lothar, greetings to you.
May the love of Christ join you and your brothers
    So that no enemy can approach.
May you maintain the rule of the world in earthly regions
    Such that the supernal realms will embrace you after death.

79.   [no title — Prudens to Prudentius]

The final poem in Dümmler's collection is included not because it is by Theodulf but because it borrows some of his conceits and refers to him in verse thirty-four. It is a strange and incoherent piece ending with an abrupt obscenity. Karl Liersch (1880:28–31) devoted the greatest attention to it and identified the recipient of the verse epistle as a certain Galindo who became the bishop of Troyes between 843 and 846 and died in 861. The writer does not identify himself but addresses Galindo as a boy; Liersch guesses at a date of composition shortly after Theodulf's death, written by an adherent of Theodulf's living in Orléans since he

Poems of Doubtful Attribution 191

mentions the church of Saint Anianus (Aignan). The writer addresses and commissions his epistle in the style of Theodulf, then recounts the vision of a man who visited the world below and of a girl who visited both the heavenly and infernal regions (compare Boniface, Letters 10 and 115 [MGH Epp. Sel. 1:8–15, 247–50]). He suggests that "our kindly Theodulf" may have been among those observed in these visions, although, interestingly enough, he does not specify in which region. (For Theodulf on dreams see Dutton 1994:41–44.) Perhaps he is positioning himself carefully between Theodulf's friends and enemies. Finally, he excuses the imperfect diction with the haste of an importunate messenger and sends greetings to three named persons—an Irish *magister*, a teacher, and perhaps a chief cook—with a request for reciprocal verses.

> He who is dearer to me among all my students,
>   Bring to his sweet self, little letter, a sweet melody.
> He who is bright with the name of his father and mine also,
>   On the one hand shines with "Prudens," on the other with Galindo's name.
> A Prudentius is rightly resplendent in his own distinction,
>   A boy certain of perpetual merit and certain in all respects.
> When his right hand touches your own with delicate fingers,
>   Convey uninterrupted the words of my mouth.
> Add: "Greetings, warm greetings, he offers two thousand greetings,
> 10   He who is my lord, and, lo, your father as well.
> I am supported only with the growth of a tiny body,
>   Even poorer in talent and poorer in the aid of art.
> He wishes that you should do well and strive more to be learned
>   And advises that you attain the heights of the mind."
> The rumor persists and circulates in our city
>   That a certain man perchance ascended to heaven's realm,
> And to the Stygian shades below covered by the darkness of nighttime,
>   That he approached the gloomy infernal gods;
> He sees the marvels of the gods and the fleeting shadows in death's semblance,
> 20   Where, fearful, he views the lower regions of Pluto below.
> He recognizes known figures tormented in the waves of Acheron
>   And that the blessed and godly are resplendent on high.
> But others tell that a certain girl in the nighttime
>   Rose to heaven by chance with a migration of mind
> And penetrated the lake of Cocytus and the Stygian marshes
>   And dire . . . . . . desiccated places . . . . . .
> Who at the same time relates she saw the punishments of many
>   And that she saw the godly shining on high.
> Questioned on all these things with great moderation
> 30   So that, with your reporting, I may bring certain news to my lord

And that with your reporting, my boy, I may grasp it as a faithful Clio,
    So that my words may sound in her guise.
If in all these visions great and godly is deservedly remembered
    Our kindly Theodulf, O friend,
I would bring to you with a modest heart and lyric meter
    Poems, believe me, excellent boy,
If an inept messenger had not suddenly beset my superior,
    Who was setting out in a rush to tread a long road.
When he should reach the holy halls, as so often,
40   Where, Anianus, your holy remains are housed,
Stopping before the holy portals in the center of the threshold,
    He quickly spoke these things to the importunate page:
"In this shape my speech is undeveloped,
    In which a boy well trained in the arts is addressed,
Nor does it shine with a little headband or accustomed purple,
    Nor does a pleasant little scroll run its round."
Our kindly circle of poets always true to your friendship
    Sends greetings most goodly to you who are most devout.
Greet your lord with reciprocal language,
50   I ask, and convey greetings to our friends
And many a . . . . . . illumine a poetic . . . . . . which . . . . . .
    Which cheerfully obeys the imperial commands,
Which swift in talent and with sharpness of brilliant perception
    Thrives endowed with all art.
Above all greet Clement, deserving of a name of such meaning,
    Who is famous and of proven worth;
Then Thomas, and likewise powerful Gondacharus,
    Whose mind, O Homer, is akin to yours.
Prepare to add the ranks of young people
60   With a resonant hand contriving other verse.
Thus may your mind offer all my lord's greetings
    And be happy and the body be crowned with good.
I ask that you load me with your poems as I retrace
    My steps, since my own skiff can hardly bear a great weight,
And carry it safely since I am so loaded with meters
    When my ship will be full of verse.
But with these matters forewarned and done, with a bright visage
    Look, boy, now knowingly at the meaningful song.
You will see, friend, what little is compacted in it,
70   It holds back much more than its words reveal.
A matter quite marvelous and with divine meaning,
    A matter that devours and is never satiated with food,

Poems of Doubtful Attribution

Which often chews food with mad jaws grinding,
    And gluttony for food grows all the more.
It spends the night eating in bed and covering itself with ordure,
    And its bed is all covered with shit.

Textual Notes

2.13–14   Fundamen fidei, fabricae incrementa salubris,
    Hi bene componunt, dant pia iura loco.
Alexandrenko (1971:61n5) understood "loco" in "dant pia iura loco" in the medieval sense of 'monastery' (see J. F Niermeyer, *Mediae latinitatis lexicon minus* [Leiden: Brill, 1976], 1: 619), but Theodulf is remarkably free of specifically medieval usage, and the meaning may be more general.

2.31   Parva sed in magna cum sim levitide turba
Alexandrenko provides a helpful note (1971:62n10) on whether this line should be understood to mean that at the time of writing Theodulf was a deacon or perhaps a newly ordained bishop. See the headnote to poems 1–2.

2.149–50   Aurea pontificis cingebat lamina frontem,
    Qua bis binus apex nomen herile dabat.
Alexandrenko (1971:68n38) explains that the "fourfold crown" ("bis binus apex") refers to the YHWH (Yahweh) of the Hebrew Bible. Cf. Freeman 1957:692; and compare the high priest's headdress in Exodus 39:30.

2.171–72   Ut sua deplorent quae nunquam crimina pravis
    Adfore, quae nunquam sollicitando beat.
Dümmler (456n) viewed the line as corrupt. Schaller (1962:69) suggested reading:
Et sua deplorat quae numquam crimina pravis
    Adfore, quae numquam sollicitando beat.
The "quae" refers to the "ista (turba)" of line 165. Thus: "Which never deplores the crimes found in the wicked and which never gives joy by encouraging." See also Alexandrenko 1971:69n42.

7.3   Huius erit promptus capiendi semper Avernus.
Alexandrenko (1971:79n2) refers to and accepts Schaller's emendation of "Avernus" to "avarus" in his dissertation (168) with reference

to Ecclesiastes 5:9: "avarus non implebitur." The dissertation is not available to us, but we adopt the emendation and translate accordingly.

10.9–10   Flava quid horrendis prosunt date mella lacunis,
        Quid litor aut olei stercore mixtus aget?
Schaller (1962:71) noted that the form of "litor" is nowhere recorded and must be an error for *licor* ('liquor').

14.7–8   Copia deest solis torrendo aestate labori,
        Verna nec officio sunt modo laeta suo.
Alexandrenko (1971:96) translated: "There is not enough sunlight in the hot summertime for work, and the serfs are not happy with their duties now." But serfs should be *vernae*. Is it possible that "verna" refers to the spring season and is short for "verna tempora"? It would then fit into the sequence of seasons—winter, summer, spring, autumn.

17.41–42   Hoc agit ut rapidis queat infercire crumenis
        Turpe lucrum, et cupidos rerum onerare sinus.
"Rapidis" should perhaps read *rabidis* with the characteristic interchange of "p" and "b" in Theodulf (see Freeman 1988:3).

17.107   Caelebs et monachus viget in Daniele choreus,
The *Mittellateinisches Wörterbuch bis zum ausgehenden 13. Jahrhundert*, vol. 2 (Munich: Beck, 1999), col. 546, takes note of this line in Theodulf and defines "choreus" as "qui conventus monasterii est—zur Klostergemeinschaft gehörig."

21.18   Ignis Achaeminii vincens incendia, victus
This is presumably the fire that consumes Sodom, but why it should be "Persian" is unclear.

23.29   Schaller 1960:40 suggests that Charlemagne may have prescribed not only the composition of the poem but the exact form as well, the "prolatus tractus."

23.41   Nobilis o lector, rutilisque per omnia cantor,
Schaller 1960:41 reads "rutilusque" for Dümmler's "rutilisque." There is thus a "rutilus cantor," a compliment that Schaller takes as a deferential reference to Alcuin.

Textual Notes 197

25.167–168   Hic poenasve dabit fugietve simillimus Austro,
       Utque sit hic aliud nil nisi Scottus erit.
The joke at the expense of the Irishman has been commented
on a number of times (e.g., Godman 1985:158–59 and Blakeman
1990:159–60). Part of the joke is that he pronounces "Scottus" with
a soft "c" so that it sounds like the soughing of the wind, "naught
but a whistling gust."

25.183–84   Quam saepe ingrediens, pistorum sive coquorum
       Vallatus cuneis, ius synodale gerit.
Alexandrenko (1971:141n96) suspected a pun in "ius synodale" and
translated "fish soup." A hypothetical *jus could mean 'broth' (see
Niermeyer, *Mediae latinitatis lexicon minus*, vol. 1 [2002]):744.

25.188   Pulchraque vasa manu, vinaque grata vehat.
"vasa . . . vinaque" can be hendiadys meaning 'goblets of wine.'

27.8   Brigenses silvas nunc habitare solet.
Liersch (1880:48) located the pagus Brigensis northeast of Orlé-
ans on the left bank of the Marne between Châlons-sur-Marne
(Châlons-en-Champagne) and Paris. Blakeman (1990:206) locates
the forests of Brie to the east of Paris between Seine and Marne.

27.69   Tres pueri circum Danielis fercula gaudent
Liersch (1880:52n6) identified the three boys as Charlemagne's
sons Charles, Pippin, and Louis. Neither Liersch nor Blakeman
(1990:224) could locate a Daniel at Charlemagne's court.

28.211–12   Alter ait: "Mihi sunt vario fucata colore
       Pallia, quae misit, ut puto, torvus Arabs."
Freeman (1957:699) noted an echo in the *Libri Carolini*, ed. eadem,
510:18.

28.527–28   Et caro quae musco redolenti et flagrat amomo,
       Quaeque peregrini tergore muris holet,
The "mus" ('field mouse' or other rodent) must be a beaver. Alex-
andrenko (1971:183n156) compares the "virosa . . . castorea" of Vir-
gil's *Georgics* (1.58–59) and notes the medical and cosmetic uses. He
also points out the use of "mus" ('beaver') in Theodulf 29.21.

28.591   On the use of associates by the *missi dominici* in the Carolingian
period see Monod 1887:7–8 and notes.

28.725 "Ne rogo, sperne preces mihi quantas ast ego vobis,
Me audacem pietas nam facit, ecce, tua."
Alexandrenko (1971:192n200) considered this passage to be corrupt and noted other solutions.

28.879 Nostra minesterii legis conplere securis
Debet, et obsequium, non scelus illud erit.
Hagen 1882:29 and Collins 1950:218 read *minesterium* for "minesterii": "Our ax is obligated to fulfill the office of the law."

29.53–54 Vile datur pretium tanti pro crimine facti
Aut nummi aut pecudis aut rude saepe metum.
Verse 29.54 seems particularly intractable. Traube 1888:67 suggested "aut rude saepe merum" for "aut rude saepe metum."

34.16 Decolor hunc Indus, hunc Agarenus habet.
Alexandrenko (1971:221n9) refers to Isidore's *Etymologies* 9.2.6 and 57, where the Agareni are identified as the descendants of Hagar and Abraham. "Hagareni" became a common locution for "Arabs."

41.31–32 Nam moecham et prolem et Joseph creber intonat Ose,
Samariam, Effraim, Gezdrahel et viduam.
The interpretation of Hosea is sufficiently vexed to require a reading of the commentaries even to identify the persons (or personifications). Gezdrahel is an unusual form of "Israel."

41.59–60 The names Ididia and Cohelet for Solomon are found in Isidore's Etymologies 7.6.65.

41.155–56 Cui si quam cupias sensu conferre vel arte,
Ut caelo tellus, haec ita caedet ei.
"Caedet" may stand for "cedet" ('will yield') as Sirmond has it (*PL* 105, 303) and as Alexandrenko (1971:242n59) approves. Alexandrenko also refers to Huemer (1882:247), who opts for "cedit" ('yields'). See also Schaller 1962:81.

41ii.7–10 Scilicet initio sumens exordia ab ipso
Per partum et regum nomina texit opus.
Et notat annorum numerum, notat ordine regna,
Eracli princeps, tempus ad usque tuum.
Dümmler (539n2) identifies the "opus" in line 8 as *Chronographia beati Isidori*, presumably a reference to a combination of Isidore's *De*

Textual Notes

ortu et obitu partum and his *Historia de regibus Gothorum, Vandalorum et Suevorum*. The latter did indeed carry the history down to the time of the eastern emperor Heraclius, who died in 641. The following works are identified by Dümmler as *Eucherii opusculum de interpretatione Hebraicorum nominum et Graecorum* and *Melitonis episcopi Sardensis clavis*. See Eucherius of Lyons and Melito of Sardes in the *New Catholic Encyclopedia*.

45.23   Proteus the truth-teller goes back to Homer's *Odyssey* 4.399–480 and is referred to by Virgil, *Georgics* 4.387–414. On the Virgin representing justice see Franz Bömer's commentary P. Ovidius Naso. *Metamorphosen*, vol. 1 (Heidelberg: Winter, 1969), 69–70.

52.4   Dümmler lists "ortivagus" in his "Index vocum rariorum" (649), but we have been unable to trace a word ortivagus or hortivagus.

52.9   The form "elluo" must be helluo 'glutton,' but it does not produce very good sense.

72.119–20   Sirmond (PL 105.34, note "c") calculated the date to be February 8, 1820. See also Dümmler (566n2) and Alexandrenko (1971:305n36).

72.196   Dümmler read "Arlaldo," but Schaller (1962:52) could find no trace of such a name and argued for Sirmond's "Arbaldo."

72.213–14   The reference is to the Battle of Pharsalus, in which Caesar (the son-in-law) defeated Pompey (the father-in-law). The Emathian expanses are the plains of Pharsalus (Lucan, *Pharsalia*, 1.1).

Appendix

To his edition Sirmond (*PL* 105:333–34) added a set of eight poems on personified figures of the seven liberal arts plus Sapientia, from MS Vat. Lat 341; Dümmler printed them as an "Appendix ad Theodulfum" (629–30). After Sapientia at the head, the arts are described in downward order, from Astronomy (at the top of the quadrivium) to Grammar (at the bottom of the trivium). Could these be Theodulfian ekphraseis of an actual work of art? Compare poem 46. The verses are here translated by Leslie MacCoull as follows:

1.   Wisdom

The unbegotten Father begot me, coeval with his Word,[1]
    Whom the body does not nourish, nor any place contain,
But I bring the earthborn to the Father's banquets,[2]
    For they lack the sun who are too lazy to proceed.

2.   Astronomy

I have a marvelous face and expressive spirit;
    I have as many eyes as the heaven has stars.
Having five breasts, one burning like fire,
    Two medium, and two ice-cold.

3.   Music

I, the increaser of sweetness, flow from the founxtain of joy,
    And no part of me is without joy.
And harmonious song, varied with threefold interplay,
    If it resounds without me, it is quite useless.

---

[1] Wisdom 10:1; Proverbs 8:22–31
[2] Proverbs 9:1–5

4.   Geometry

Whoever happens zealously to want to penetrate my secrets
　　Has first to approach the various gates.
I shine with ancient eyes and with threefold faces,
　　And with my measuring rod I measure six-sided areas.

5.   Arithmetic

I am delicate of face, and with many swift wings:
　　Whoever wants to know me, let him always attend to me lovingly.
I am born variable, yet will set down marvelous diagrams,
　　Remaining the fount and origin for the three brothers.

6.   Rhetoric

An experienced and eloquent tongue gave me my name,
　　Yet still I often visit unlearned men.
For if someone who has never seen me wins by means of me,
　　How much more can he who knows my laws do?

7.   Dialectic

I allow nothing to be spoken ambiguously, but define certainties,
　　Knowledgeable to confine broad locutions in specified places.
I determine all that exists in five modes,
　　Neither less nor more, but uttering everything.

8.   Grammar

I become a beautiful remedy when I give speech to the stammering,
　　For I am a strong medicine for mistakes in utterance.
I put together a sweet taste out of six leaves,
　　Then I add the saving work in a thousand ways.

BIBLIOGRAPHY*

Primary Sources and Reference Works:

Alcuini Epistolae. Ed. Ernst Dümmler. In *Epistolae karolini aevi* 2, 18–481. MGH: Epistolarum Tomus 4, karolini aevi 2. Berlin: Weidmann, 1895.

Analecta hymnica medii aevi. Ed. Clemens Blume and Guido M. Dreves. 55 vols. Leipzig: 1886–1922; repr. New York and London: Johnson Reprint Corporation, 1961.

Capitula Episcoporum, vol. 1. MGH. Ed. Peter Brommer. Hannover: Hahn, 1984.

Du Cange, Charles Dufresne. *Glossarium Mediae et Infimae Latinitatis.* 7 vols. Paris: Firmin Didot, 1840–1850; repr. Graz: Akademische Druck- und Verlagsanstalt, 1954.

The Etymologies of Isidore of Seville. Trans. Stephen A. Barney, W. J. Lewis, J. A. Beach, Oliver Berghof, with the collaboration of Muriel Hall. Cambridge: Cambridge University Press, 2006.

Hagen, Hermann, ed. *Theodulfi epicopi aurelianensis De judiciis versus. Sollemnia anniversaria conditae Universitatis (Bernensis).* Bern: Typis S. Collini.

Hugh of Fleury. *Ex historia ecclesiastica.* MGH: Scriptorum , vol. 9. Ed. Georg Heinrich Pertz. Hannover: Hahn, 1851.

The Hymnal According to the Use of the Episcopal Church. New York: The Church Hymnal Corporation, 1940.

The Jerusalem Bible. Ed. Alexander Jones et al. Garden City, NY: Doubleday & Company, 1966.

Karolus Magnus et Leo Papa. Ein Paderborner Epos vom Jahre 799. Ed. Helmut Beumann, Franz Brunhölzl, and Wilhelm Winkelmann. Paderborn: Bonifacius Druckerei, 1966.

Opus Caroli Contra Synodum (Libri Carolini). Ed. Ann Freeman in collaboration with Paul Meyvaert. MGH: Concilia. Vol. 2, suppl. 1. Hannover: Hahn, 1998.

---

* Addendum: June-Ann Greeley's unpublished Fordham dissertation "Social Commentary in the Prose and Poetry of Theodulf of Orléans: A Study in Carolingian Humanism" (2000) came to our attention only after proofreading had been completed. We regret the omission

Poetae Latini Aevi Carolini. Ed. Ernst Dümmler. Vols. 1–2. MGH. Berlin: Weidmann, 1881–1884.

Thegan. *Die Taten Kaiser Ludwigs*; Astronomus. *Das Leben Kaiser Ludwigs.* MGH: Scriptores rerum germanicarum in usum scholarum separatim editi 64. Ed. and trans. Ernst Tremp. Hannover: Hahn, 1995.

Secondary Works:

Adamik, Tamás. 2001. "Theodulfs Palmsonntagshymnus." *Acta Antiqua Academiae Scientiarium Hungariae* 41:165–74.

Alexandrenko, Nikolai A. 1971. "The Poetry of Theodulf of Orleans: A Translation and Critical Study." Ph.D diss. Tulane University.

Allott, Stephen. 1974. *Alcuin of York: His Life and Letters.* York: William Sessions Ltd.

Arcari, Paola Maria. 1952. "Un goto critico delle legislazioni barbariche." *Archivio storico italiano* 110:3–37.

Barbero, Alessandro. 2004. *Charlemagne, Father of a Continent.* Berkeley: University of California Press.

Barthès, Louis. 1992. *L'abbaye et la cité d'Aniane de Saint-Benoît à la révolution.* Aniane: Foyer Rural d'Aniane (Hérault).

Baunard, Louis. 1860. *Théodulfe, évêque d'Orléans et abbé de Fleury-sur-Loire.* Paris: Charles Douniol.

Bischoff, Bernhard. 1955/1967. "Theodulf und der Ire Cadac-Andreas." *Historisches Jahrbuch* 74:92–98; repr. idem, *Ausgewählte Aufsätze zur Schriftkunde und Literaturgeschichte,* 2:19–25 (Stuttgart: Anton Hiersemann).

Blakeman, Christopher John. 1990. "A Commentary with Introduction, Text and Translation, on Selected Poems of Theodulf of Orléans (Sirmond III. 1–6)." Ph.D. diss., University of St. Andrews.

Bretzigheimer, Gerlinde. 2004. "Der Herkules-Mythos als Gefässdekor: Eine 'descriptio' des Theodulf von Orléans." *Mittellateinisches Jahrbuch* 39:183–205.

Brommer, Peter. 1974. "Die bischöfliche Gesetzgebung Theodulfs von Orléans." *Zeitschrift der Savigny-Stiftung für Rechtsgeschichte* 91, Kanonistische Abteilung 60:1–120.

Bruce, Scott G. 2007. *Silence and Sign Language in Medieval Monasticism: The Cluniac Tradition c. 900–1200.* Cambridge: Cambridge University Press.

Brugnoli. G. 1959. "Ovidio e gli esiliati carolingi." In *Atti del convegno internazionale ovidiano. Sulmona, maggio 1958.* Vol. 2:209–16. Rome: Istituto di studi romani.

Brunhölzl, Franz. 1975. *Geschichte der lateinischen Literatur des Mittelalters,* Vol. 1: *Von Cassiodor bis zum Ausklang der karolingischen Erneuerung.* Munich: Fink.

Bullough, Donald A. 2004. *Alcuin: Achievement and Reputation.* Leiden and Boston: Brill.

Bibliography

Caro Baroja, Julio. 1935. *Los vascones y sus vecinos*. Estudios vascos 13. San Sebastián: Editorial Txertoa.

Cavadini, John C. 1993. *The Last Christology of the West in Spain and Gaul, 785–820*. Philadelphia: University of Pennsylvania Press.

Chekhov, Anton. 1967. *The Image of Chekhov: Forty Stories in the Order in Which They were Written*. Trans. Robert Payne. New York: Alfred Knopf.

Chevalier-Royet, Caroline. 2007. "Les révisions bibliques de Théodulf d'Orléans et la question de leur utilisation par l'exégèse carolingienne." In *Etudes d'exégèse carolingienne*, ed. S. Shimahara, 237–56. Turnhout: Brepols.

Chiri, Giuseppe. 1954. *Poesia cortese Latina (profilo storico dal v al xii secolo)*. Rome: Edizioni dell'Ateneo.

Collins, S. T. 1950. "Sur quelques vers de Théodulfe." *Revue Bénédictine* 60:214–18.

Cuissard, Charles. 1892. *Théodulfe évêque d'Orléans. Sa vie et ses œuvres*. Orléans: H. Herluison.

Dahlhaus-Berg, Elisabeth. 1975. *Nova antiquitas et antiqua novitas. Typologische Exegese und isidorianisches Geschichtsbild bei Theodulf von Orléans*. Cologne and Vienna: Böhlau.

Delisle, Léopold. 1879. "Les bibles de Théodulfe." *Bibliothèque de l'Ecole des Chartes* 40:5–47.

de Riquer [Permanyer], Alejandra. 1990. "El árbol de las siete artes liberales descrito por Teodulfo de Orleans." In *Las Abreviaturas en la enseñanza medieval y la transmissión del saber*. 347–54. Barcelona: Publicaciones de la Universitat de Barcelona.

———. 1992a. "Ovidius magister Theodulfi (ecos del *Ars Amatoria* en el Carmen XXVIII de Theodulfo de Orleans)." *Anuari de filologia* 115:99-106.

———. 1992b. "El 'Scottus-sottus' en Teodulfo de Orleans: un ejemplo de burla y invectiva en la literatura carolingia." *Cultura neolatina* 52:201–29.

———. 1994. *Teodulfo de Orleans y la epístola poética en la literatura carolingia*. Barcelona: Real Academia de Buenas Letras.

Dronke, Peter. 1974. *Fabula*. Leiden: Brill.

Duby, Georges. 1980. *The Three Orders*. Chicago: University of Chicago Press.

Dupont, André. 1965. "L'aprision et le régime aprisionnaire dans le Midi de la France (fin du VIIIe-début du Xe siècle)." *Le moyen âge* 71:179–213, 375–99.

Dutton, Paul Edward. 1994. *The Politics of Dreaming in the Carolingian Empire*. Lincoln: University of Nebraska Press.

Ebert, Adolf. 1878. "Kleine Beiträge zur Geschichte der karolingischen Literatur." In *Berichte über die Verhandlungen der Königlich Sächsischen Gesellschaft der Wissenschaften zu Leipzig*, Philol.-hist. Cl, 30:95–112. Leipzig: Hirzel.

———. 1880. *Allgemeine Geschichte der Literatur des Mittelalters im Abendlande*. Vol. 2: *Lateinische Literatur vom Zeitalter Karls des Grossen bis zum Tode Karls des Kahlen*. Leipzig: F. C. W. Vogel.

Esmeijer, Ank C. 1973. "De VII liberalibus artibus in quadam pictura depictis. Een reconstructie van de arbor philosophiae van Theodulf van Orléans." In *Album Amicorum J. G. van Gelder*, ed. J. Bruyn, J. A. Emmens, E. de Jongh, and D. P. Snoep, 102–113. The Hague: Nijhoff.

Estey, F. N. 1943. "Charlemagne's Silver Celestial Table." *Speculum* 18:112–17.

Fichtenau, Heinrich. 1957. *The Carolingian Empire*. Trans. Peter Munz. Oxford: Blackwell.

Freeman, Ann. 1957/repr. 2003. "Theodulf of Orléans and the *Libri Carolini*." *Speculum* 32:663–705.

———. 1965. "Further Studies in the *Libri Carolini*." *Speculum* 40:203–89.

———. 1971/repr. 2003. "Further Studies in the *Libri Carolini* III: The Marginal Notes in Vaticanus Latinus 7207." *Speculum* 46:597–612.

———. 1985/repr. 2003. "Carolingian Orthodoxy and the Fate of the *Libri Carolini*." *Viator* 16:65–108.

———. 1987/repr. 2003. "Theodulf of Orléans and the Psalm Citations of the *Libri Carolini*." *Revue Bénédictine* 97:195–224.

———. 1988/repr. 2003 "Additions and Corrections to the *Libri Carolini*: Links with Alcuin and the Adoptionist Controversy." In *Scire litteras. Forschungen zum mittelalterlichen Geistesleben*, ed. Sigrid Krämer and Michael Bernhard, 159–69. Bayerische Akademie der Wissenschaften, neue Folge, 99. Abhandlungen, Philos.-hist. Kl., neue Folge, 99. Munich: Verlag der Bayerischen Akademie der Wissenschaften.

———, with Paul Meyvaert. 1998. *"Opus Caroli Regis contra synodum*: An Introduction." In eadem, *Theodulf of Orléans: Charlemagne's Spokesman against the Second Council of Nicaea*, 1–123. Variorum Collected Studies Series. Aldershot: Ashgate Publishing Ltd.

———. 1992/repr. 2003. "Theodulf of Orléans: A Visigoth at Charlemagne's Court." In *L'Europe héritière de l'Espagne wisigothique. Colloque international du C. N. R. S. tenu à La Fondation Singer-Polignac (Paris, 14–16 Mai 1990)*. Ed. Jacques Fontaine and Christine Pellistrandi. Madrid: Casa de Velázquez.

———. 1994/repr. 2003. "Scripture and Images in the *Libri Carolini*." In *Testo e immagine nell'alto medioevo. Settimane di studio del Centro italiano di studi sull'alto medioevo* 41, 1:163–95. Spoleto: Presso la Sede del Centro.

———, and Paul Meyvaert. 2001. "The Meaning of Theodulf's Apse Mosaic at Germigny-des-Prés." *Gesta* 40:125–39; repr. in Paul Meyvaert, *The Art of Words: Bede and Theodulf*, 1–28. Aldershot: Ashgate Publishing Ltd., 2008.

———. 2003. *Theodulf of Orléans: Charlemagne's Spokesman against the Second Council of Nicaea*. Variorum Collected Studies Series. Aldershot: Ashgate Publishing Ltd.

Fried, Johannes. 1990. "Ludwig der Fromme, das Papsttum und die fränkische Kirche." In *Charlemagne's Heir: New Perspectives on the Reign of Louis the Pious (814–840)*, ed. Peter Godman and Roger Collins, 231–73.

Bibliography

Fritsch, Andreas. 1990. *Materialien zum Lateinsprechen im Unterricht. Geschichte-Probleme-Möglichkeiten.* Bamberg: C. C. Buchners Verlag.

Fuhrmann, Manfred. 1980. "Philologische Bemerkungen zu Theodulfs Paraenesis ad iudices." In *Das Profil des Juristen in der europäischen Tradition. Symposion aus Anlass des 70. Geburtstages von Franz Wieacker,* ed. Klaus Luig and Detlef Liebs, 257–77. Ebelsbach: Verlag Rolf Gremer.

Geary, Patrick. 2008. "Judicial Violence and Torture in the Carolingian Empire." In *Law and the Illicit in Medieval Europe,* ed. Ruth M. Karras, Joel Kaye, and Ann E. Matter, 79–88. Philadelphia: University of Pennsylvania Press.

Godman, Peter. 1985. *Poetry of the Carolingian Renaissance.* Norman: University of Oklahoma Press.

———. 1987. *Poets and Emperors: Frankish Politics and Carolingian Poetry.* Oxford: Clarendon Press.

———. 1990. "The Poetic Hunt: From Saint Martin to Charlemagne's Heir." In *Charlemagne's Heir,* ed. idem and Roger Collins, 565–89.

———, Jörg Jarnut, and Peter Johanek, eds. 2002. *Am Vorabend der Kaiserkrönung. Das Epos "Karolus Magnus et Leo papa" und der Papstbesuch in Paderborn 799.* Berlin: Akademie Verlag.

Greeley, June-Ann. 2006. "Raptors and Rebellion: The Self-Defence of Theodulf of Orleans." *Journal of Medieval Latin* 16:28–75.

Hauréau, Barthélemy. 1861. "Théodulfe." In idem, *Singularités historiques et littéraires,* 37–99. Paris: Michel Lévy frères.

Hentze, Wilhelm, ed. 1999. *De Karolo rege et Leone papa. Der Bericht über die Zusammenkunft Karls des Grossen mit Papst Leo III. in Paderborn 799 in einem Epos für Karl den Kaiser. Mit vollständiger Farbeproduktion nach der Handschrift der Zentralbibliothek Zürich, Ms. C78, und Beiträgen von Lutz E. v. Padberg, Johannes Schwind und Hans-Walter Stork.* Paderborn: Bonifatius.

Hubert, Jean, Jean Porcher, and Wolfgang Fritz Volbach. 1970. *The Carolingian Renaissance.* Trans. James Emmons, Stuart Gilbert, and Robert Allen. New York: George Braziller.

Huemer, Johannes. 1882. Review of Dümmler's *Poetae latini aevi carolini,* vol. 1. *Deutsche Litteraturzeitung* 3:246–48.

Kränzle, Andreas. 1996. "Theodulf." In *Biographisch-Bibliographisches Kirchenlexikon,* ed. Friedrich Wilhelm Bautz, 11:1003–8. Herzberg: Verlag Traugott Bautz.

Ledru, A. 1926. "Théodulfe évêque d'Orléans et l'hymne *Gloria laus.*" *La Province du Maine* 6:60–72.

Lendinara, Patrizia. 1998. "Mixed Attitudes to Ovid: The Carolingian Poets and the Glossographers." In *Alcuin of York: Scholar at the Carolingian Court,* ed. L. A. J. R. Houwen and A. A. MacDonald, 171–213. Groningen: Egbert Forsten.

Lewis, C. S. 1964. *The Discarded Image.* Cambridge: Cambridge University Press.

Liebeschütz, Hans. 1957. "Theodulf of Orléans and the Problem of the Carolingian Renaissance." In *Fritz Saxl: 1890–1948. Memorial Essays from His Friends in England*, ed. D. J. Gordon, 77–92. London, etc.: Thomas Nelson and Sons Ltd.

Liersch, Karl. 1880. *Die Gedichte Theodulfs, Bischofs von Orléans.* Halle: E. Karras.

Mähl, Sibylle. 1969. *Quadriga virtutum. Die Kardinaltugenden in der Geistesgeschichte der Karolingerzeit.* Archiv für Kulturgeschichte, Beiheft 9. Cologne and Vienna: Böhlau.

Manitius, Max. 1886. "Zu karolingischen Gedichten." *Neues Archiv der Gesellschaft für ältere deutsche Geschichtskunde* 11:553–63.

———. 1911–1931. *Geschichte der lateinischen Literatur des Mittelalters.* 3 vols. Munich: Beck.

Meens, Rob. 2007. "Sanctuary, Penance and Dispute Settlement under Charlemagne: The Conflict between Alcuin and Theodulf of Orléans over a Sinful Cleric." *Speculum* 82:277–300.

Megivern, James J. 1997. *The Death Penalty: An Historical and Theological Survey.* New York and Mahwah, NJ: Paulist Press.

Meyvaert, Paul. 1979. "The Authorship of the 'Libri Carolini': Observations Prompted by a Recent Book." *Revue Bénédictine* 89:29–57.

———. 2001. "Maximilien Théodore Chrétin and the Apse Mosaic at Germigny-des-Prés." *Gazette des Beaux-Arts* 137: 203–20; repr. in idem *Art of Words: Bede and Theodulf,* 1–26. Aldershot: Ashgate Publishing Ltd., 2008.

———. 2002. "Medieval Notions of Publication: The 'Unpublished' *Opus Caroli Regis contra Synodum* and the Council of Frankfurt (794)." *Journal of Medieval Latin* 12:78–98; repr. in his *The Art of Words: Bede and Theodulf,* 78–89.

———, and Anselme Davril. 2003. "Théodulfe et Bède au sujet des blessures du Christ." *Revue Bénédictine* 113:71–79; repr. in Meyvaert, *The Art of Words,* 71–79.

———, and A. Freeman. See Freeman.

Monod, Gabriel. 1887. "Les mœurs judiciaires au VIIIe siècle; d'après la *Paraenesis ad judices* de Théodulfe." *Revue historique* 35:1–20.

Nees, Lawrence. 1987. "Theodulf's Mythical Silver Hercules Vase, *Poetica Vanitas,* and the Augustinian Critique of the Roman Heritage." *Dumbarton Oaks Papers* 41:443–51.

———. 1991. A *Tainted Mantle: Hercules and the Classical Tradition at the Carolingian Court.* Philadelphia: University of Pennsylvania Press.

Noble, T. F. X. 1981. "Some Observations on the Deposition of Archbishop Theodulf of Orléans in 817." *Journal of the Rocky Mountain Medieval and Renaissance Association* 2:29–40.

———. 2009. *Images, Iconoclasm, and the Carolingians.* Philadelphia: University of Pennsylvania Press.

Nowell, I. 2003. "Psalms, Book of." *New Catholic Encyclopedia* 11:794. Detroit: Thompson/Gale.

Ohlers, Norbert. 2004 (first edition 1986). *Reisen im Mittelalter.* Düsseldorf and Zürich: Artemis & Winkler.

Ommundsen, Åslaug. 2002. "The Liberal Arts and the Polemic Strategy of the *Opus Caroli Regis Contra Synodum (Libri Carolini)." Symbolae Osloenses* 77:175–200.

Orlandis, José. 2003. *Historia del reino visigodo español. Los acontecimientos, las instituciones, los protagonistas.* Madrid: Ediciones Rialp.

O'Sullivan, Sinéad. 2004. *Early Medieval Glosses on Prudentius'* Psychomachia. Leiden: Brill.

Parisse, Michel, with Jacqueline Leuridan. 1994. *Atlas de la France de l'an mil. État de nos conaissances.* [Paris]: Picard.

Raby, F. J. E. 1957. *A History of Secular Latin Poetry in the Middle Ages.* 2nd ed. Oxford: Clarendon Press.

Riché, Pierre. 1992. "Les réfugiés wisigoths dans le monde carolingien." In *L'Europe héritière de l'Espagne wisigothique. Colloque international du C. N. R. S. tenu à la Fondation Singer Polignac (Paris, 14–16 Mai 1990).* Ed. Jacques Fontaine and Christine Pellistrandi, 177–83. Madrid: Casa de Velásquez.

Ross, Werner. 1954. "Die 'Ecbasis captivi' und die Anfänge der mittelalterlichen Tierdichtung." *Germanisch-romanische Monatsschrift* 35:266–82.

Rouche, Michel. 1979. *L'Aquitaine des Wisigoths aux Arabes 418–781. Naissance d'une région.* Paris: Ecole des Hautes Etudes en Science Sociale et Editions Jean Touzot.

Rzehulka, Ernst. 1875. *Theodulf, Bischof von Orléans, Abt von St. Aignan in Orléans.* Diss. Breslau: R. Grosser.

Schaller, Dieter. 1960. "Die karolingischen Figurengedichte des Cod. Bern. 212." In *Medium aevum vivum. Festschrift für Walther Bulst*, ed. Hans Robert Jauss and idem, 22–47. Heidelberg: C. Winter.

———. 1962. "Philologische Untersuchungen zu den Gedichten Theodulfs von Orléans." *Deutsches Archiv für Erforschung des Mittelalters* 18:13–91.

———. 1970a. "Lateinische Tierdichtung in frühkarolingischer Zeit." In *Das Tier in der Dichtung,* ed. Ute Schwab, 91–113, 272–76. Heidelberg: Winter.

———. 1970b. "Vortrags- und Zirkulardichtung am Hof Karls des Grossen." *Mittellateinisches Jahrbuch* 6:14–36.

———. 1971. "Der junge 'Rabe' am Hof Karls des Grossen (Theodulf carm. 27). In *Festschrift Bernhard Bischoff zu seinem 65. Geburtstag dargebracht von Freunden, Kollegen und Schülern*, ed. Johanne Autenrieth and Franz Brunhölzl, 123- 41. Stuttgart: Anton Hiersemann.

———. 1992a. "Theodulfs Exil in Le Mans." *Mittellateinisches Jahrbuch* 27:91–101.

———. 1992b. "Briefgedichte als Zeitzeugen: Theodulfs Sturz 817/818." In *Aus Archiven und Bibliotheken. Festschrift Raymund Kottje zum 65. Geburtstag*, ed. Hubert Mordek, 107–19. Frankfurt a. M.: Peter Lang.

———. 1995. *Studien zur lateinischen Dichtung des Frühmittelalters*. Quellen und Untersuchungen zur lateinischen Philologie des Mittelalters 11. Stuttgart: Anton Hiersemann.

Schieffer, Rudolf. 2002. "Das Attentat auf Papst Leo III." In *Am Vorabend der Kaiserkrönung. Das Epos "Karolus Magnus et Leo Papa" und der Papstbesuch in Paderborn 799*, ed. Peter Godman, Jörg Jarnut, and Peter Johanek, 75–85. Berlin: Akademie Verlag.

Schwartz, Gerhard. 1914. Review: "A. Vidier 'La mappemonde de Théodulfe et la Mappemonde de Ripoll' . . . ." *Neues Archiv der Gesellschaft für ältere deutsche Geschichtskunde* 39:589–91.

Sears, Elizabeth. 1990. "Louis the Pious as *Miles Christi*." In *Charlemagne's Heir*. Ed. Godman and Collins, 605–28.

Shaffer, Jenny H. 2006. "Letaldus of Micy, Germigny-des-Prés, and Aachen: Histories, Contexts, and the Problem of Likeness in Medieval Architecture." *Viator* 37:53–83.

Sidwell, Keith. 1992. "Theodulf of Orléans, Cadac-Andreas and Old Irish Phonology: A Conundrum." *Journal of Medieval Latin* 2:55–62.

Stella, Francesco. 1993. *La poesia carolingia latina a tema biblico*. Spoleto: Centro Italiano di Studi sull'alto Medioevo.

Strecker, Karl. 1922. "Studien zu karolingischen Dichtern." *Neues Archiv der Gesellschaft für ältere deutsche Geschichtskunde* 43:479–511.

Szövérffy, Josef. 1964. *Die Annalen der lateinischen Hymnendichtung. Ein Handbuch*. Vol. 1: *Die lateinischen Hymnen bis zum Ende des 11. Jahrhunderts*. Berlin: Erich Schmidt Verlag.

Tiraboschi, Girolamo. 1822–26. *Storia della letteratura italiana*. 9 vols. Milan: Società tipografica de'classici italiani. Vol. 3 (1823).

Tougher, Shaun. 2004. "Social Transformation, Gender Transformation: The Court Eunuch, 300–900." In *Gender in the Early Medieval World: East and West, 300–900*, ed. Leslie Brubaker and J. Smith, 70–82. Cambridge: Cambridge University Press.

Traube, Ludwig. 1888. *Karolingische Dichtungen*. Schriften zur germanischen Philologie 1. Berlin: Weidmann.

Treffort, Cécile. 2007. "Une consécration 'à lettre': Place, rôle et autorité des textes inscrits dans la sacralisation de l'église." In *Mises en scène et mémoires de la consécration de l'église dans l'occident médiéval*, ed. Didier Méhu, 219–51. Turnhout: Brepols.

Umiker-Sebeok, Jean, and Thomas A. Sebeok. 1987. *Monastic Sign Languages*. Berlin: Mouton de Gruyter.

Vidier, A. 1911. "La mappemonde de Théodulfe de Ripoll." *Bulletin de géographie historique et descriptive du Ministère de l'Instruction et des Beaux-arts*, 285–313.

Waddell, Helen. 1947. *Poetry in the Dark Ages*. Glasgow: Jackson.

Wallach, Luitpold. 1959. *Alcuin and Charlemagne: Studies in Carolingian History and Literature*. Cornell Studies in Classical Philology 32. Ithaca: Cornell University Press.

———. 1951. "Alcuin's Epitaph of Hadrian I: A Study in Carolingian Epigraphy." *American Journal of Philology* 72:128–44.

Weinberger, Stephen. 1982. "Cours judiciaires, justice et responsabilité sociale dans la Provence médiévale: IXe-XIe siècle." *Revue historique* 542:273–88.

Werner, Karl Ferdinand. 1990. "*Hludovicus Augustus*: Gouverner l'empire chrétien—idées et réalités." In *Charlemagne's Heir*, ed. Godman and Collins, 3–123. Oxford: Clarendon Press.

Willeumier-Schalij, J. M. 1953–1954. "De spreuk van de doden tot de levenden." *Neophilologus* 37:227–33; part 2: *Neophilologus* 38:200–6.

Williams, Burma P., and Richard S. 1995. "Finger Numbers in the Greco-Roman World and the Early Middle Ages." *Isis* 86:587–608.

Ziolkowski, Jan M. 1993. *Talking Animals: Medieval Latin Beast Poetry, 750–1150*. Philadelphia: University of Pennsylvania Press.

General Index

A

Aachen, 7
Aaron, 59
Aaron (Hildebald), 78
Abel, 58
Abraham, 58
Acedia, 17, 25–26, 45
Acheron, 14, 84, 191
Adam (first man), 23, 58
"Ad Carolum regem," 3–4, 15, 75, 113, 161, 171
Adamik, Tamás, 161
"Ad Corvinianum," 15
"Ad episcopos," 3, 10, 12, 17, 34, 40, 171
"Ad Gislam," 67
Adoptionism, 3, 121
Adultery, 25
Aeneid, 81, 140
Agareni (Hagareni), 119, 198
Agde, 80, 87
Aiulf (bishop in Bourges), 7, 11–13, 167, 170
Aix-en-Provence, 80, 87
Albinus (Alcuin), 72
Albinus (patron saint of a monastery in Angers), 163, 165, 187, 190
Alcuin, 2–4, 57, 62, 66, 73, 75–77, 79, 127–28, 140, 150, 187, 196
Alexandrenko, Nikolai A., 6, 8, 35–36, 57, 66, 73, 76, 122, 126, 137, 139, 148, 152–53, 164, 177, 183, 187, 195–99
Allier (river), 86
Allott, Stephen, 4
Ambrose (archbishop of Milan), 140
Amphitrite, 148
Anger, 10, 17, 19–21, 25

Angers, 8, 161, 163, 170, 174
Anglican *Hymnal*, 161
Angoulême, 150
Aniane, 2, 111
Anianus (Saint), 156, 159, 163, 191–92
Anselm of Milan, 7
Antichrist, 36
Antaeus, 88
Aquitaine, 1, 86, 148
Arabs, 68, 89, 109, 119, 126, 198
Arator, 141
Arbaldus (a priest), 176, 199
Argos, 87
Arles, 80, 87
Ars Amandi (Ovid), 18–19
Ars Numerorum, 142, 144, 202
Assyrians, 119
Astronomer (author of *Vita Hludowici Imperatoris*), 6–7, 122
Astronomy, 201
Aude (river), 80, 86
Augustine (Saint), 140, 156
Auredus (companion of Theodulf), 148–49
Ausonia, 111–12
Avarice, 17, 25–26, 91
Avars, 3, 39, 65, 68
Avernus, 14, 23
Avignon, 80, 87, 139
Avitus, 141

B

Bacchus, 72, 94
Bagao (a court eunuch), 78
Balaam, 77
Barbero, Alessandro, 119
Barthès, Louis, 111

Baunard, Louis, 34, 36, 57, 65, 111, 117, 119, 126, 137, 148, 150, 156, 162, 177
Bede, 35
Bellona, 20
Benedict of Aniane, 2, 5
Benedict of Nursia, 111–12
Benedictine Rule, 111
Bernard (nephew of Louis the Pious), 6–7, 119
Berta (daughter of Charlemagne), 69–70
Bezaleel (Einhard), 75
Béziers, 80, 87
Bischoff, Bernhard, 66, 76
Blakeman, John, 76, 197
Blume, Clemens, 161
Boethius, 177, 179
Bömer, Franz, 199
Boniface, 80, 191
Bourges, 167
Bretzigheimer, Gerlinde, 81, 140
Bribery, 10, 81–83, 94, 103–4
Brie (pagus Brigensis), 76, 197
Britain, 160
Brommer, Peter, 13, 156
Bullough, Donald A., 3, 62, 66

C

Cacus, 81, 88, 140–41
Cadac-Andreas, 15, 66, 71–72, 75–76, 78
Caesar, Julius, 199
Cahors, 174
Calydon, 88
Cannae, 176
Capitularies, 10, 13, 15
Carcassonne, 80, 87
Cardinal sins, 10, 17
Carmen figuratum, 1
Caro Baroja, Julio, 148
Carthaginians, 175
Cassino, 112
Cassiodorus, 143
Castelnau-le-Lez, 80
Catalogue poem, 35, 57, 119, 140, 177
Catalonia, 146
Cavadini, John C., 121
Cavaillon, 80–81, 87
Ceres, 72

Chalon-sur-Saône, 7
Châlons, Council of, 8
Châlons-sur-Marne (Châlons en Champagne), 197
Cerberus, 23
Charlemagne, 1–4, 6, 8, 10, 13, 62–63, 65, 73–75, 79, 81, 86, 113–14, 116, 119–22, 124–25, 127, 137, 161, 196–97
Charles (eldest son of Charlemagne), 6, 69, 120, 197
Charles Martel, 124–25
Charroux, 150–51
Chekhov, Anton, 152
Chevalier-Royet, Caroline, 128
Chiri, Giuseppe, 137
Christina (queen of Sweden), 146
Chruodtrud (daughter of Charlemagne), 69–70
Circe, 43
Clement (unidentified), 192
Clio, 192
Cocytus, 14, 84, 95, 191
Cohelet (Solomon), 198
Collins, S. T., 75, 198
"Consolation of a Certain Brother," 177
Constantine (emperor), 62
"Contra iudices," 1, 3, 10–12, 14, 18, 34, 58, 66, 74, 108, 142, 161, 171, 183
Cordoba, 68, 89
Corvinianus, 66
Cuissard, Charles, 1–3, 5–8, 34, 36, 57, 65, 119–20, 127, 137, 150, 161–62, 164, 170, 177
Cupid, 140–41
Cupidity, 91
Cyprian, 140

D

Dahlhaus-Berg, Elisabeth, 7–8, 18, 128
Damaeta or Damoetas (Riculf, archbishop of Mainz), 75, 78
Damasus (pope), 156, 160
Daniel (unidentified figure at Charlemagne's court), 197
Daniel, 54–55, 60, 78
Daniel, Pierre, 79

Index

Danube, 13, 39, 68, 86
David (King), 34, 40, 59, 61, 63, 68, 84, 162, 188
David (appellation of Charlemagne), 77–78
Davril, Anselme, 35
Deceit, 35–36, 38, 51
Deianira, 88
Delia (appellation of one of Charlemagne's daughters?), 75, 77
Delisle, Léopold, 128
De Riquer [Permanyer], Alejandra, 1, 3–4, 6, 9, 66–67, 111, 137, 143
Desiderius (King), 116
De spiritu sancto, 121
Dialectica, 142–43, 202
Die (south of Grenoble), 139
Disputes, 48
Divisio Regnorum, 6, 8, 119
Donatus (the grammarian), 141
Dordogne (river), 81, 148–49
Dreves, Guido M., 161
Dronke, Peter, 140
Dümmler, Ernst, 2–3, 9, 17–18, 34–35, 45, 57, 62, 65, 73, 75, 79, 116, 119, 122, 127–28, 148, 150, 153, 164, 170, 177, 183, 187, 190, 195–96, 198–99, 201
Dupont, André, 1
Durand, Guillaume, 161
Dutton, Paul Edward, 171, 191
Duty, 15

E

Eberhard, 78
Ebert, Adolf, 164
Ebro, 86
Eden, 26, 132
Effraim (figure in Hosea), 198
Egeus (a court eunuch), 78
Egyptians, 119
Einhard, 65–66, 75, 77, 114
Elbe, 86
Elegy, 36
Elijah, 59, 78
Elisha, 59
Elysium, 183–85
Emathia, 176, 199

Enoch, 58
Envy, 17, 25–26, 48
Ephraim (rescues Theodulf), 148–49
Eppinus (a courtier), 72, 78
Erato, 139, 170
Ercambald (a courtier), 71
Ermengarde (Louis the Pious's queen), 187, 190
Ermoldus Nigellus, 164
Esmeijer, Ank C., 143
Esther, 60
Ethica, 142, 144
Ethiopians, 119
Eucherius of Lyons, 199
Eufrasia (wife of Rotharius), 151
Euphorbus, 112
Euphrates, 13, 39, 68
Eve (first woman), 26
Ezekiel, 60
Ezra, 60

F

Facetiae, 10
Fallen angel, 23, 25
Fardulf (abbot of Saint-Denis), 6, 116
Fastrada (Charlemagne's queen), 3, 65, 73, 113
Fichtenau, Heinrich, 137
Flaccus (appellation of Alcuin), 70
Fleury, 3
France, 1, 161
Francia, 116, 160
Frankfurt, Council of, 3
Fraud, 48, 84, 91–92, 104
Fredegis (a courtier), 71
Freeman, Ann, 1–5, 8, 35, 128, 137, 195–97
Fried, Johannes, 7, 170
Fritsch, Andreas, 117
Fuhrmann, Manfred, 2, 79, 82
Fulrad (abbot of Saint Quentin), 124–26
Furies, 21

G

Gairardus (an informant), 174
Galindo (bishop in Troyes), 190–91
Ganges, 13, 68, 90
Gard (river), 86

Garonne, 86
Gaul, 2, 40, 189
Gave (river), 86
Geary, Patrick, 83
Geometria, 142, 145, 202
Georgics, 140, 197, 199
Germanus (a saint), 163
Germigny-des-Prés, 4–5, 35
Geryon, 119
Getae, 119
Gisla (daughter of Charlemagne), 69–70
Gisla (unidentified), 13, 137
"Gloria, laus," 8
Gondacharus (unidentified), 192
Gluttony, 17, 25–26, 54, 193
Godman, Peter, 3, 6–8, 62, 65–66, 79,
    108, 115, 119–20, 167, 171, 177, 197
Goliath, 59
Gomis (a messenger), 120
Gorgon, 21
Grace, 37, 48, 158, 168–69
Grammatica, 142–43, 201–2
Greed, 35, 39, 48, 52, 86, 90–92, 149
Greeks, 119
Gregory the Great (pope), 140
Greeley, June-Ann, 4, 119, 167, 171, 178

H

Hadrian (pope), 3, 73–74
Hagen, Hermann, 17, 79, 198
Haggai, 60
Haman, 60
Hannibal, 176
Hardberd, 78
Hauréau, Barthélemy, 137
Heavenly bliss, 14
Hebrews, 119
Heine, Heinrich, 15
Hellfire, 14, 44, 57
Helmengald (palace prefect), 127
Hentze, Wilhelm, 115
Heraclius, 135, 198–99
Hercules, 81, 88, 119, 140–41
Hero, 173
Hesperia, 1–2
Hezekiah, 85
Hilary of Poitiers, 140, 177, 179

Hildebald (palace chaplain), 6, 78
Hiltrud (daughter of Charlemagne), 70
Hiram, 79
Hispania, 1
Homer (the Greek poet), 192, 199; *see also*
    Odyssey
Homer (appellation of Angilbert), 71, 76
Hrabanus Maurus, 75
Huemer, Johannes, 198
Hugh of Fleury, 161
Huisne (river), 8, 170, 174
Humor, 15, 66
Huns, 68, 119
Hyrcania, 90

I

Ididia (Solomon), 198
Indians, 119
Inn (river), 86
Isaac, 58
Isaiah, 59
Isidore of Seville, 2, 75, 119, 140, 142–43, 198
Israel, 31, 162, 198

J

Jacob, 58
Jericho, 173
Jerome (Saint), 36, 137, 140
Jerome (father of Fulrad), 125, 149
Jerusalem, 60, 78
Job, 22, 41, 54, 78, 98
John of Arles, 6
John Chrysostom, 140
John (the apostle), 61
John the Baptist, 60, 163, 177, 179
Jonah, 59
Jonas of Orléans, 6, 122
Joseph (student of Alcuin), 62
Joseph (son of Jacob), 59, 68, 169, 188
Joseph (figure in Hosea), 198
Joshua, 59
Josiah, 59, 85
Jove, 72
Judah, 123
Judas, 43, 115
Judith, 60
Justice, 11, 15

Justitia, 142, 144
Juvencus, 141

K

Karolus Magnus et Leo Papa, 114–15

L

Lacedemonia, 120
Lady Ethica, 11; *see also* Ethica
Laidradus, 79–81, 86
Langobards, 7, 116
Latium, 86
Leander, 173
Ledru, A., 161, 170
Lemuel, 76
Lendinara, Patrizia, 18, 81, 140, 143
Lentulus (a courtier), 71
Le Mans, 8, 161, 170, 173
Leo I (pope), 140
Leo III (pope), 4, 114–15, 127
Le Perche, 173
Lérins, 149
Lès (river), 86
Lewis, C. S., 143
Libri Carolini, 1–5, 8, 142, 183, 197
Libya, 86, 160
Liebeschütz, Hans, 150
Liersch, Karl, 76, 126, 164, 190, 197
Limoges, 81, 148, 150
Lindisfarne, 57
Liutgard (Charlemagne's queen), 13, 69, 113–14
Logica, 142, 144–45
Loire, 76, 86, 163
Lorsch, 2, 150
Lot, 59
Lot (river), 86
Lothar (eldest son of Louis the Pious), 6, 119, 124, 187, 190
Louis the Pious, 2, 6, 8, 69, 119–20, 122–26, 161, 164, 174, 187–89, 197
Lucan (*Pharsalia*), 199
Lucius (unidentified courtier), 75, 77
Lupus (Theodulf?), 77
Lust, 17, 26, 48, 54
Lychas, 88
Lyons, 79–81, 86–87

M

MacCoull, Leslie S. B., 201
Maas, 67, 86
Maguelone, 80, 87
Mähl, Sibylle, 142–43
Mancio (or Mantio), 148–49, 175
Manitius, Max, 34, 137
Marcellus of Die, 139
Marne, 86, 197
Marseille, 80, 87
Martianus Capella, 143
Martha (John 11), 160
Martin (Saint), 163, 189
Matfrid (count in Orléans), 7–8, 180
Mauricius (Saint), 163
Maurilius (Saint), 163
Maximinus (abbot at Micy), 112
Mayenne (river), 163, 173
Meens, Rob, 4, 8, 167
Megivern, James J., 12, 83
Melito of Sardis, 199
Menalcas (Audulf—a courtier), 72, 75–76, 78
Mercury, 143
Metamorphoses (Ovid), 199
Meyvaert, Paul, 3–6, 35, 127
Michael (archangel?), 163
Micy (Mitiacus), 5, 112
Missus dominicus, 1, 4, 79, 116, 124, 149, 197
Moderatio, 142, 144
Modoin (bishop in Autun), 7, 35, 57, 148, 170–71, 177–78, 181
Monod, Gabriel, 82, 197
Moors, 119, 126
Mordecai, 60
Mosel, 86
Moses, 18, 27, 32, 59, 84, 108
Mount of Olives, 36
Mozarabic Psalter, 137
Musica, 142, 144, 201

N

Narbonne, 1, 80–81, 87
Nardus or Nardulus (Einhard), 71
Nazareth, 149
Nazarius (Saint), 149

Nees, Lawrence, 81
Nehemiah, 60, 78
Nemias (Nehemiah), 78
Nessus, 88
Nero, 179
New Law, 81, 107, 112, 122, 131, 136
New Testament, 128, 132
Nicene Acts, 3
Niermeyer, J. F., 195, 197
Nile, 13, 40, 68
Nîmes, 80, 87
Nimrod, 76, 79
Noah, 54, 58
Noble, Thomas F. X., 3, 7–8
Noricus, 86
Novempopulania, 148
Nowell, I., 137
Nun (father of Joshua), 59

O

Oaths, 82
Ohlers, Norbert, 80, 124
Old Law, 81, 84, 110, 112, 122, 131, 136
Old Testament, 81–82, 107–8, 128, 132
Ommundsen, Åslaug, 142
Odyssey, 199
Optatianus Porfyrius, 62
Opus Caroli Regis contra Synodum, 1
Orange, 87
Ordinatio Imperii, 6, 8, 119
Orlandis, José, 2
Orléans, 3–4, 112, 122–23, 146, 156, 164, 190, 197
Orpheus, 77
Osulf (a courtier), 71
O'Sullivan, Sinéad, 17
Ovid (Publius Ovidius Naso), 18–19, 34, 140–41, 177, 179, 199; *see also Metamorphoses*

P

Padberg, Lutz E. von, 115
Paderborn, 114–15
Palm Sunday, 161; *see also* "Gloria, laus"
Pannonia, 68
Paradise, 84, 86, 183, 186

Parma, 3
Parthians, 119
Pascasius (an informant), 174
Paul (Saint), 36, 46, 48, 61–62, 75, 177, 179, 185
Paulinus of Aquileia, 3, 141
Pavia, 116
Pentateuch, 128
Périgord, 148–49
Périgueux, 81
Persians, 119
Personal relations, 15
Personified verse epistles, 18, 27, 111, 121, 170, 191
Peter (Apostle), 56, 60, 75, 115, 163, 169, 177, 179
Pharsalus, Battle of, 199
Phlegethon, 14, 21, 43, 95
Phoebus, 76
Phrygians, 120
Physica, 144–45
Pippin (father of Charlemagne), 74
Pippin (son of Charlemagne), 7, 197
Pluto, 191
Po, 67, 86
Poitiers, 150
Polyphemus, 76, 79
Pompeius Trogus, 141
Pompey (Gnaeus Pompeius Magnus), 199
"Populana Gallia," 148–49
Potiphar (a court eunuch), 78
Proteus, 140–41
Provence, 4
Prudens, 190–91
Prudentia, 142–44
Prudentius, 2, 17, 141
Prudentius (recipient of a verse epistle), 190–91
Pyrenees, 86
Pythagoras, 112

R

Raby, F. J. E., 15, 139
Raphael, 60
Razès (or Le Razès), 80, 87
Rheims, 6

Index

Rhetorica, 142–43, 202
Rhine, 67, 81, 86, 149–50
Rhône, 67, 79–81, 86, 176
Richbod of Trier, 3
Riculf (archbishop of Mainz), 71, 75
Ripoll (in Catalonia), 146
Rochemaure, 79, 87
Roer (river), 86
Romans, 119, 175–76
Rome, 74, 114, 116, 149–50, 152, 158,
    160, 176, 179
Ross, Werner, 170
Rothaid (daughter of Charlemagne), 70
Rotharius (a count), 151
Rouche, Michel, 1
Rutulians, 175
Rzehulka, Ernst, 1, 7, 137

S

Saint Quentin (abbey), 10, 124–25
Samaria (figure in Hosea), 198
Samuel (high priest), 59, 84
Santa Maria Maggiore, 4
Saône, 67, 86, 176
Sapphics, 122–23, 187
Sarmatians, 126
Sarthe (river), 8, 163, 170, 173–74
Satan, 18, 25, 82
Saturninus, 163
Schaller, Dieter, 3, 6–8, 57, 62, 65–67, 73,
    75–76, 146–47, 150, 153, 156, 164,
    170, 177, 183, 187, 195–96, 198
Schieffer, Rudolf, 115
Scylla, 102
Sears, Elizabeth, 62
Sebeok, Thomas A., 36
Second Council of Nicaea, 3
Sedulius, 141
Seine, 86, 197
Seneca, 177, 179
Septimania, 1, 3
Sergius (martyr), 163
Shaffer, Jenny H., 6, 35
Shem, 58
Sibyl, 140
Sidwell, Keith, 66

Sign language, 50
Silenus, 77
Sintegaudus (protégé of Theodulf), 167–68
Sirmond, Jacques, 8, 147, 183, 198–99, 201
Sodom, 59, 196
Solomon (King), 43, 59, 68, 85, 99, 188
Sophia (Sapientia), 142–43, 201
Soutancion, 80, 87
Spain, 1–2, 40, 126, 160
Spanish Bible redactions, 2, 128
Spanish liturgy, 2
Spanish orthography, 2
Stella, Francesco, 128
Stephen IV (pope), 6
Strecker, Karl, 139
Strife, 48
Styx, 21, 39, 42, 54, 84, 95, 191
Suavericus (husband of an unidentified
    Gisla), 138
Syria, 90
Szövérffy, Josef, 161

T

Tartarus, 14, 25, 60, 68
Tetrada (Charlemagne's daughter), 70
Teucri, 175
Thalia, 170
Thegan, 7
Theodulf Bibles, 127
Thomas (unidentified), 192
Thracians, 120
Thyrsis (Meginfred—a courtier), 70, 75, 77
Tiber, 67, 150
Tiphys, 178
Tiraboschi, Girolamo, 137
Tiryns, 88
Tityrus, 77
Tougher, Shaun, 76
Toulouse, 86, 148, 174–75
Tours, 4, 158, 176, 187, 189
Traube, Ludwig, 198
Treffort, Cécile, 6, 35
Truth in the pagan poets, 140

U

Ulysses, 43
Umiker-Sebeok, Jean, 36

V

Vacuousness, 91
Vanity, 25
Valence, 79, 87
Venantius Fortunatus, 62, 67, 141
Via Domitia, 80
Vidier, A., 146
Vienne, 79, 87
Virgil, 77, 81, 140–41, 177, 179, 197, 199;
    see also Aeneid, Georgics
Virgin Mary, 26, 163
Vis (Fortitude), 142, 144
Vulcan, 72, 88
Volturno, 86

W

Waal, 86
Waddell, Helen, 35
Wallach, Luitpold, 4, 73

Weinberger, Stephen, 15
Weser, 86
Werner, Karl Friedrich, 4, 7
Wibod (a courtier), 66, 72, 76
Wicked shepherds, 31–32
Williams, Burma P., 36
Williams, Richard S., 36
Willeumier-Schalij, J. M., 74
Wolfhold of Cremona, 7
Worms, 150
Wulfinus, 139–40

Z

Zaragoza, 2
Zechariah, 60
Zerubbabel, 60
Ziolkowski, Jan, 150
Zirkulargedichte, 66–67
Zodiac, 145

Index of Countries and Regions Listed in Poem 7

("De eo quod avarus adglomeratis diversis opibus satiari nequit")

Africa, 40
Agarenian (goods), 39
Arabia Felix, 39
Araxes, 39
Arcadia, 39
Argyra (in Asia), 39
Assyria, 39
Asturias, 40
Athens, 39
Bactria, 39
Baghdad, 39
Black Sea, 39
Bosphoran (land), 39
Britain, 40
Calabria, 40
Caspian regions, 39
Ceylon, 39
China, 39
Chryse (North Malaya), 39
Constantinople, 39
Cordoba, 40
Dacia, 39
Don (river), 39
Ethiopians, 40
Galauli, 40
Galicia, 40
Garden of the Hesperides, 40
Gelonians, 39
Gepids, 39
Germany, 39
Geta (Goth), 39

Greece, 39
Hungary, 39
Hydaspes, 39
Hyperborean people, 39
Hyrcania, 39
India, 39
Ireland, 40
Jerusalem, 39
Jordan (river), 39
Jugurtha, 40
Latium, 40
Libya, 40
Ligurians, 40
Mauritania, 40
Moors, 40
Ophir, 39
Palestine, 39
Pannonia, 39
Persia, 39
Po, 40
Rhodopeian Hebrus, 39
Riphaean (frost), 39
Sarmatia, 39
Scythia, 39
Sheba, 39
Swabia, 39
Thrace, 39
Thule, 40
Tigris, 39
Troglodytes, 40
Veneti, 40

INDEX OF PROMINENT THEMES IN THEODULF'S VERSE

Apparent injustice, 35–36, 40–42, 46

Capital justice, 10, 83, 105, 108–9

God's omniscience, 14, 35, 41, 46, 52, 85, 92, 104, 156, 158, 160

Honesty, 11, 15, 24, 36–38, 46, 51, 94, 168

Humility, 11, 18, 24–25, 33, 62, 95, 98, 134, 168

Hypocrisy, 33–36, 38, 51–52

Kindness, 12, 31, 83, 110

Learning, 13, 35, 43, 57, 69–70, 133–34, 139, 167

Memento mori, 10, 82, 96–97, 183

Mercy, 12, 36, 42, 83, 105, 107, 156

Moderation, 14, 83–84, 94, 99

Patience, 17, 22–23, 26, 31, 41, 49

Perjury, 48

Poor people, 10, 12, 30, 35, 38, 82–83, 85, 91, 93, 98–99, 106–7, 127, 156, 159, 164

Pride, 10–11, 17–18, 23–26, 29, 82, 95–96, 134, 168

Rising to heaven, 14, 32, 36, 44, 49, 98, 107, 112, 121, 124, 127, 136, 155, 162, 183–85

Social values, 10, 14–15, 36, 66

Superiority of the spirit over the flesh, 18, 20, 29, 97, 146, 148, 183–84, 187

Teaching, 13, 18, 24, 33–35, 42, 51, 62, 70, 72, 134, 141, 167–68, 171, 189

Vainglory, 23, 25, 30, 134